What Parents Are Saying

"Dr. Monteiro's approach with my son g[ave me the sense that here was someone] (other than me) who understood my chi[ld,] and that she had gotten a representative diagnosis of autism and of the paths we needed to pursue to get help for him. Her simple to understand visual diagrams kept my husband and me focused while our heads were swimming and our hearts were breaking at the undeniable news of our son's diagnosis. Believe me, her simple drawings were worth a thousand words during those heavily emotional times.

"Dr. Monteiro's diagnosis methodology and approach to children recognizes and affirms each child's uniqueness. This appreciation of individuality is very reassuring to parents. My son is not a label or a category. He is Drew. Dr. Monteiro understands this. I am heartened to know that more families may benefit from her approach with the publication of this book."

Kitsy Shelton Haiman, *Parent of a child with autism*

"WOW! Really wish there would have been a book like this when my son was younger. Dr. Monteiro speaks in terms that are understandable for parents, educators, and the medical profession and explains in detail significant information relating to autism. Parents want to know that someone understands them and their child's diagnosis and is listening to their concerns. They want affirmation that their child's unique qualities are understood and make them special. This book gives the tools to deliver that."

Beth Ann Susens, *Parent of a child with autism*

"*Autism Conversations* is easy to read and comprehend even for those that are just beginning the autism journey. I was especially appreciative of the concern and consideration toward the parental emotions that go along with this devastating diagnosis. Also, I was struck by the fact that so much respect is shown for the individuality of each precious child. If only I had had access to this book before the evaluation of my then four-year-old son. Having this preparation would have certainly eased the stress of the evaluation process for both him and me. I feel very strongly that *Autism Conversations* should and will become the number one guide and handbook for all involved in the evaluation of autism. Bravo, Dr. Monteiro."

Julie Collier, *Parent of a young adult with autism*

"Dr. Monteiro brings a warm and human approach to evaluating children who may have autism spectrum disorders. During my son's assessment, I could tell she really saw him as a person—instead of checking off boxes and categorizing his differences. Her genuine passion for helping children with autism spectrum disorders and their families shines through in person and in this book. Readers will find Dr. Monteiro's book reassuring, supportive, and brimming with fabulous information, resources, and ideas."

Laura Schieber, *Parent of a child with PDD-NOS*

"I love this book.

"As a parent, I am delighted to have this new perspective on how to have a meaningful conversation with my own child. Dr. Monteiro points out parents need to 'tell their stories.' *Autism Conversations* is a valuable resource for connecting with and articulating our own stories, allowing us to offer our insight to the people in our children's lives.

"As a parent advocate, I am excited to see this step-by-step approach to engaging and supporting parents through the evaluation process. Because of the unique experience of raising a child on the spectrum, parents don't often get a chance at a meaningful conversation with or about their child. Education professionals can use these techniques to pull together a solid team for each child and point the way to a hopeful future for each family."

Pam Seeger, *Parent of a child with autism*

Autism Conversations

Evaluating Children on the Autism Spectrum through Authentic Conversations

By **Marilyn J. Monteiro**

Foreword by Tony Attwood

PUBLISHED BY

Test with Confidence

*www.*wpspublish*.com*

*www.*MarilynMonteiro*.com*

*www.*AutismConversations*.com*

Western Psychological Services, Los Angeles, CA 90025

Copyright © 2010 by Marilyn J. Monteiro, Ph.D.

All rights reserved.

Not to be reproduced, adapted, and/or translated in whole or in part without prior written permission of WESTERN PSYCHOLOGICAL SERVICES.

ISBN: 978-087424-4939

First Printing: February 2010

Printed in the United States of America

10 9 8 7 6 5 4 3 2 1

This book is dedicated to my multidisciplinary colleagues in schools throughout Texas and to the many children and parents with whom I have had the privilege of having "autism conversations."

Contents

List of Figures viii

List of Tables viii

Acknowledgments ix

Foreword by Tony Attwood xi

Author's Note xiii

An Initial Conversation 1

Chapter 1. Understanding Autism Spectrum Disorders: Setting the Context for
the Conversations 7

    The Visual Framework for Understanding Autism Spectrum Disorders 8

    The Conversational Approach 9

    The Visual Framework 9

        The Descriptive Triangle 10

        The Degree of Involvement 12

    Applying the Visual Framework 13

    Developmental Differences Across the Autism Spectrum 15

    *How does the visual framework fit with traditional diagnostic
categorization systems like the DSM-IV-TR?* 21

    Using the Visual Framework: A Case Example 21

    *How does the visual framework help clinicians make differential diagnoses
among autism spectrum disorders?* 28

        Comparing Behaviors in Each of the Three Areas Across the
Autism Spectrum 29

    Best Practices 29

        Why Multidisciplinary Evaluation Teams Are Important 33

        Information That Should Be Collected Prior to the Sensory-Based
Diagnostic Interview 34

        The Sensory-Based Diagnostic Interview 35

        After the Sensory-Based Diagnostic Interview Has Been Completed ... 36

    *How does the sensory-based diagnostic interview fit in with the use of
standardized autism evaluation measures such as the ADOS and the PEP-3?* .. 37

    The Best Practices Components of Team-Based Autism Evaluations 38

Chapter 2. Conversations With Children: The Sensory-Based Diagnostic Interview 39

    The Neuro-Atypical Conversation in the Context of the Sensory-Based
Diagnostic Interview 40

    The Neuro-Atypical Conversation 41

        Starting the Conversation in the Middle 41

What are sensory toys and how do you select them? 42

The Sensory-Based Diagnostic Interview 43

How was the sensory-based diagnostic interview developed? 44

A Conversation With a 7-Year-Old Child Suspected of Having
Asperger's Syndrome 45

A Conversation With a Neuro-Typical Child 51

A Conversation With a Child With Autistic Disorder 52

A Conversation With a Child With Pervasive Developmental
Disorder Not Otherwise Specified (PDD-NOS) 59

A Valuable Addition to the Evaluation Process 64

*How does the sensory-based diagnostic interview change when
an adolescent is evaluated?* 64

The Team Evaluation Process for the Sensory-Based Diagnostic
Interview 65

Chapter 3. Conversations With Parents: The Parent Interview 67

The Conversational Approach to Interviewing Parents 68

Parents Need to Tell Their Stories 69

    Conversations Versus Checklists 69

*How does the conversational approach to interviewing parents
differ from a traditional parent interview?* 71

An Interview With Jonathon's Parents 71

Features of the Parent Interview Process Using the
Conversational Approach 79

Guidelines for Conducting the Parent Interview Using the
Conversational Approach 82

Chapter 4. Conversations With Teachers: The Teacher Interview 83

The Conversational Approach to Interviewing Teachers 84

Teachers Need to Share Their Concerns 85

*Is it okay to bypass the teacher interview and only ask the teacher
to fill out behavior checklists?* 86

An Interview With Evan's Teacher 87

Features of the Teacher Interview Process Using the
Conversational Approach 93

Guidelines for Conducting the Teacher Interview Using the
Conversational Approach 96

Chapter 5. Collaborative Team Conversations: From Interview to Diagnosis ... 97

Collaborative Team Conversations and the Sensory-Based
Diagnostic Interview 98

A Team Conversation About Brian 99

    Preparing for the Sensory-Based Diagnostic Interview 99

A Team Conversation With Brian 103

    Conducting the Sensory-Based Diagnostic Interview 103

How important is it for evaluators to know details about the child's areas of interest? 108
A Team Conversation About Brian 108
    Reaching Consensus on Brian's Diagnosis 108
What is the difference between a quantitative and a qualitative vocabulary? 114
    Linking Brian's Diagnosis to His Educational Plan 114
An Example of a Differential Diagnosis 118
    A Team Conversation With Felix 118
    A Diagnosis for Felix 122
The Collaborative Team Process 127
How difficult is it to form an autism evaluation team, and how do newly formed teams learn to work together? 128
Collaborative Team Conversations: Discussing the Diagnosis 129

Chapter 6. Conversations With Parents: The Diagnostic Feedback Conversation 131
The Diagnostic Feedback Conversation 132
Preparing for the Diagnostic Feedback Conversation With Parents 133
Delivering the Diagnosis 134
What is the nonfinite grief process? 135
A Sample Diagnostic Feedback Conversation 137
Is it common for parents to observe their child's autism evaluation? 137
What if the parents disagree with the team's diagnosis? 158
When should a child's diagnosis be shared with him or her, and how should it be discussed? 159
Facilitating the Diagnostic Feedback Conversation 160

Chapter 7. Written Conversations: Constructing a Narrative Report 161
Written Conversations: The Narrative Report 162
The Narrative Report: A Parent's Reaction 163
The Structure of the Narrative Report 163
An Excerpt From Gabriela's Narrative Report 166
Report Writing Essentials 176
    Essentials for the Background Information Section 176
    Essentials for the Behavioral Observations and Results Section 177
    Essentials for the Summary and Recommendations Section 182
Written Conversations: Report Writing Essentials 189

A Final Conversation 191

Appendix: Questionnaires Specific to Autism Spectrum Disorders 193

Glossary 195

References 207

FIGURES

1. The Visual Framework for Understanding Autism Spectrum Disorders: The Descriptive Triangle 11
2. The Visual Framework for Understanding Autism Spectrum Disorders: The Degree of Involvement 12
3. Understanding Autistic Disorder in the Context of Autism Spectrum Disorders 17
4. Understanding Pervasive Developmental Disorder Not Otherwise Specified (PDD-NOS) in the Context of Autism Spectrum Disorders 18
5. Understanding Asperger's Syndrome in the Context of Autism Spectrum Disorders 19
6. Using the Visual Framework to Depict Neuro-Typical Development 20
7. Brian's Autistic Disorder Behavioral Profile 112
8. Suggested Educational Supports for Brian 117
9. Felix's Language Learning Differences Behavioral Profile 125
10. Suggested Educational Supports for Felix 126
11. Eric's Autistic Disorder Behavioral Profile 138
12. Gabriela's Autistic Disorder Behavioral Profile 168
13. Suggested Educational Supports for Gabriela 169

TABLES

1. Clinical Behavior Features for Autism Spectrum Disorders: Language and Communication 30
2. Clinical Behavior Features for Autism Spectrum Disorders: Social Relationships and Emotional Responses 31
3. Clinical Behavior Features for Autism Spectrum Disorders: Sensory Use and Interests 32
4. Key Topics to Cover During the Parent Interview 81
5. Key Topics to Cover During the Teacher Interview 94
6. Language and Communication: General Areas to Include in the Narrative Report 184
7. Social Relationships and Emotional Responses: General Areas to Include in the Narrative Report 185
8. Sensory Use and Interests: General Areas to Include in the Narrative Report 186
9. Five Basic Educational Areas to Include in the Narrative Report 187

Acknowledgments

Thanks to my husband, Timothy Allen, for encouraging me to write this book. Our ongoing conversations throughout this process were helpful. Thanks also to my son Bennett for his support. I'm glad Jeff Manson approached me about publishing the book with Western Psychological Services and thank him for his support. My Project Director, Sheri Stegall, has done a great job guiding the manuscript through the publication process and I am grateful for our ongoing professional dialogue. I appreciate Kathy Tootle's talents with the cover art and book layout. Thanks also to Tony Attwood, who generously read the manuscript and wrote a lovely foreword. I very much appreciate his support of my work. I also want to thank the following people who read the manuscript and offered their feedback: my sister Marguerite Cavett, James Ball, Lisa Bower, Julie Collier, Michael DuPont, Susan Girvin, Gail Griswold, Kitsy Shelton Haiman, Deborah Johnson, Carol Kranowitz, Leigh Lane, Nancy Mabrey, Leigh Mann, Gale Roid, Pam Seeger, Laura Schieber, Leslie Sharp, Elissa Kay Stover, Beth Susens, and Melanie Wells. I hope readers enjoy this finished product.

Foreword

By definition, a child who has autism is different from other children of the same age. Sometimes the difference is quite obvious, in that the child's behaviour and abilities are conspicuously different from those of his or her peers. But autism is a very complex developmental disorder. There are some children for whom it is difficult to determine whether the unusual profile of abilities is due to autism, another developmental disorder, or a reaction to unusual circumstances. Some children, especially girls who have Asperger's syndrome, have developed strategies that camouflage the characteristics of the disorder, making diagnosis particularly difficult. Information from parents provided during the diagnostic assessment may be subjective and need validating by an experienced clinician.

Conducting a diagnostic assessment requires extensive knowledge of the development of typical children and a recognition of what is, and is not, normal for a child of that age. By creating the right situation, the clinician is able to elicit, identify, and quantify the characteristics of an autism spectrum disorder (ASD). This is achieved by observation and direct interaction or "conversation" with the child, and additional information from parents, teachers, and colleagues.

Each clinician develops a personal diagnostic style and script using standardized instruments that determine whether the child has autism. *Autism Conversations* provides a best practice script and procedure, advice on materials to use during the diagnostic assessment, and a structure to explain and quantify the nature of autism as expressed by a particular child. Clinicians who have recently decided to specialize in the diagnosis and treatment of ASDs will greatly enhance their expertise using the advice provided within *Autism Conversations*. Advanced clinicians will also benefit from the ideas and explanations. There were many instances as I read the manuscript that I thought, "What a great idea!"

Clinicians need such a text, not simply to improve diagnostic accuracy but also to cope with the recent deluge of referrals for a diagnostic assessment for autism. When I started my professional career as a specialist in autism in the late 1970s, ASD was considered a relatively rare condition, occurring in 1 in 2,500 children. Recent research suggests that autism, including Asperger's syndrome, occurs in 1 in 150 children. There are several reasons for this increase in diagnosis. In part, there is greater accuracy, such that children who would have previously been simply diagnosed with mental retardation are now more accurately diagnosed with autism. There is also an acceptance of dual diagnoses: for example, children with Down's syndrome can also have autism. And finally, there is a greater understanding of the continuum, or spectrum, of autism that includes the more recently defined Asperger's syndrome.

There are many pathways to a diagnosis of ASD that include the initial diagnosis of an associated disorder such as Attention-Deficit Disorder, developmental delay in language abilities, or a mood disorder such as Obsessive-Compulsive Disorder or depression. Thus, psychologists, paediatricians, psychiatrists, and speech pathologists, who may not be considered specialists in autism, need to be aware that a percentage of the children they see may have autism, and they will need a resource such as *Autism Conversations* to determine whether the child has a combination of disorders that includes autism.

I use as a metaphor for the diagnostic assessment the completion of a 100-piece jigsaw. The assessment identifies how many pieces of the autism puzzle are recognizable in the child's abilities and behaviour. The approach of *Autism Conversations* enables the assessment of all the characteristics or parts of the autism puzzle, including those parts such as sensory sensitivity that may not be given great prominence in the current diagnostic criteria. However, as a clinician, I know sensory sensitivity has a great impact on the child's quality of life. *Autism Conversations* describes and provides strategies to examine aspects of autism that are not explained adequately in the current diagnostic criteria.

Once the diagnostic assessment is completed, it is extremely important that the parents receive a coherent and accurate explanation about whether or not the child has autism and what the implications might be. The clinician needs to develop a sense of rapport with parents such that the information will be accepted, and must write reports that provide more practical information than simply whether or not the child has autism. Autism is a complex disorder and each child is unique. The clinician needs to have a degree of expertise or special interest in the area of autism, as well as a natural ability to understand the perspective and experiences of both the child and his or her parents. In addition, the ability to communicate explanations and strategies in conversation and in report writing is essential. Thus, the dimensions used to determine whether a child has autism are dimensions that make a good clinician.

I know that *Autism Conversations* will be read for advice, before and during a diagnostic assessment, and used to provide guidance when writing the report and discussing the results and implications with parents, teachers, and colleagues. I recommend that each clinician have his or her own copy, because if this book is shared, whoever has *Autism Conversations* will be reluctant to part with it.

Tony Attwood, Ph.D.

Author's Note

The individuals described in this book represent composites of children, parents, teachers, and professional evaluators with whom I have worked during the past 25 years. The specific examples given in this book, including the physical descriptions of individual children, are literary devices. They are based on my cumulative experience and are used to help the reader experience "conversations" while protecting the confidentiality of individual children and their families.

An Initial Conversation

Autism Conversations describes an innovative way to evaluate children suspected of having autism spectrum disorders. A conversation first develops when parents and others in the child's life discuss the differences they notice in the child and decide to seek help. The diagnostic conversation begins as evaluators encourage parents to tell stories about their child; a bond is forged between the parents and the evaluators, and a nuanced description of the child emerges. The conversation continues when evaluators invite the child to share his or her unique interests, and a rich and detailed understanding of the child's worldview unfolds. This process of evaluating children through authentic conversations is the focus of *Autism Conversations*.

If you evaluate children with suspected autism, this book will help you have effective conversations with children, their parents, their teachers, and your colleagues. If you are a parent of a child with suspected autism, this book will help you understand the evaluation process. Additionally, this book will help both evaluators and parents learn to recognize the unique worldview held by children on the autism spectrum and to understand and talk about each child's worldview in practical and accessible language.

The conversations in the first chapter focus on teaching evaluators and parents to use a *visual framework* to understand and talk about autism spectrum disorders in specific but nontechnical terms. The visual framework provides a common reference point to discuss the profile of behaviors that make up a diagnosis of an autism spectrum disorder. Instead of focusing exclusively on the diagnosis itself, you will learn how to recognize the pattern of developmental differences that characterize autism spectrum disorders in the three key areas of language and communication, social relationships and emotional responses, and sensory use and interests. Throughout the book, you'll be shown how to apply the visual framework to discuss individual children and their specific behavioral profiles.

My approach to evaluating children focuses on inviting the child into an authentic conversation. Getting to know a child who has developmental differences involves understanding that the entry point into the child's unique worldview is distinctly different for children with autism spectrum disorders. To reflect the distinctive nature of this exchange, I refer to the conversations I have with children on the autism spectrum as *neuro-atypical* conversations. Instead of asking the child to conform to my expectations and my point of view, I watch and listen for clues to the child's point of view and start the conversation there.

I introduce toys that have interesting and appealing sensory qualities so the child can have a pleasant shared experience with me; for example, many times the conversation begins as the child explores a toy that lights up and spins when a button is pushed. At other times, conversation is initiated when the child is encouraged to talk about a favorite topic, such as facts about space or information about a favorite movie. Children who have the unique worldview that comes with an autism spectrum disorder seldom have opportunities to share their interests and to experience time with others in an authentic way. They respond in a positive way when the evaluation begins with a neuro-atypical conversation.

In this book, I show you how to enter the child's sensory-driven world and effectively engage the child in a neuro-atypical conversation that reveals his or her authentic style of relating to the world. A unique focus of this book is the emphasis on teaching evaluators to use toys and materials with appealing sensory qualities to start a conversation with a child on the autism spectrum. I use vivid narrative examples to teach the use of sensory-based conversational techniques. Methods of working effectively with nonverbal children who have significant autism are covered, as well as specific conversational techniques that work best with children with Asperger's Syndrome.

A crucial part of evaluating children is taking the time to form meaningful connections with their parents. Parents entering the evaluation process for their child face an oftentimes confusing and stressful situation. Few books are available to guide either the parents of children suspected of having a form of autism or the professionals who evaluate children through this complicated process. *Autism Conversations* provides a framework for evaluation specialists to effectively work with children, talk with parents and teachers, and summarize the diagnosis in a narrative report. This book also provides parents with information to help them through this complicated and emotionally demanding process.

Throughout the book, I discuss the skills involved in forming a trusting relationship with parents. In my experience, well-meaning evaluation specialists frequently have difficulty engaging in an effective conversation with parents. Too often, evaluators rely on giving parents checklists to complete instead of spending time with them in an informal but structured conversation. I teach evaluators how to let parents and teachers not only tell their stories about the child, but through those conversations to also lay the groundwork for becoming a collaborative team. From the initial parent interview to the follow-up session when a professional shares the diagnosis with a child's parents and teachers, I provide guidelines and specific conversational techniques to help structure the important relationship between the professionals who evaluate a child and the child's parents and teachers.

Finally, this book provides evaluators with a framework for writing compelling narrative reports. Most evaluation reports contain information from checklists and standardized scores for developmental, cognitive, and learning skills. These are important and valuable parts of a comprehensive evaluation, but often a nuanced description of the individual child is missing. A significant aspect of report writing addressed in this book is the need for evaluators to write about the child's behavioral profile in a narrative or conversational format that uses specific examples of the child's behavior. Parents have told me repeatedly through the years that they valued and appreciated having an evaluation report that described their child's unique qualities and distinguished that child as an individual.

Equally important, parents have expressed their appreciation when the report includes specific recommendations for the child's educational program. The link established between the diagnosis and educational strategies helps teachers develop instructional supports for the child in the school setting and helps parents work with the child at home. This book teaches evaluators how to link the child's diagnosis to practical educational recommendations.

The framework for gathering qualitative information about children through the structured, sensory-driven conversations presented in this book comes from my years of working with thousands of children and their families. I found that the information gained about the child through the conversational techniques described here could not be gathered using more formal testing methods. Many evaluation specialists have already been trained in the strategies covered in this book. They report that their ability both to make difficult differential diagnoses and to work with the parents of children being evaluated has improved significantly by using the techniques described in *Autism Conversations.*

If you are an evaluation specialist reading this book, you will learn how to have authentic conversations with:

- The children you evaluate
- The parents of the children you evaluate
- The teachers of the children you evaluate
- Your multidisciplinary colleagues

This book will provide you with the tools to become more competent, confident, and effective in your diagnostic work with this ever-increasing population of children.

If you are the parent of a child with a suspected autism spectrum disorder, this book was written to help you anticipate what to expect from a "best practices" autism evaluation of your child. The process of seeking a diagnosis for a child can be stressful, frightening, and emotional. In this book, I wanted to share stories about children and families to help make the diagnostic process less daunting. After reading this book, you will have a better understanding of what a diagnosis on the autism spectrum means and how the diagnosis might relate to your child.

Autism Conversations focuses on the process of forming authentic connections with children on the autism spectrum, and with their parents and teachers. Meaningful connections are formed when people talk with one another. Now, let's begin our conversations about autism spectrum disorders.

CHAPTER 1

Understanding Autism Spectrum Disorders

Setting the Context for the Conversations

The Visual Framework for Understanding Autism Spectrum Disorders

What is the visual framework?

- The visual framework organizes the child's differences in development across the three key areas of language, social, and sensory development.
- The framework includes a descriptive triangle that provides a visual means to understand the key behavioral features associated with autism spectrum disorders.
- The framework provides an intuitive way to discuss the behaviors listed in the formal diagnostic systems used by physicians and clinicians.

Why is it useful?

- It provides a practical way to discuss the developmental differences inherent in a diagnosis of an autism spectrum disorder with parents, teachers, and diagnostic teams.
- It allows evaluators to discuss the diagnosis with parents using a visual talking point that depicts a triangle of developmental differences.
- The organization of the framework helps guide discussion among evaluators when they are trying to determine the most appropriate diagnosis for a child.

What are the benefits?

- The descriptive triangle directs evaluators to focus on the pattern of developmental differences that define children with autism spectrum disorders as they discuss the specific behavior patterns seen in individual children.
- The framework guides evaluators to systematically discuss a child's behavioral profile instead of focusing on checklists or quantitative scores to arrive at a diagnostic label.
- The framework guides evaluators to describe the behavioral profiles of individual children in an authentic and accessible way by using specific but nontechnical language.

THE CONVERSATIONAL APPROACH

Autism is a word that is difficult for parents to hear in relation to their child. When parents receive a diagnosis of an autism spectrum disorder, they search beyond the label to understand what the diagnosis means for their child. Traditionally, parents are left to understand this diagnosis with the technical language that results from standardized measures and formal diagnostic criteria, and they struggle to see how the label fits their individual child. While standardized testing and the use of formal diagnostic criteria are critical parts of an autism evaluation, relying solely on those procedures results in critical gaps in our understanding of the child. The opportunity to help parents and teachers understand the child's diagnosis, and to develop the specific educational supports the child needs, is lost.

In this book, you will learn a conversational approach to autism evaluations that is being put forth as an integral part of best practice. The techniques described throughout this book are essential for obtaining an accurate understanding of each child and for enhancing communication with each child's parents and teachers. This approach to understanding autism spectrum disorders begins with a visual framework that uses nontechnical but highly specific language that makes intuitive sense to parents and teachers.

THE VISUAL FRAMEWORK

The visual framework was developed as a distinct way to approach the autism evaluation process while enhancing the use of traditional autism evaluation measures. The visual framework described in this book gives evaluators and parents a more accessible way to organize and understand diagnostic information about children with possible autism spectrum disorders. The figures presented in this chapter allow evaluators to discuss the authentic and unique behavioral profile of a child in a very compelling way.

The traditional approach to diagnosing autism spectrum disorders involves the use of checklists and observation of the child, along with the use of tests that require the child to respond to adults and materials following a standardized set of procedures. Once the information is gathered, numbers are tallied and scores are derived, indicating the degree to which the child's measured behavior matches the diagnostic criteria for autism. Useful information is gained from using this traditional approach, but there are limitations that come with using technical diagnostic language and standardized measures.

Over the years, as I evaluated children using the traditional approach to diagnosing autism spectrum disorders, I encountered two obstacles that led me to develop the visual framework.

The first obstacle involved the limitations placed on the child when I used standardized evaluation tests. Standardized tests require children to conform to the agenda of the examiners. The evaluation methods described in this book were developed so evaluators would have a set of tools that would help children relax and explore the testing toys in a way that conforms to their autism-driven agenda. When examiners enter into a conversation with a child based on that child's interests, a detailed and authentic profile of the individual emerges. The child enjoys the time shared with the evaluation team, and the evaluators gain an appreciation for the child's unique way of relating to the world.

The second obstacle I faced involved the lack of an intuitive and straightforward way to discuss the diagnosis with parents. The visual framework provides a way to organize and talk about autism spectrum disorders using nontechnical but specific language. When evaluators use the visual framework to discuss a child's diagnosis with the parents, the focus shifts from the diagnostic label to a detailed description of how the child relates to the world. When a child's behavioral profile is discussed using the visual framework, the diagnostic label makes more sense and is often less overwhelming to parents.

Throughout this book, when I refer to autism spectrum disorders, I am talking about the three major forms of autism that are commonly the focus during diagnostic evaluations. The first diagnostic label on the autism spectrum is Autistic Disorder, also referred to as *classic autism* or simply *autism*. The second diagnostic label is Pervasive Developmental Disorder Not Otherwise Specified, often referred to by the initials PDD or PDD-NOS. The third diagnostic label is Asperger's Syndrome. As you read this chapter, you will learn how to recognize the behaviors that are commonly associated with each of these forms of autism and to understand them in the context of the visual framework. You will also learn to talk about each type of autism spectrum disorder using nontechnical but specific language.

Let's begin our conversation about the visual framework by talking about the descriptive triangle.

The Descriptive Triangle

All children with autism spectrum disorders display a behavioral profile marked by a pattern of developmental differences, or disruptions, in three key areas: (1) language and communication, (2) social relationships and emotional responses, and (3) sensory use and interests. Figure 1 shows how a child's behavioral profile can be organized around a descriptive triangle to provide a visual depiction of this pattern of developmental differences.

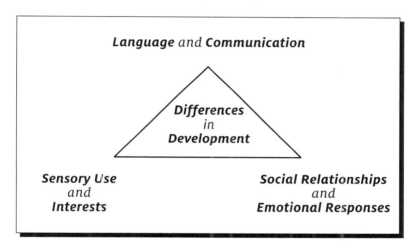

FIGURE 1
The Visual Framework for Understanding Autism Spectrum Disorders:
The Descriptive Triangle

The descriptive triangle has the words *Differences in Development* in the center. The word *differences* is used to highlight the fact that children with autism spectrum disorders have a pattern of disruptions, or differences, or atypicalities, in their development. The triangle draws attention to the three key areas in which distinctive developmental disruptions occur across the autism spectrum. At the top of the triangle, the words *Language and Communication* remind us that one of the key areas where disruptions in development occur is the manner in which the child develops and uses language and communication. At the bottom right corner of the triangle, the words *Social Relationships and Emotional Responses* direct us to understand that the manner in which the child relates to other people and manages emotions is another key aspect of the pattern of developmental differences seen in children with autism spectrum disorders. Finally, at the bottom left corner of the triangle, the words *Sensory Use and Interests* focus our attention on the key area of sensory differences and how sensory issues affect a child's play and interests.

The Degree of Involvement

In addition to considering the child's functioning within each of the three key areas, it is useful to consider the overall severity of those differences and their impact on an individual child's learning patterns. Autism spectrum disorders cover a wide range of developmental differences and ability levels, and can have mild to significant impact on a child's ability to learn. The severity with which an individual is affected by an autism spectrum disorder can be referred to as the *degree of involvement* of the disorder. The concept of degree of involvement can be used to answer the following question: How much is the child's pattern of developmental differences getting in the way of his or her ability to learn? When a child is diagnosed with an autism spectrum disorder, it is helpful to discuss the degree of involvement of the disorder so that parents and teachers can understand how much the diagnosis is likely to affect the child educationally and functionally.

Figure 2 shows how the continuum of the degree of involvement can be depicted in the visual framework by a line drawn above the descriptive triangle, with a mild degree of involvement indicated at the far left of the continuum and a significant degree of involvement indicated at the

FIGURE 2
The Visual Framework for Understanding Autism Spectrum Disorders:
The Degree of Involvement

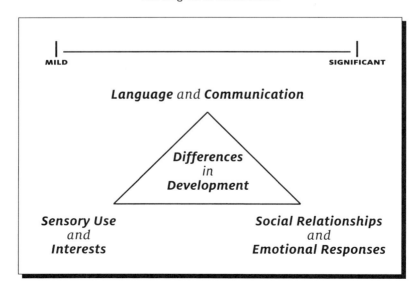

far right. When applying the visual framework to a specific child, the child's diagnosis can be written above the continuum line and a circle can be drawn at the place along the continuum that represents the disorder's degree of involvement.

APPLYING THE VISUAL FRAMEWORK

Children who have an autism spectrum disorder show a neuro-atypical pattern of development, which means they show a pattern of distinctive differences in development in the three key areas depicted in the descriptive triangle. The term *neuro-atypical* has come to be used by professionals and individuals with autism spectrum disorders to help understand and describe their differences in development. The meaning of this term has evolved over time, sometimes referring only to those with autism spectrum disorders, and other times referring to those who show any atypicalities in their neurodevelopment. The opposite term, *neuro-typical,* has been used to describe those who do not have autism spectrum disorders, or those who do not show any atypicalities in their neurodevelopment.

In this book, neuro-atypical is used to refer specifically to those individuals who show a pattern of distinctive differences in development in the three key areas that are affected by autism spectrum disorders, and neuro-typical is used to refer to individuals who do not show this characteristic pattern of developmental differences. I use the term neuro-atypical because I believe it succinctly captures the quality of unusual development inherent in children with autism spectrum disorders. The term *neuro* is fitting because autism spectrum disorders have a neurobiological base, and *atypical* refers to being different from the norm. After having countless conversations with children on the spectrum where I started the conversation "in the middle," either with sensory toys or topics, I found myself thinking that there was a distinctively different, neuro-atypical quality to our conversations. I use the term *neuro-atypical conversation* to highlight this distinctively different nature of the conversations with these fascinating children.

Children with autism spectrum disorders approach social interactions in a neuro-atypical, sensory-driven way. This different perspective on the world can be seen when these children are invited into a neuro-atypical conversation. Evaluators can engage children in such a conversation through the use of the sensory-based diagnostic interview. In contrast to a traditional clinical interview that gathers information from the examiner's perspective, the sensory-based diagnostic interview is a neuro-atypical conversation that draws out the child's autism-driven agenda. In the sensory-based diagnostic interview, a team of evaluators meets with the child and uses sensory-based toys and a focus on the child's preferred topics to experience the child's worldview. The visual framework helps evaluators structure their observations of the child during the interview and also discuss their observations after the interview. An example of the sensory-based diagnostic interview is provided later in this chapter, and the sensory-based diagnostic interview is discussed in detail in chapter 2.

Thinking about a child's behavioral profile in the three key areas affected by autism spectrum disorders also provides a natural entry point for a conversation about how autism affects that child's learning style and life. Describing the child's behavioral profile within the visual framework helps parents and teachers understand that *autism* is a compelling way to describe the child's worldview, or the child's unique way of relating to the world. When evaluation specialists inform parents their child "has autism" or "meets the diagnostic criteria for Asperger's Syndrome," the delivery of the diagnosis without a corresponding visual framework to help the parents understand how the label directly applies to their child can be alarming and confusing, and an opportunity to forge a working relationship is lost. It can be difficult for parents to trust the diagnosis if it is based on checklist results and a review of medical diagnostic criteria, because labels, checklists, and standardized test results fail to adequately describe individual children in an accessible way. Using the visual framework to talk about a child's pattern of developmental disruptions, or differences, makes intuitive sense to parents and educators.

Let's compare two ways to discuss the behavioral profile of a child with classic autism. Using a traditional clinical model, one might talk about "qualitative impairments in communication" or a "lack of development of spoken language." Using the visual framework, one is more likely to discuss how the child uses language to label objects he or she is holding or looking at instead of making social comments, securing attention, or responding to direct requests. Evaluators might also talk about how the child responds better to verbal requests when they are accompanied by visual contextual cues. In this way, the child's pattern of disruptions in the area of language and communication can be described using nontechnical but specific language that resonates with the way parents and educators understand the child.

The visual framework helps diagnostic evaluation teams because it provides an organized way to observe, describe, and discuss a child's behavioral profile once the diagnostic evaluation with the child has been completed. It provides evaluators with an accessible means to organize their observations about a child so they can arrive at the most compelling way to discuss that child's pattern of developmental differences. When evaluation teams learn to discuss and describe a child's behavioral profile using the visual framework, they are more likely to communicate effectively with the child's parents and teachers. The use of the framework also helps evaluation teams link practical instructional suggestions to the key developmental differences seen in the child during the evaluation process.

DEVELOPMENTAL DIFFERENCES ACROSS THE AUTISM SPECTRUM

Since all children with autism spectrum disorders display a pattern of developmental differences in the three key areas of language and communication, social relationships and emotional responses, and sensory use and interests, how does one distinguish among the diagnostic labels of Autistic Disorder, Pervasive Developmental Disorder Not Otherwise Specified (PDD-NOS), and Asperger's Syndrome? The visual framework provides a way to organize the distinct behavioral profiles associated with each of these forms of autism. The information presented here comes from my clinical experience as well as from formal diagnostic systems (e.g., *Diagnostic and Statistical Manual of Mental Disorders, Fourth Edition, Text Revision [DSM-IV-TR]*, American Psychiatric Association, 2000; *International Classification of Diseases, 10th Revision [ICD-10]*, World Health Organization, 1993). To gain an understanding of how the visual framework applies to the three forms of autism, refer to Figures 3, 4, and 5.

Figure 3 uses the descriptive triangle to highlight the behaviors and developmental differences seen in children with Autistic Disorder. Notice that the way in which children with Autistic Disorder show disruptions in their language, social, and sensory development is detailed under each of the three headings. Specific but nontechnical language is used to describe behaviors. For example, under *Language and Communication*, instead of talking about the child's "prosody," the words "intonation and inflection" are used. Furthermore, examples of unusual types of intonation and inflection often used by children with Autistic Disorder, such as "lilting," "exclamatory," and "high-pitched," are provided.

Figure 4 shows the visual triangle emphasizing the behaviors commonly seen in children with PDD-NOS. The behaviors listed under each of the three headings describe the specific developmental disruptions associated with this milder form of an autism spectrum disorder. Notice how the ability to initiate social contact with others is emphasized and contrasted with the inability to participate in reciprocal social exchanges with others.

Figure 5 uses the visual triangle to lay out the behaviors associated with Asperger's Syndrome in each of the three key areas. Emphasis is placed on describing the unique communication, social, and sensory differences associated with Asperger's Syndrome, including a drive to discuss preferred topics, anxiety surrounding social situations, and general body clumsiness.

Evaluation teams are encouraged to carefully review the behaviors as they are organized and presented in Figures 3, 4, and 5. The visual framework depicted in these figures provides a detailed and organized way to think about the pattern of differences in development associated with each of the major forms of autism spectrum disorders.

What about children who experience neuro-typical development? What would the descriptive triangle reflect in the areas of language and communication, social relationships and emotional responses, and sensory use and interests for a child who does not show a characteristic pattern of developmental differences in these areas? To help evaluators distinguish between the behavioral profiles of children who have an autism spectrum disorder and those who do not, Figure 6 uses the descriptive triangle to depict neuro-typical development.

FIGURE 3
Understanding Autistic Disorder in the Context of Autism Spectrum Disorders

Language and Communication

- Often functionally nonverbal
- May use spontaneous words, but use is random or unpredictable
- Common to acquire a few words by age 18 months and then stop talking
- Atypical verbal language features:
  - used primarily to label objects
  - not directed to a listener
  - unusual intonation and inflection:
    - lilting or exclamatory cadence
    - high-pitched tone of voice
  - jargon interspersed with meaningful utterances
  - utterances are repetitive, scripted, and rote
  - expressive language better developed than receptive language
- Atypical nonverbal communication features:
  - extremely limited or absent nonverbal language, as shown by:
    - lack of eye contact to gain social information
    - failure to use facial expressions to communicate social information
    - unresponsiveness to eye gaze, facial expressions, or vocal changes made by caregiver

Sensory Use and Interests

- Captured by a drive to complete repetitive sensory routines
- Focused on visual details
- Responds inconsistently to auditory input; may have pronounced taste, touch, or smell sensitivities
- Usually has good gross motor skills; likes to climb
- Play is sensory-seeking and solitary; uses objects for sensory input
- Play lacks social component, lacks representational or symbolic elements
- Unusual body movements and mannerisms, including hand flapping, hand and body posturing, peripheral eye gaze, running back and forth, holding breath, rocking, and vocalizing to self

Social Relationships and Emotional Responses

- Neutral facial expression; occasional facial grimacing or laughing to self
- Eye gaze limited and fleeting; used mostly to "check in" to determine source of demands (i.e., to gauge information about what is coming next rather than to gain or communicate social information)
- Does not initiate social exchanges and is not responsive to social play
- Moves away from people when social or language demands are made
- Seeks out people mainly to use them as a means to obtain a desired object
- Social praise not meaningful as a source of motivation
- Limited awareness of and interest in others
- Inconsistent and limited response to voices

FIGURE 4
Understanding Pervasive Developmental Disorder Not Otherwise Specified (PDD-NOS) in the Context of Autism Spectrum Disorders

Language and Communication

- Some use of verbal language is present
- Perseverative use of phrases, topics, and questions is common
- Not able to participate in reciprocal verbal exchanges
- May initiate conversations in the form of questions, but has difficulty maintaining or extending conversations
- Prompt-dependent on adults to structure a conversation
- Questions are repeated despite being answered as the child becomes more anxious
- Able to use and respond somewhat to nonverbal communication cues and requests

Differences in Development

Sensory Use and Interests

- Highly sensitive to changes in visual environment
- May have general motor clumsiness
- Sensitive to auditory input; may have pronounced taste, touch, or smell sensitivities
- Play is a mixture of approaching peers and staying by self on the perimeter
- Does not know how to respond to peers in social situations
- Seeks out repetitive play
- Likes to act out scenes from videos or cartoons
- Solitary play directed by sensory-seeking drive, but can be redirected
- Unusual body movements and mannerisms less pronounced than with classic autism

Social Relationships and Emotional Responses

- Neutral affect, but makes more eye contact than children with classic autism
- Initiates social interactions but has difficulty responding in a reciprocal way
- Seeks out and is responsive to people, but interactions are limited
- Transitions are highly stressful, resulting in anxiety responses
- Difficulty regulating anxiety once it has escalated
- Unstructured social and language interactions are experienced as highly stressful

FIGURE 5
Understanding Asperger's Syndrome in the
Context of Autism Spectrum Disorders

Language and Communication

- Although early language delays may be present, language skills have developed
- Atypical speech features:
  - intonation and inflection have a nasal or otherwise unusual tone and cadence
  - formal, rote, or scripted quality of speech
  - fluency and flow become disrupted when child responds to questions
  - speech is most fluent and vocabulary most developed when child is in charge of the topic
- Has one or more preferred topics of conversation; prefers facts and information
- Misses conversational cues for reciprocal conversation
- Corrects others frequently
- Literal and rule-bound
- Relies on repetitive phrases to start sentences ("Well, actually...")

Differences in Development

Sensory Use and Interests

- Poor body awareness results in clumsiness and awkward gait
- Rule-bound and controlling in play with others; will continue to play game alone according to rules rather than accommodate peers
- Handwriting often is difficult and frustrating
- Sensory sensitivities include clothing and food preferences
- Sensitive to sounds and visual details
- Unusual and subtle body movements and mannerisms, including picking at lips and face, body tensing, pacing, and hand posturing

Social Relationships and Emotional Responses

- Neutral facial expression
- Eye contact limited, but will stare at a listener when talking about a preferred topic
- Looks away when spoken to
- May have superficial social skills but misses subtle context cues
- Usually has a desire for social relationships; seeks out adults and younger children
- Anxious in social situations
- Has difficulty self-regulating when anxious or distressed
- Transitions and unexpected changes are stressful
- Rule-bound and rigid in interpretation of social rules

FIGURE 6
Using the Visual Framework to Depict Neuro-Typical Development

Language and Communication

- Nonverbal language features:
  - pointing
  - use of specific gestures
  - use of eye contact to gain attention of a listener
  - use of a range of facial expressions to communicate
  - searches faces of others during communication exchanges
  - responds to facial expressions and voice intonation during communication with others
- Verbal language features:
  - varies intonation and inflection to match circumstances
  - addresses a listener when speaking
  - seeks out responses from a listener and indicates receipt of response
  - participates in shared conversations or exchanges
  - changes topics as appropriate without undue stress
  - includes social information among topics
  - asks questions to establish a context or reference point during conversations with unfamiliar people
  - initiates, reciprocates, and extends conversations with others in a flexible way

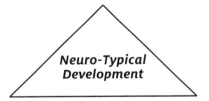

Sensory Use and Interests

- May have some sensory preferences or sensitivities, but is not restricted in activities or exploration of the world
- When exploring toys or materials, is not driven to examine sensory details; uses materials as intended
- Play includes a natural social component
- May sustain interest in toys longer when play is shared with others
- Play is primarily social rather than sensory-seeking in nature
- Play includes spontaneous use of representational and symbolic elements
- Has a range of age-appropriate interests
- Uses body in natural way; absence of unusual or repetitive body movements or mannerisms

Social Relationships and Emotional Responses

- Seeks out social contact with adults and peers
- Responsive to and uses social gestures, including:
  - eye contact
  - range of facial expressions
  - body gestures
- Has and seeks out reciprocal, genuine relationships with peers and adults
- Can regroup when upset by something
- Recognizes emotions in self and others
- Displays a range of emotions congruent with circumstances

How does the visual framework fit with traditional diagnostic categorization systems like the DSM-IV-TR?

Traditional diagnostic categorization systems, such as the *DSM-IV-TR*, provide sets of criteria for diagnosing psychiatric disorders, such as autism spectrum disorders. In the visual framework, the distinct behavioral features of autism spectrum disorders that are described in traditional diagnostic categorization systems are organized into the three key areas clinicians look at when evaluating children for suspected autism spectrum disorders: language and communication, social relationships and emotional responses, and sensory use and interests. The three key areas form a behavioral profile, organized around a descriptive triangle, that provides an accessible way to understand the challenges associated with autism spectrum disorders. Clinicians are better able to recognize the pattern of developmental differences a child presents in an evaluation setting when they use the visual structure and translate the key behaviors into nontechnical but specific language, as opposed to using the technical language found in diagnostic categorization systems. They are also better equipped to talk to parents and teachers about the child, using terms that are instantly recognizable as qualities the child displays.

When clinicians evaluate children for suspected autism spectrum disorders, they refer to the *DSM-IV-TR* criteria for Autistic Disorder, PDD-NOS, or Asperger's Syndrome. By using the visual framework, clinicians have an organized and structured way to gather the information needed for these formal diagnoses. If they approach the evaluative process by organizing their understanding of the child's pattern of developmental differences in this manner, their clinical observations and understanding of the diagnostic process, as well as their ability to communicate a diagnosis to parents and others, will substantially improve.

USING THE VISUAL FRAMEWORK: A CASE EXAMPLE

To give you an example using the visual framework as an organizational tool when determining a child's diagnosis, I'd like to describe the team process of evaluating Alexander with a sensory-based diagnostic interview.

Alexander, a 3-year-old boy with sandy brown hair and a constant, serious expression on his face, was referred for an autism evaluation through his private preschool. Local public school special education representatives met with Alexander's parents to explain the evaluation process and gain their consent for testing prior to setting up the date for his autism evaluation.

Shelly, the speech therapist, and Margaret, the educational diagnostician, were the other members of the evaluation team with me on the day of our play-based evaluation of Alexander. Alexander came to the play-based evaluation session with his mother. A wooden train engine was nestled securely under his arm as he entered the room. Although there were several toys on the table directly in front of Alexander as he walked into the room, Alexander spotted a figurine of a house on a shelf located on the opposite side of the room from the table and the adults in the room. As he approached the shelf, he gazed intently at the figurine and said in a lilting, high-pitched voice, "It's a house." He did not point to the figurine or glance toward his mother to secure her attention but labeled the house several times as he spoke to himself.

I approached Alexander, stood next to him, and said, "It's a house." I held a plastic water ring toss game in my hands and said, "Look, Alexander," then pushed the button on the toy, which caused the colored rings to swirl in the water. Without looking at me, Alexander directed his gaze intently toward the water toy I held in front of him. I pushed the button on the front of the toy again, causing the colored rings to swirl, but did not say a word.

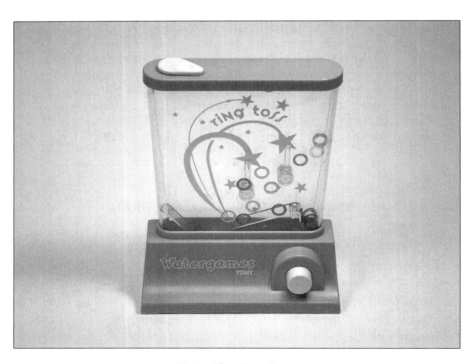

Water Ring Toss Game

Alexander reached for the toy with one hand while his other hand continued to grasp his train. "It's a green one," he said, as he labeled the color of one of the swirling rings.

I pushed the button quickly several times in succession as Alexander and I both held the toy.

"Push the button," I said, using a lilting tone of voice similar to Alexander's. He extended his index finger to push the button.

"It's a red one," I said, mirroring Alexander's pattern of labeling the colors of the swirling rings, as a red ring settled onto one of the pegs. As we both held the toy, I guided Alexander to the table, where he sat down, his attention intently focused on the visual details provided by the water and the rings. I let go of the toy and sat beside Alexander at the table, where the other adults were already seated. He carefully placed his train on the table so he could use both hands to grasp the water toy.

Our conversation had begun.

"Yellow, it's a yellow one," Alexander intoned.

"Green, it's a green one," I replied, as I tapped the transparent side of the plastic toy.

> In the area of **language and communication,** Alexander was verbal but used his language primarily to label objects in his visual environment. He did not direct his language to a listener. When he spoke, he used a high-pitched intonation and a lilting inflection.

I placed two blocks on the table that fit together to form the pictures of a vehicle. When the two pictures matched, the sound of the vehicle was triggered. I placed the blocks next to each other, making the image of a train. I slid the blocks into Alexander's view.

"It's a train," he said, shifting his attention from the water game to the train. I pointed to the outer sides of each block to prompt Alexander to push them together. He did, and leaned closer to the blocks when he heard the sound of a train engine emerge from the blocks. Alexander placed his face close to the blocks and examined the details of the pictures by tilting his head to one side and gazing peripherally at the lines created by the blocks. He became focused on manipulating the blocks to match up the other vehicles. Although Alexander accepted my help to align the blocks, he did not request help directly by asking, making eye contact, or gesturing. He did not respond when his mother, Shelly, Margaret, or I praised him or commented on his play.

The session continued, and Alexander worked with us to complete various puzzles. A pattern emerged, showing his response to toys and materials. Each time a toy or a developmental task was introduced, Alexander went through a process of visually labeling properties, such as color or shape. He placed the objects in a line as he systematically touched and looked at them. Once the objects were organized in a line, Alexander took the time to examine the visual properties of his line. He became quite captured by this routine. We were able to learn how Alexander organized his world, and we also learned how long he needed to organize objects and visually examine them before he could shift from his agenda to ours. He was able to cooperate with us and to work with a range of developmental toys and puzzles after he was given the opportunity to initially explore the sensory properties of the novel materials in his systematic way. When we used social language or praise, Alexander consistently ignored and resisted our attempts to enter into his play.

> In the area of **social relationships and emotional responses,** Alexander had a neutral facial expression, made limited eye contact, and was not responsive to social play. He moved away from us when social or language demands were made.

We knew that at home Alexander enjoyed rough and tumble play with his father and that he liked to be given tight hugs and squeezes by his mother. To invite Alexander into a social exchange with me, I handed him the end of a strip of bright yellow Lycra material. He was reluctant to grasp it at first, but I formed his fist around the material and simultaneously pulled on the other end of the fabric, creating tension before I let go. He was quick to understand the game and responded by holding his end of the fabric while I created tension and released it, causing the band of fabric to release toward him. During this exchange, Alexander looked at me for the first time. He made eye contact, showing his anticipation of this sensory game, and laughed when the band was released. Unlike most young children, Alexander never released his end of the fabric strip in imitation to "surprise" me. He was dependent on me to maintain the game by releasing my end of the fabric strip.

"Give Mommy a turn," I said, as I handed my end of the band to him and pointed toward his mother. Alexander handed one end of the band to his mother and proceeded to play with her for several exchanges before he crawled into her lap. He took her arms and placed them around his body, prompting her to embrace him in a secure squeeze. Each time she released the pressure, Alexander took her arms and pressed them until he felt the desired deep pressure on his body.

> In the area of **sensory use and interests,** Alexander focused on visual details and preferred sensory-seeking, solitary play. He sought out ways to create or feel deep pressure on his body as a way to self-regulate.

After about an hour of working and playing with Alexander, we were ready to give him a break while we discussed his behavioral profile. While he and his mother went for a walk, we took out our visual framework diagram and began discussing our impressions of Alexander. Using the framework allowed us to systematically describe his behavior.

"Let's talk about his language and communication profile first," I said.

"Well, Alexander used most of his language to label visual details, and most of his talking was self-directed rather than toward a listener," Shelley, the speech therapist, commented. "He used the same lilting cadence each time he spoke. I noticed that he referred to himself in the third person and confused his pronouns. He repeated or echoed some of our verbal directions. I heard some jargon interspersed with his meaningful speech. Most of his talking consisted of two- and three-word phrases."

"He responded best to verbal directions when we used visual contextual cues," Margaret, the educational diagnostician, noted. "When you said his name, he didn't respond, but when you put the train blocks in his line of vision, he followed your directions well. The need for visual prompts was a pattern throughout the session."

"Even though Alexander has acquired a solid vocabulary of words to label visual properties, he has difficulty using his language in a social context," I added. "He has some nice emerging language, but he was really on his own agenda throughout the session."

We moved on to discuss his behavioral profile in the area of social relationships and emotional responses. Margaret remarked that Alexander had a close and positive bond with his mother. I noted that his mother intuitively understood her son's needs and did a great job of structuring his world so it made sense to him. We all agreed that despite his obvious bond with his mother, Alexander had difficulty using and understanding basic social exchanges. He did not make eye contact, change his facial expression, or use gestures to initiate social interactions during our session, with the exception of the Lycra strip pulling game. Even then, he depended on the adults to set up the interaction. Once the structure or prompts were gone, it was difficult for him to start up a social exchange.

"Alexander consistently moved away from me when I was the source of social or language demands. He only approached me when I was a source of gaining sensory input—with the sound blocks and the Lycra strip," I recalled. "Except for showing us a delightful smile during the pull game, Alexander maintained a neutral expression throughout the session. When we showed him his reflection in the mirror, he used the mirror to look at the reflection of the line of sensory balls on the table rather than his own reflection."

"Social praise was not motivating for him," Margaret said. "He hasn't developed a sense of himself in relation to others yet. Social and language-based exchanges made him agitated and somewhat distressed."

"It was as if I wasn't even at the table," noted Shelly. "I spent an hour with him yesterday completing his language testing and he didn't react to me as someone he'd met before. He didn't respond to my presence at all during today's interview session."

"Alexander is definitely organizing his world around sensory information," I said, as we began discussing his behavioral profile in the third area of the visual framework. "His play was sensory-seeking rather than social."

"Most definitely," added Margaret. "He preferred exploring the materials on his own rather than including any of us in his play. In fact, he consistently resisted our attempts to involve us in his play. He focused on visual details and derived immense satisfaction from his prolonged inspection of the way things looked after he lined them up. He used peripheral eye gaze almost every time he created a visually interesting pattern. I noticed some body tensing and holding his breath when he was intensely captured by visual routines."

I said, "I also noticed that he pressed many of the sensory balls that had a dense texture up to his lips to experience the deep pressure feedback. He really wanted deep pressure input from his mom as well. The Lycra pull game was definitely driven by the sensory rather than the social aspects of the game. When he felt the sensory input created by the tension from the fabric strip, he was able to give me a genuine social connection. The rest of the time, his play was sensory-driven and solitary, and definitely followed his agenda.

"He was pretty resistant to shifting from his agenda to mine," I continued. "I needed the visual, manipulative materials to help him organize his behavior and to tolerate my instructional demands. But once he became interested in a task, he learned quickly. He has a lot of potential to learn, but his autism learning style interferes with his ability to follow the agenda of others.

> *The information we gained from our sensory-based diagnostic interview was only part of our comprehensive autism evaluation. Information obtained from Alexander's parents through the parent interview and standardized testing results obtained through the use of observational checklists and developmental measures were also included in our team evaluation process.*

"Let's talk about our thoughts on Alexander's diagnosis," I said. "It sounds like we're in agreement that Alexander's behavioral profile falls on the autism spectrum."

"Definitely," said Margaret.

Shelly added, "He showed differences in each of the key areas during his time with us, and our experience was consistent with the information we gathered from his parents and our other testing."

"Alexander's behavioral profile is best described as Autistic Disorder rather than PDD-NOS or Asperger's Syndrome," I commented.

"I agree," said Margaret. "He organizes his world around sensory routines and uses his language primarily to label visual objects. He followed his agenda and was resistant to social exchanges with others. His use of language is not developed enough to consider a diagnosis of Asperger's Syndrome at this point, and he lacked the social initiation qualities we see in young children with PDD-NOS."

"For me, the differential diagnosis is between Autistic Disorder and PDD-NOS," Shelly added. "I see his profile under the category of Autistic Disorder rather than PDD-NOS. His use of language and his sensory play routines were repetitive and visually based, and he resisted attempts to engage him in social exchanges. Children with PDD-NOS are more responsive to social prompts and generally use some social language during the sensory-based diagnostic interview."

"I agree," I said. "The high-functioning aspects of his profile are his ability to learn and his solid developmental skills. The most compelling way to talk about Alexander's differences in development is to talk about his high-functioning Autistic Disorder behavioral profile."

After we discussed his behavioral profile within the visual framework, it was clear that Alexander was organizing his world in terms of communication, social, and sensory development in a pattern that is best described as an autism spectrum disorder. Specifically, Alexander showed a pattern of developmental disruptions that is often seen in young children with Autistic Disorder. Our visual framework helped us describe his Autistic Disorder learning profile in a nontechnical, authentic, and individualized way.

> Alexander's pattern of differences in development was suggestive of Autistic Disorder rather than PDD-NOS or Asperger's Syndrome. He displayed the pattern of developmental differences in the areas of language and communication, social relationships and emotional responses, and sensory use and interests that are depicted in Figure 3.

We were able to gain consensus about his specific behaviors and learning pattern before we approached the label of autism. We referred to his profile as "high-functioning" Autistic Disorder because he was using verbal language and was able to complete many developmental tasks at his age level. The sensory-based diagnostic interview was a critical part of our comprehensive evaluation process and helped us determine the most compelling way to describe Alexander's developmental differences. Although we considered all of the information gathered through the comprehensive evaluation process, including standardized checklists and testing, it was only through the sensory-based diagnostic interview that we were able to establish the authentic behavioral profile described in this example.

Because we used our visual framework, we were able to discuss Alexander's pattern of development in terms that would make intuitive sense to his parents. Our suggestions for teaching Alexander would make more sense because we could link the strategies with each of the three areas of developmental disruptions depicted in our descriptive triangle. We would write a report that described Alexander's individual behavioral profile rather than simply citing technical terms such as Autistic Disorder. In chapter 6, you will read a detailed description of how the visual framework can be applied when discussing the diagnosis with parents. Writing nontechnical narrative reports is covered in a chapter 7.

How does the visual framework help clinicians make differential diagnoses among autism spectrum disorders?

When evaluation teams use the descriptive triangles provided in this chapter as part of their discussion of the child's behavioral profile during the evaluation process, they are more likely to make an accurate diagnosis. The subtle but significant differences—for example, in the child's use of language with a diagnosis of Autistic Disorder, PDD-NOS, or Asperger's Syndrome—become clearer when teams review the descriptive terms provided alongside each of the triangles. The description of differences in development provided by the visual framework helps clinicians recognize when the most compelling way to describe the child is consistent with a form of autism and when it is not. If an autism spectrum disorder diagnosis is ruled out, clinicians are left with a clear and detailed behavioral profile that will inform alternative diagnostic considerations.

Comparing Behaviors in Each of the Three Areas Across the Autism Spectrum

One of the biggest challenges for evaluation teams is how to determine where a child's behavioral profile falls on the autism spectrum. Is it best to talk about the child as having Autistic Disorder or PDD-NOS? Is the child's language more reflective of high-functioning Autistic Disorder or Asperger's Syndrome?

To assist evaluation teams in their discussion of a child's behavioral profile in the three key areas of the descriptive triangle, a comparison of behavioral characteristics across the spectrum is provided in Tables 1, 2, and 3. Table 1 organizes the behavioral features in the area of language and communication, contrasting the behaviors seen in children with Autistic Disorder, PDD-NOS, and Asperger's Syndrome. The ability to see a list of the key language characteristics for each of the three forms of autism spectrum disorders on a single page helps guide discussion about which form of autism is most descriptive of a child's behavioral profile. Table 2 provides a contrast of behaviors across the spectrum in the area of social relationships and emotional responses. Table 3 does the same in the area of sensory use and interests.

BEST PRACTICES

Autism evaluations are done in many different settings for many different purposes. Although there are numerous possible approaches to evaluating children on the autism spectrum, it is generally considered best practice when an evaluation includes the following: a review of relevant background information, interviews with parents and other caregivers, direct observation of the child, cognitive assessment, and an assessment of adaptive functioning. Looking at general emotional and behavioral concerns, as well as concerns specific to autism spectrum disorders, is important. A comprehensive medical evaluation is usually recommended as well. In an evaluation of the child, the use of both standardized and informal assessment procedures, as well as structured and unstructured methods, are considered necessary to obtain a full picture of the child. (For a more complete description of practice parameters, see the American Academy of Child & Adolescent Psychiatry Web site.)

The autism conversation techniques described in this book are an essential part of meeting best practice guidelines, because they not only result in a nuanced and richer understanding of the child, but also foster clear, helpful communication about results, prognosis, and treatment. The following sections focus on how the conversational approach is applied within the context of a best practices autism evaluation.

Table 1
Clinical Behavior Features for Autism Spectrum Disorders: Language and Communication

Autistic Disorder

Often functionally nonverbal

May use spontaneous words, but use is random or unpredictable

Common to acquire a few words by age 18 months and then stop talking

Atypical verbal language features:
- used primarily to label objects
- not directed to a listener
- unusual intonation and inflection:
  - lilting or exclamatory cadence
  - high-pitched tone of voice
- jargon interspersed with meaningful utterances
- utterances are repetitive, scripted, and rote
- expressive language better developed than receptive language

Atypical nonverbal communication features:
- extremely limited or absent nonverbal language, as shown by:
  - lack of eye contact to gain social information
  - failure to use facial expressions to communicate social information
  - unresponsiveness to eye gaze, facial expressions, or vocal changes made by caregiver

Pervasive Developmental Disorder Not Otherwise Specified (PDD-NOS)

Some use of verbal language is present

Perseverative use of phrases, topics, and questions is common

Not able to participate in reciprocal verbal exchanges

May initiate conversations in the form of questions, but has difficulty maintaining or extending conversations

Prompt-dependent on adults to structure a conversation

Questions are repeated despite being answered as the child becomes more anxious

Able to use and respond somewhat to nonverbal communication cues and requests

Asperger's Syndrome

Although early language delays may be present, language skills have developed

Atypical speech features:
- intonation and inflection have a nasal or otherwise unusual tone and cadence
- formal, rote, or scripted quality of speech
- fluency and flow become disrupted when child responds to questions
- speech is most fluent and vocabulary most developed when child is in charge of the topic

Has one or more preferred topics of conversation; prefers facts and information

Misses conversational cues for reciprocal conversation

Corrects others frequently

Literal and rule-bound

Relies on repetitive phrases to start sentences ("Well, actually...")

Table 2
Clinical Behavior Features for Autism Spectrum Disorders: Social Relationships and Emotional Responses

Autistic Disorder

Neutral facial expression; occasional facial grimacing or laughing to self

Eye gaze limited and fleeting; used mostly to "check in" to determine source of demands (i.e., to gauge information about what is coming next rather than to gain or communicate social information)

Does not initiate social exchanges and is not responsive to social play

Moves away from people when social or language demands are made

Seeks out people mainly to use them as a means to obtain a desired object

Social praise not meaningful as a source of motivation

Limited awareness of and interest in others

Inconsistent and limited response to voices

Pervasive Developmental Disorder Not Otherwise Specified (PDD-NOS)

Neutral affect, but makes more eye contact than children with classic autism

Initiates social interactions but has difficulty responding in a reciprocal way

Seeks out and is responsive to people, but interactions are limited

Transitions are highly stressful, resulting in anxiety responses

Difficulty regulating anxiety once it has escalated

Unstructured social and language interactions are experienced as highly stressful

Asperger's Syndrome

Neutral facial expression

Eye contact limited, but will stare at a listener when talking about a preferred topic

Looks away when spoken to

May have superficial social skills but misses subtle context cues

Usually has a desire for social relationships; seeks out adults and younger children

Anxious in social situations

Has difficulty self-regulating when anxious or distressed

Transitions and unexpected changes are stressful

Rule-bound and rigid in interpretation of social rules

Table 3
Clinical Behavior Features for Autism Spectrum Disorders: Sensory Use and Interests

Autistic Disorder

    Captured by a drive to complete repetitive sensory routines

    Focused on visual details

    Responds inconsistently to auditory input; may have pronounced taste, touch, or smell sensitivities

    Usually has good gross motor skills; likes to climb

    Play is sensory-seeking and solitary; uses objects for sensory input

    Play lacks social component, lacks representational or symbolic elements

    Unusual body movements and mannerisms, including hand flapping, hand and body posturing, peripheral eye gaze, running back and forth, holding breath, rocking, and vocalizing to self

Pervasive Developmental Disorder Not Otherwise Specified (PDD-NOS)

    Highly sensitive to changes in visual environment

    May have general motor clumsiness

    Sensitive to auditory input; may have pronounced taste, touch, or smell sensitivities

    Play is a mixture of approaching peers and staying by self on the perimeter

    Does not know how to respond to peers in social situations

    Seeks out repetitive play

    Likes to act out scenes from videos or cartoons

    Solitary play directed by sensory-seeking drive, but can be redirected

    Unusual body movements and mannerisms less pronounced than with classic autism

Asperger's Syndrome

    Poor body awareness results in clumsiness and awkward gait

    Rule-bound and controlling in play with others; will continue to play game alone according to rules rather than accommodate peers

    Handwriting often is difficult and frustrating

    Sensory sensitivities include clothing and food preferences

    Sensitive to sounds and visual details

    Unusual and subtle body movements and mannerisms, including picking at lips and face, body tensing, pacing, and hand posturing

Why Multidisciplinary Evaluation Teams Are Important

Diagnosing a child with an autism spectrum disorder is a serious job that requires the input and expertise of a team of qualified professionals. Although children with a diagnosis of an autism spectrum disorder share the pattern of developmental differences outlined in the previous section, each child has an individualized and complex behavioral profile. It helps to have a team of qualified professionals sort out and interpret the behavioral profile presented by the child during the evaluation process. Complex behavioral profiles can be detected when professionals from different disciplines of training participate in the evaluation process. Evaluators are less likely to make an inaccurate diagnosis when they work together as a team and discuss the child's behavioral profile.

Exactly who are the members of a multidisciplinary team? A multidisciplinary evaluation team includes professionals from various areas of training, all of whom have experience working with children with an autism spectrum disorder. Professionals trained as psychologists, speech and language pathologists, psychometricians, educational diagnosticians, and occupational therapists typically form the core of such teams. In clinical or hospital settings, psychiatrists, pediatricians, and pediatric nurses may participate as members of the team. Job titles vary from state to state and from country to country, so it is important to keep in mind that a multidisciplinary team should include professionals with the credentials and expertise to conduct autism evaluations. All team members should be familiar with the diagnostic criteria listed in current editions of formal diagnostic systems.

Because autism evaluation teams are often called upon to differentiate between a child's pattern of global developmental delays versus a pattern of developmental differences specific to autism, it is important that the team have experience recognizing and working with children with developmental disabilities as well as children with a range of typical and atypical development. Multidisciplinary teams are well equipped to play and interact with a child with a possible autism spectrum disorder in a dynamic way during the sensory-based diagnostic interview because they can work together to draw out the child's unique behavioral profile. They also are more likely to be familiar with the practical teaching strategies that need to be included in the evaluation report.

Skilled evaluation teams learn to work together and share their areas of expertise. The most effective evaluations include at least one session with the child where all of the team members participate in playing with and observing the child as part of the evaluation process. When professionals from various disciplines interact with the child during the sensory-based diagnostic interview, they are able to discuss their shared experience with the child in the three key areas depicted in the descriptive triangle. How did the child communicate with the multiple adults in the room? How did the child respond to attempts by the various adults to participate in shared play experiences? Did the child use the toys in a sensory-driven or social way? The shared experience gives professionals a basis to discuss the qualitative aspects of the child's behavioral profile in the key areas that distinguish children with autism spectrum disorders, because the evaluation team participates in an experience that encourages the child to explore his or her autism-driven agenda. Additionally, some team members notice things that others might not, so the group approach strengthens the assessment beyond each participant's particular area of expertise.

Teams that omit the group session and follow the format of having each professional work with the child individually miss this valuable opportunity to gain a rich sample of the child's behavioral profile. Time spent with the child conducting standardized speech, cognitive, and academic testing provides important information. However, in addition to the information gathered from standardized testing of the child by various professionals, applying the conversational approach to a best practices autism evaluation necessitates including a sensory-based diagnostic interview session with the child and a team of evaluators. Only the team evaluation format gives evaluators detailed information about a child's specific behavioral profile. Chapter 2 provides detailed guidelines on how a multidisciplinary team of evaluators can conduct a sensory-based diagnostic interview with a child.

The process of interviewing parents, and later discussing the child's diagnosis with them, requires evaluators to possess a wide range of interpersonal skills. Just as each child presents the evaluation team with a unique behavioral profile, each parent has his or her own communication style, and evaluators must be skilled at having meaningful conversations with parents. Chapters 3 and 6 discuss how to communicate effectively with parents during the evaluation process.

Information That Should Be Collected Prior to the Sensory-Based Diagnostic Interview

Before the members of an evaluation team can make an accurate diagnosis regarding the child's behavioral profile, they need to collect and review a range of information. A thorough parent interview, conducted in person, provides key information about the child at home. In addition, it provides the evaluators with an opportunity to have a conversation with the child's parents and to start the process of establishing the trust to work together. Both the *Autism Diagnostic Interview–Revised* (ADI-R; Rutter, LeCouteur, & Lord, 2003) and the *Monteiro Interview Guidelines for Diagnosing Asperger's Syndrome* (MIGDAS; Monteiro, 2008) can assist evaluators in conducting interviews with parents and caregivers that are specifically focused on behaviors relevant to autism spectrum disorders. The MIGDAS is designed to collect this information using a conversational approach. If the child is already in a school program, a thorough teacher interview needs to be completed as well. Conducting a teacher interview in-person allows the teacher to be included as a valuable member of the evaluation process. The MIGDAS can assist evaluators in conducting conversational autism spectrum–focused interviews with teachers as well. Once the parent and teacher interviews have been completed, the evaluation team may want to have the parents and teacher complete a general behavior checklist, an adaptive behavior form, and questionnaires specific to screening for autism spectrum disorders. A list of questionnaires specific to autism spectrum disorders can be found in the appendix.

Along with obtaining background information from parents and teachers, the evaluation team will need to conduct formal testing and informal observations of the child. Formal testing should include intellectual, achievement, and speech and language testing, as well as any standardized measures of autism spectrum disorders that the evaluation team wishes to use, such as the *Psychoeducational Profile, Third Edition* (PEP-3; Schopler, Lansing, Reichler, & Marcus, 2005), the *Autism Diagnostic Observation Schedule* (ADOS; Lord, Rutter, DiLavore, & Risi, 1999), and the *Childhood Autism Rating Scale, Second Edition* (CARS2; Schopler, Van Bourgondien, Wellman, & Love, 2010). Both the PEP-3 and the ADOS are designed to provide a standardized measure of behavior through the use of various tasks. The CARS2 is a rating scale focused on behavior relevant to autism spectrum disorders that can be completed by trained observers. Informal observations of the child should occur in school or day care settings, as they provide useful information about the child's behavior during daily routines. Whenever possible, evaluation team members should complete formal testing and informal observations prior to conducting the sensory-based diagnostic interview, as the results can help to guide the interview.

The Sensory-Based Diagnostic Interview

Once all of the aforementioned evaluation pieces have been gathered, the evaluation team is ready to conduct the sensory-based diagnostic interview. The techniques described in chapter 2 will help evaluators to conduct this interview. In addition, the MIGDAS is explicitly designed to guide evaluators through the qualitative process of conducting a sensory-based diagnostic interview with verbal children that draws out the child's autism-driven agenda.

The sensory-based diagnostic interview process provides evaluators with a way to gather information about the child's distinctive behavioral profile by encouraging the child to explore the testing toys while following his or her own agenda rather than the agenda of the examiner. It is difficult to draw out a child's authentic behavioral profile while adhering to the constraints that are an integral part of standardized measures, checklists, and observations. Including a sensory-based diagnostic interview session as part of a comprehensive evaluation process allows the evaluation team to develop a behavioral profile of the child that is difficult to obtain during standardized testing or observations. The sensory-based diagnostic interview differs from standardized evaluation situations because it is based on following the child's lead. The introduction of sensory toys and materials that are of high interest to most children with an autism spectrum disorder draws out the child's specific behavioral profile in a way that does not occur in a standardized testing situation.

The presence of a team of evaluators during the sensory-based diagnostic interview provides important social information about the child. Social referencing challenges are part of the pattern of developmental differences that make up autism spectrum disorders. In a social situation with multiple adults and one child, the social differences in a child with an autism spectrum disorder become readily apparent. Children who have an autism spectrum disorder focus on the one adult who is providing sensory toys or facts about specific topics of interest to them. They have difficulty socially referencing the team of adults or responding to social questions and interactions. The structure of the sensory-based diagnostic interview provides a sample of the child's behavioral profile based on a dynamic exchange between the child and the evaluation team.

An accurate diagnosis of Autistic Disorder, PDD-NOS, or Asperger's Syndrome depends on the ability of the evaluation team to gain access to the child's unique way of relating to the world. A sensory-based diagnostic interview allows the evaluation team to obtain a detailed sample of the child's neuro-atypical responses to sensory toys, social exchanges, and social communication opportunities. The sensory-based diagnostic interview provides a way for evaluators to have a genuine conversation with a child on the autism spectrum. The dialogue occurs when the evaluators and the child share the exploration of toys that have visual, tactile, or auditory properties. It also occurs when the evaluators follow the child's lead and discover the entry point to understanding and sharing the child's worldview.

Adding a sensory-based diagnostic interview to the use of standardized measures, or conducting one on its own, provides authentic information about the child's pattern of developmental differences. Keep in mind that no evaluation measure can determine a diagnosis. Professionals who use evaluation measures must integrate multiple sources of information and use their clinical judgment to make a diagnosis.

After the Sensory-Based Diagnostic Interview Has Been Completed

Once all of the information for the evaluation has been gathered and the team has completed the sensory-based diagnostic interview with the child, the team should meet to discuss their diagnostic conclusions and ideas for educational supports. After the team reaches a consensus on a diagnosis, an informal meeting should be held with the child's parents to discuss the results of the evaluation, including the child's specific diagnosis. Finally, a comprehensive evaluation report should be written, including specific recommendations for educational supports. Chapters 5, 6, and 7 describe how to use the conversational approach when conducting collaborative team conversations, providing diagnostic feedback to parents, and writing narrative evaluation reports.

Now that we've discussed applying the conversational approach to a best practices autism evaluation, let's discuss the specifics of how an evaluation team engages in a sensory-based conversation with a child who has an autism spectrum disorder.

How does the sensory-based diagnostic interview fit in with the use of standardized autism evaluation measures such as the ADOS and the PEP-3?

Standardized autism evaluation measures, such as the ADOS and the PEP-3, provide important information that helps evaluators recognize the pattern of behaviors associated with autism spectrum disorders. However, because the presentation of the presses, or tasks, is standardized, the examiners set the agenda and the child is required to follow it. The emphasis is placed on the quantitative scoring criteria, and subtle details about the child's responses are lost. As a result, evaluators may often feel that they have obtained a score but not a sample of behaviors that capture the child's autism-driven agenda and unique way of organizing information when relating to the world. A clear, individualized profile has not emerged, making it difficult for evaluators to describe the child in an authentic way.

The sensory-based diagnostic interview, described in detail in chapter 2, is a unique evaluation tool in that the child is encouraged to explore sensory toys and to interact with the adults by following his or her own autism-driven agenda. The toys and materials recommended for use during the sensory-based diagnostic interview were selected for their sensory properties, and children with autism spectrum disorders respond in uniquely sensory-driven ways to these materials in comparison to their neuro-typical peers. Conducting a sensory-based diagnostic interview with young children allows evaluators to experience the child's natural drive for sensory-driven play and to assess how difficult it is for the child to participate in social communication exchanges, which is not inherently possible when standardized autism evaluation measures are administered.

Because the sensory-based diagnostic interview allows evaluators to probe in more detail for language, social, and sensory interactions, they gain access to a richer and more defined behavioral profile. This additional information helps evaluators better understand and describe the child they are evaluating and facilitates individualized instructional planning. For these reasons, evaluation teams are encouraged to add a sensory-based diagnostic interview to their autism evaluation process. The sensory-based diagnostic interview can also be used as a stand-alone tool. The MIGDAS provides detailed guidelines for using a sensory-based diagnostic interview when evaluating children for possible Asperger's Syndrome, high-functioning Autistic Disorder, or high-functioning PDD-NOS.

The Best Practices Components of Team-Based Autism Evaluations

What are the best practices components?

- Ideally, the autism evaluation is conducted by a multidisciplinary team of specialists with experience in the area of autism. The following are possible areas of specialization of evaluation team members: psychology, educational testing, speech and language pathology, occupational therapy, psychiatry, and child development.
- Prior to the sensory-based diagnostic interview, the following steps are completed: a detailed face-to-face parent interview, a teacher interview, behavioral checklists (including general behavior, adaptive functioning, and autism-specific concerns), formal testing of the child (addressing intellectual, achievement, speech-language development, and autism-specific concerns), and classroom observation of the child.
- The team participates in a sensory-based diagnostic interview with the child. Sensory toys are used and topics of interest to the child are introduced to allow the team to follow the child's lead and understand and share the child's autism-driven agenda.

How is a best practices team evaluation structured?

- The autism evaluation team reviews all available information prior to evaluating the child.
- The autism evaluation team completes a sensory-based diagnostic interview with the child, in addition to any standardized autism assessments that may be used. Evaluation team members participate in a dynamic interaction with the child during the diagnostic interview.
- Once the evaluation team comes to a consensus on the diagnosis, an informal meeting is held with the child's parents to discuss the diagnosis. A comprehensive evaluation report is written, including educational recommendations that are directly linked to the child's autism spectrum disorder behavioral profile.

What are the benefits of a best practices team evaluation?

- The multidisciplinary approach allows the team to obtain a more detailed, authentic understanding of the individual child's behavioral profile.
- The face-to-face meetings with parents prior to and following the team evaluation provide opportunities to build a trusting relationship between the parents and the school. In clinical settings, the meetings provide an opportunity to discuss the diagnosis and to develop a personalized and comprehensive plan to teach the child critical skills.
- Including the sensory-based diagnostic interview as an integral part of the team evaluation process allows evaluators to develop a thorough understanding of the child's pattern of developmental differences. The information gleaned from the sensory-based diagnostic interview leads to a more accurate, accessible, and individualized diagnosis.

CHAPTER 2

Conversations With Children

The Sensory-Based Diagnostic Interview

The Neuro-Atypical Conversation in the Context of the Sensory-Based Diagnostic Interview

What is the neuro-atypical conversation?

- It is a sensory-based conversation between the evaluation team and the child.
- Sensory toys and the child's special interest topics provide the entry point for the conversation.
- Evaluation team members interact with the child throughout the session.

How is it structured?

- The conversation starts in the middle, with sensory objects or topics.
- Team members mirror the content of the child's actions or topics.
- Team members prompt social exchanges and structure transitions from the child's agenda to the agenda of the evaluation team.

What are its benefits?

- It reveals the child's authentic style of relating to the world.
- It allows for a comparison with responses by neuro-typical peers in a similar situation.
- It provides an opportunity for the evaluation team to compare their experiences.

THE NEURO-ATYPICAL CONVERSATION

Children with autism spectrum disorders structure their conversations with others in a neuro-atypical way. Compared with their neuro-typical peers, children with autism spectrum disorders follow a sensory-driven agenda rather than a social one, and the way they participate in conversations with others reflects this sensory focus. To have a shared conversation with a child on the spectrum, I've found that it works best if I begin the conversation on the child's terms. A neuro-atypical conversation is sensory-based, and sensory toys and special interest topics provide the entry point.

Understanding how to participate in a neuro-atypical conversation is the key to unlocking a child's perspective on the world during the sensory-based diagnostic interview. Rather than opening with an exchange of social information, neuro-atypical conversations start in the middle, either by exploring the sensory properties of selected toys and materials or discussing a child's favorite topics (areas of special interest). Because neuro-atypical children are sensory focused, beginning the conversation in a sensory way, rather than a social one, helps to draw out their unique worldview. The conversation unfolds best when the evaluator mirrors the content of the child's actions and topics. For children with autism who have developed verbal skills, the conversation begins in the middle by focusing on an area of special interest to the child. For children with autism who do not have fluid verbal skills, the conversation begins in the middle with the introduction of toys with sensory properties.

A neuro-atypical conversation jumps right into the child's worldview. Children who have an autism spectrum disorder react to these immediate references by relaxing and responding to the person who addresses them in this comforting way. Most children with an autism spectrum disorder rarely have an experience in which another individual initiates a conversation on such familiar terms. More commonly, either the child on the spectrum introduces a preferred topic but doesn't find a person to participate in a discussion about that topic or the child is expected to respond to social questions and comments that either hold little interest or are a source of stress. My experience has been that children with autism spectrum disorders truly enjoy the experience of having a conversation that begins on familiar terms.

Starting the Conversation in the Middle

Starting the conversation in the middle refers to the deliberate process of omitting social banter and instead introducing sensory-based materials or topics of interest to the child as the starting point for the exchange. For verbal children, I often introduce a comparison question about the child's preferred topic as the conversational entry point. Sometimes merely stating that I've heard that the child is interested in a specific topic is enough to start the conversation. Children who have an autism spectrum disorder react in a positive way to starting the conversation in the middle.

Neuro-typical children who are verbal tend to respond by quickly broadening the scope of topics to include social and reference questions. They want to know some social and background information about the adult who is speaking with them. Many neuro-typical children ask questions about why the adult is interested in the specific topics, and they want to know where the adult learned about the topics. Children on the autism spectrum typically do not ask the adult referential questions. In fact, when I ask children on the spectrum if they have any questions to ask of the adults in the room, most of the time the children ask a question about their own preferred topic rather than a social or reference question.

Even nonverbal children are capable of participating in conversations with others. For many nonverbal children with autism, the entry point into having a shared experience is through the use of sensory toys. I've found that limiting my verbalizations at the beginning of the sensory conversation with a nonverbal child with autism creates a more relaxed atmosphere for the child. Knowing in advance what types of sensory experiences the child enjoys or seeks out will help the evaluation team because they can make sure to have toys available that will be of high interest to the child when starting the sensory conversation.

> ## *What are sensory toys and how do you select them?*
>
> Sensory toys are toys that provide some form of clear sensory input. Usually the toys provide a way for the child to set up repetitive sensory routines to obtain visual, auditory, or tactile input. Conversely, sensory toys also allow evaluators to observe when the child has an aversion or sensitivity to sensory input.
>
> When searching for sensory toys, I look for toys that fall into at least one of four categories: visual cause-and-effect toys, noisemakers, tactile objects, and science toys. *Visual cause-and-effect toys* include water games, spinning light-up toys that require the child to push a button to operate them, magnetic puzzles, and other toys of that nature. *Noisemakers* include the Thunder Tube percussion instrument, plastic tubes that make a squawking sound when they are tilted back and forth, musical toys, and plastic microphones that produce an echo when one speaks into them. *Tactile objects* that are useful during the sensory-based diagnostic interview include sensory stress balls with various textures and animal pull toys that vibrate. *Science toys* include magnets, a robot arm that can be used to grasp objects, a small robot that lights up and moves, and an expanding sphere. I also like to have books or figurines of popular cartoon characters available to trigger the child's specific areas of interest. I am constantly adding new sensory toys to use during the interviews. It's amazing to me how easy it is to find sensory-based toys once you look for them.

It is helpful to have several identical toys to use as you engage in imitation and shared play routines. Having toys that are exactly the same or that fall into the same category allows you to gather more diagnostic information about the child in the area of social play. When every member of the evaluation team is spinning a light-up toy along with the child, but the child is intently focused only on the toy he or she is holding, that is powerful diagnostic information. With nonverbal children, having identical toys allows you to model actions with the toy without having to take the toy away from the child. My experience has been that children with autism spectrum disorders are more likely to carefully watch and imitate my actions with a toy when they are relaxed because they understand that I won't be taking the toy they are holding away from them.

Nonverbal children who do not have an autism spectrum disorder respond to the sensory conversation by including social referencing that children with autism do not include. For example, nonverbal children who do not have autism use eye contact, social gestures, and shared play in ways that children with autism do not.

As you can see, starting the conversation in the middle yields a great deal of qualitative information about the child's thought processes and sensory needs. This approach helps the evaluation team gather descriptive information as they compare the child's responses to those of typical children.

THE SENSORY-BASED DIAGNOSTIC INTERVIEW

As we've discussed, the neuro-atypical conversation takes place between the child and a team of evaluators during the sensory-based diagnostic interview. This interview format provides evaluators with a powerful qualitative experience of the child's worldview. One of the key features of the sensory-based diagnostic interview is the use of sensory toys and special topics of conversation to create a dynamic and interactive exchange between the child and the evaluation team. The qualitative information that is gathered when team members interact with the child provides tangible insight into how the child organizes information and relates to the world. During the interview, team members also spend time observing the child. The result is a rich and detailed sample of the child's behavioral profile.

Let's contrast the dynamic approach created by the sensory-based diagnostic interview with the more traditional clinical observational method. Presenting a child with tasks or activities and observing that child's response creates a static environment. The child is asked to follow the lead of the examiner, and the examiner remains neutral while recording the child's responses. While this observational method yields useful information, it prevents the evaluators from gaining the level of insight into the child's autism-driven agenda that a more dynamic and interactive approach yields. Since the goal of conducting an autism evaluation is to gather as much information as possible about the child, including the sensory-based diagnostic interview means adding critical information to the diagnostic process.

The sensory-based diagnostic interview works best when it is the last step in the process of gathering diagnostic information about the child. If the parent and teacher interviews have been completed, then the team will know what types of sensory toys they need to have available for the interview with the child. If all of the standardized testing has been completed, the evaluation team will have a comprehensive understanding of the child's learning profile and can select appropriate toys and materials to use during the diagnostic interview. In addition, the sensory-based diagnostic interview is the only part of the autism evaluation process that requires the entire team to be present. If all other parts of the evaluation process have been completed beforehand, the team can discuss the child's behavioral profile and come to a consensus about the child's diagnosis in their discussion immediately following the completion of the session with the child.

How was the sensory-based diagnostic interview developed?

I developed the sensory-based diagnostic interview method out of necessity. As a consulting psychologist to many school districts, my role on the autism evaluation team typically required me to assimilate a great deal of information about a child in a relatively short period of time. I found that it was difficult to draw out an individualized behavioral profile of a child during our team evaluation when we relied solely on standardized autism measures. I began gathering unusual toys with sensory properties to take to my team interviews with children as a way to engage the children in the evaluation process in a natural way.

What I found was that the children were much more likely to actively participate in the evaluation process when I started out with sensory-based play. My colleagues began to comment on how much information we were able to gather about each child's behavioral profile during the sensory-based play portions of the evaluation process. Eventually, my method of evaluating children using the sensory-based diagnostic interview became systematic enough that I was able to develop it into a structured method of working with children on the spectrum. I continue to use these methods when I evaluate children and have taught many colleagues to use the sensory-based diagnostic interview method in their work on autism evaluation teams.

Let's review several conversations that illustrate the dynamics of the sensory-based diagnostic interview between a child and a multidisciplinary autism evaluation team.

A CONVERSATION WITH A 7-YEAR-OLD CHILD SUSPECTED OF HAVING ASPERGER'S SYNDROME

This section provides an example of how to conduct a sensory-based diagnostic conversation with a child suspected of having Asperger's Syndrome. It is based on my first meeting with Paul, a second-grade student. Paul had completed standardized intellectual and achievement testing with Sharon, the educational diagnostician on the team, and Sharon accompanied me to Paul's classroom on the day of our diagnostic interview. Sharon described Paul as a quiet, serious, and polite child who did not talk much during their formal testing sessions. She had not observed a pattern of developmental differences in Paul's responses during their time together. Paul had been referred for the autism evaluation by his mother. She told the team that Paul had always seemed different from her other two sons and that after she read about Asperger's Syndrome, she wanted to pursue a professional evaluation.

> *Before you conduct your sensory-based diagnostic interview with the child, be sure to complete the parent interview, the teacher interview, and all standardized testing.*

Paul's mother told the team her son preferred playing indoors by himself rather than outside with his brothers. He was interested in dinosaurs, and more recently, in any information related to Godzilla, the Japanese monster. His mother noted that Paul had been looking at Japanese Web sites about Godzilla and had collected and watched all of the available Godzilla movies.

Paul's teacher reported that he was a quiet student who generally kept to himself. He did not socialize with the other children, but his teacher reported that he had started to join in with his peers on the playground when they were running around and playing chase. She noted that he did not offer information in class on his own, and he frequently needed her physical presence and prompting to begin his writing assignments. Paul's teacher also noted that unlike his peers, who often shared information about their family and friends, Paul would only discuss facts about dinosaurs or the solar system.

When we went to Paul's classroom to meet him for our interview, he came with us without hesitation after his teacher explained that he would be working with us. She did not tell him, however, exactly where we were going. Paul began to walk down the hallway slightly ahead of us. Paul was a nice-looking boy, with auburn hair that was well trimmed. He had a serious expression on his face that made him appear introspective. We noted that his gait was marked by a pattern of bouncing off the balls of his feet, with his torso leaning out in front of his lower body. We quickly caught up with him and matched his pace. Noting that he was wearing a T-shirt with a Tyrannosaurus rex on the front, I started the conversation by telling him I liked the T-rex on his shirt. Paul glanced down at the image and told me it was a new shirt. I told him I couldn't decide if my favorite dinosaur was T-rex or the velociraptor, and Paul began telling me the relative merits of each type of dinosaur. Then I asked him if Godzilla was considered to be a dinosaur, and he made a seamless transition from dinosaurs to a nonstop narrative of facts about Godzilla as we walked down the hallway and entered the evaluation room. I directed the conversation to the other topics we needed to cover to get to know Paul during the diagnostic interview session, but we always came back to his preferred topics. I learned, by the way, that Godzilla has a clone that was made from a minute piece of Godzilla's DNA.

This conversation example highlights several key pieces of information. Learning Paul's areas of interest beforehand allowed me to start a conversation—that began in the middle—right away. In other words, rather than establishing a context for the conversation with a series of questions or facts about who we were and what we would be doing, I started with Paul's areas of interest. Since children with autism spectrum disorders lack the social referencing framework that their neuro-typical peers have and even rely on, a conversation that starts in the middle is a perfect fit. I commented on his shirt, which provided a visual prompt to start his conversational flow. Next, rather than asking him what dinosaurs he liked, I set up a fact comparison between T-rexes and velociraptors. Most children with Asperger's Syndrome love to talk about comparisons and details related to their preferred topics. By making a comparison myself, I was mirroring the type of thought process that is often present in children on the spectrum. This put Paul at ease because the conversation began on familiar terms.

By the way, Paul never asked us where we were going, and once we arrived at the interview room, with toys on the interview table and no apparent structure or academic format, he never commented on this arrangement or asked any questions about the situation. This response to the diagnostic interview session is often seen in children with an autism spectrum disorder but is rarely seen when their neuro-typical peers are placed in the same situation.

> *Remember to start the conversation in the middle.*
> *Frame questions as comparisons.*
> *Focus on facts and information.*

Let's stop for a moment and compare my interaction with Paul to an interaction I might have with another second-grade student from his class. Most second-grade children would answer a question about their T-shirts, but many would use the initial exchange as a bridge to ask the adult a social context question, such as "Where are we going?", "What toys do you have?", "Do you come to my school often?", or "Are you going to talk to anybody else from my class?" Or they may share information about social relationships with their parents, siblings, friends, and teacher. Many second graders love dinosaurs and even wear dinosaur shirts. What is striking about the conversation with Paul is not so much his interest in dinosaurs, but the fact that he stuck almost exclusively to facts about dinosaurs rather than expanding the conversation to include social information. Most second-grade children are full of questions in new situations.

> *Neuro-typical children ask social questions and make social comments even when the evaluator starts the conversation in the middle.*

As is typically seen in children with an autism spectrum disorder, Paul's interaction with us was striking for the absence of his need to ask us any referential questions. If I had asked Paul social questions instead of starting our conversation with his areas of interest, it would have been more difficult to gain the rich, detailed picture of his interior world that we gained by the end of our conversation.

Paul was a bright child who was interviewed at his school. If I had first asked him how he liked school, who his friends were, and what his favorite subjects were, he would have provided brief answers to my questions. I would not have obtained the information I needed, however, to effectively describe the qualitative differences that make up Paul's language, social, and sensory responses to the world around him. I would not have been able to talk with his parents and teachers about him in a compelling and authentic way.

> At some point during the sensory-based diagnostic interview, shift the conversation from the child's agenda to your own.

By starting the conversation in the middle and moving to more conventional topics later in the interview, we were able to get a more genuine and open response from Paul. We not only got to know him better, but we could also see the marked contrast between the way he discussed his preferred topics and the way he responded to questions of a more social nature. We were able to note how his fluency faltered and how he hesitated and became less detailed when he responded to spontaneous topics other than dinosaurs and Godzilla facts. Simple requests, such as "Tell me a time when you felt happy" or "Tell me about your friends," resulted in longer pauses and very short responses. This pattern of social language challenges paired with a fluent ability to recite facts and information about a few preferred topics is one of the hallmark differences seen in children with Asperger's Syndrome.

The goal of the team evaluation process is to provide a structure for the child that will bring out a detailed picture of that child's use of language, ability to relate to others in a social context, and sensory differences. It is highly unusual for a student in school to be in a room with multiple adults and no other children. When the room contains a set of interesting but somewhat unusual toys and no demands for academic performance, children who have an autism spectrum disorder respond in a distinctively different way from their neuro-typical peers.

I mentioned that when we went to get Paul from his classroom, I was accompanied by Sharon, the educational diagnostician. Sharon had previously spent several hours with Paul completing the standardized intellectual and achievement tests that were part of his comprehensive evaluation. One would expect that when she greeted him, Paul would show some sign of recognition, acknowledgment, or familiarity with her. Sharon is an engaging adult who works well with children, easily establishing rapport. However, Paul did not respond to her with social reciprocity.

This brings up another point: the use of a team of adults yields important social information. Paul talked exclusively to me as we went down the hallway, and this continued in the interview session. Even when I deliberately included Sharon in our conversation by saying things like "Oh, Sharon, you told me you liked the first Godzilla movie the best," and she responded in some detail, Paul did not direct his statements to her. This is markedly different from the social behavior seen in most second-grade children in a conversation with two adults and no peers. Most second-grade children would direct their responses to the adult asking the question. They would offer social information about themselves and ask referential questions about the toys and the testing situation. They would spontaneously expand the conversation beyond the narrow limits of facts and information about a small range of specific topics.

> *The use of a team of adults allows for a comparison between children with autism spectrum disorders and their neuro-typical peers in a similar situation. Neuro-typical children interact with all of the adults in the room, whereas children with autism spectrum disorders focus their attention on the adult who provides the sensory topics or materials.*

To gain insight into Paul's play and interest in materials, we provided him with several unusual toys on the table in the interview room. Paul immediately began to play with a water ring toss game by pushing the button repeatedly and watching the colored rings swirl in the water as some of them landed on the plastic stakes inside the game. Like many children with an autism spectrum disorder, Paul became visually captured by the game. Even when we praised him for getting some of the rings on the stakes, Paul did not reference us or include us in his play in any way. This lack of social referencing is commonly seen in this situation among children with autism spectrum disorders, but rarely seen among neuro-typical children. Even when I placed my face on the opposite side of the toy and began talking to Paul, his eyes did not move from watching the movements of the colored rings. Paul was clearly becoming visually captured by the sensory features of the toy.

We also had six sensory stress balls that had various textures and colors. Paul was reluctant to touch or explore the softer ones, but one engaged him, a ball with smaller balls inside the latex exterior. He spent about 20 minutes manipulating it in a consistent pattern of squeezing and pulling. Paul reached for the ball when we began to ask him questions about school and other activities. It became apparent that he was using the ball as a way to regulate his anxiety during the open-ended part of our conversation.

> *Is the child's play primarily sensory-seeking or social in nature? Sensory toys and novel fidget items provide an entry point for the sensory-based conversation.*

Because many children with autism spectrum disorders show sensitivity to unexpected sounds, we took out a cylindrical tube with a coil attached to it and shook it at one point during our conversation. The tube has a pattern of lightning on the exterior and is actually a percussion instrument called a Thunder Tube. When Paul heard the rumbling sound, he visibly flinched as he searched for the source of it. Once he saw the tube, he told us that he had a "minor flinch problem" and expressed an interest in holding the tube to see how it worked. When we asked him what he thought the noise sounded like, Paul told us it sounded like "lightning." Once he was in control of the tube, Paul began to shake it repeatedly and became intensely focused on the sound being produced. He engaged in some involuntary body tensing during his exploration of the tube. When he was finally finished with it, he handed it back to me and told me that it made "a seismic sort of sound."

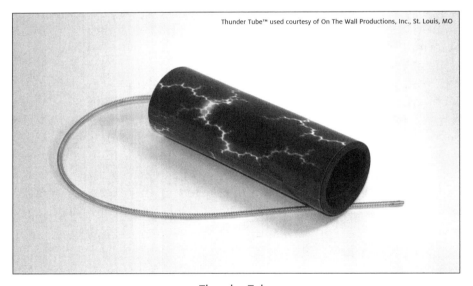

Thunder Tube

This pattern of Paul's sensory responses to the various toys during our conversation is typically seen during diagnostic interviews with children who have an autism spectrum disorder. Another common response that Paul displayed was difficulty finding the precise word to describe an object. Hence, when Paul saw the lightning picture on the tube, he told us the noise sounded like lightning instead of thunder. Paul's body tensing and repetitive squeezing of the sensory stress ball were also reflective of the sensory differences seen in children with an autism spectrum disorder.

A CONVERSATION WITH A NEURO-TYPICAL CHILD

Let's compare Paul's responses to those of Sam, a second-grade peer who had some language delays and attention and focusing challenges. Sam was an energetic boy who wore glasses and smiled often. Because Sam had a well-developed interest in the *Star Wars* movies and was socially immature with his peers, he was referred for an autism evaluation. On the morning of our scheduled sensory-based diagnostic interview, I went to his classroom to meet him and accompany him to the interview room. When Sam's teacher introduced us, Sam smiled at me and asked me where we were going. As we walked down the hallway, I started my conversation with Sam by asking him a question about *Star Wars*. "What is Luke Skywalker's home planet?" I asked. Sam responded by telling me the answer, which was Tatooine. I made the comment that now I knew where Luke was born, and Sam corrected me, telling me that Luke was not born on Tatooine but in a distant nebula. After a few more exchanges about *Star Wars*, Sam asked me what else we were going to talk about. When we arrived at the interview room, he looked at the two other adults in the room, smiling and greeting them as I introduced Sarah and George, the other members of the evaluation team.

Sam showed an immediate interest in the water game toy as he sat at the table.

"Cool!" he said. "I had one of these that had dolphins in it."

He immediately began to manipulate the water game, successfully getting the colored rings to land on the spikes inside the game. "Hey, watch this," he commented, as the rings began to pile up.

"You're good at this," Sarah said. Sam glanced up at her and nodded.

Sam continued to fiddle with the water game, but stopped his play to sit back and look at the adults in the room as he answered our questions and made comments of his own. I continued to make comments about various aspects of the *Star Wars* universe, and Sam began to smile and roll his eyes at the other adults.

"Can't you talk about anything else?" he finally said.

Sam's exploration of the sensory balls consisted of pulling and stretching each before throwing one of them back and forth from hand to hand. When I cupped my hands together, he immediately threw it to me and we started a game of catch. He threw a ball to George and another one to Sarah. George started a game of "hot potato," a fast-paced game of throwing one of the balls between people in a rather frenetic way. It was apparent that Sam delighted in the social aspects of this game. It is important to note that children with autism spectrum disorders do not typically include the examiners in social or reciprocal play.

> *The sensory toys allow for a comparison between neuro-typical and neuro-atypical responses in children when they are placed in the diagnostic interview situation.*

Children who have other types of neurological differences but who do not have the pattern of differences associated with an autism spectrum disorder show a clear social component to their play and exploration of the materials. Just as Sam did, they watch the adults to see the response to their actions and respond to comments made by the adults. They ask questions about the toys. They do not become caught up in repetitive sensory play. They are not compelled to talk about a narrow range of topics.

A CONVERSATION WITH A CHILD WITH AUTISTIC DISORDER

Now I'd like to give you an example of a sensory-based conversation I had with Taylor, a 3-year-old nonverbal child with Autistic Disorder. Taylor was an only child who had a close, positive relationship with his mother. He sought her out when he needed something and enjoyed cuddling with her on his own terms. He liked to be chased by his father and to be tickled and swung in the air. Taylor's parents described their son as a good-natured child who preferred to play alone. He liked to gather toys and objects, placing them in a pile in front of him. After he created a cluster of toys, he liked to flip them around with his fingertips. His mother stated that Taylor did not like to apply a firm touch to objects, and preferred having her open containers and manipulate toys. He frequently took her hand and directed it to the desired object, using it as a tool. Taylor's mother commented that she noticed her son did not look her in the eye or search her face for information when they interacted. Although Taylor did not talk or use words to ask for things, he frequently vocalized to himself. His vocalizations consisted of repetitive sounds, gibberish or jargon, and an occasional word or phrase. When Taylor was running back and forth across the room in a repetitive pattern, his vocalizations increased in intensity and volume.

Taylor liked to climb and preferred being barefoot. Once his shoes were off, he liked to remove all his clothes. His mother commented that he was learning to put his socks on by himself and when he had trouble getting them on his feet he placed his socks on his hands. Taylor walked on his tiptoes at times. He could be fearful of loud noises. He enjoyed watching videos and selected the ones he wanted by looking at the graphics on the disc. His mother recalled that Taylor liked to watch himself in the mirror and had recently begun to recognize photographs of himself. She remarked that Taylor resisted looking at photographs or books with her, preferring to flip the pages of the album or book while seated alone.

> *Talking with Taylor's parents before the team evaluation session allowed us to match the sensory toys to his particular interests.*

Taylor's mother saw a television show that described autism and requested the team-based evaluation after she recognized some autistic characteristics in Taylor. Both parents brought Taylor to the evaluation session. The evaluations for early childhood students in Taylor's school district were conducted in the speech-language therapist's office. Her room contained a kidney-shaped table with several chairs, bookshelves, counters with books, and a few toys.

When we met Taylor and his parents in the school office and walked with them to the evaluation room, Taylor held his mother's hand and walked on the balls of his feet with his head turned to one side. He did not look at his parents or the evaluators, but focused on taking in the visual details provided by the lines on the floor and objects on the walls. He had the round, slightly chubby cheeks of a toddler and his dark hair curled around the nape of his neck. He had striking hazel eyes that rarely focused on our faces. Since we knew Taylor liked to gather objects into clusters, we had placed several sensory balls on the table prior to his arrival.

Sensory Balls

Once we entered the room, we directed Taylor's mother to walk to the table with him so Taylor would direct his visual attention to the balls. When Taylor saw the balls, he let go of his mother's hand and stood in front of the table, his eyes transfixed on the visual details they provided. One was a Koosh ball with multicolored strings fanning out from its center. Another was a latex ball with a stubby surface and colored balls clustered inside it. A third was a smooth blue latex ball that changed to purple when it was squeezed. As Taylor stood in front of the balls, I sat in the chair to his left without speaking. I picked up the Koosh ball with the long strands and began to twirl it as I held the ball by one strand. Taylor tensed his body and moved his head closer to the ball. When it stopped spinning, I placed my hand next to it but hesitated before spinning it a second time. I was starting my conversation with Taylor. He reached up and touched my hand, pushing it toward the Koosh ball. I spun the ball again. As Taylor watched the pattern of colors move in a circle, I placed a chair behind him and he sat down. He had made a successful transition into the evaluation setting.

> *When children are nonverbal, start the conversation with sensory objects. Talk as little as possible until the sensory conversation has begun.*

I placed the Koosh ball on the table in front of him, and Taylor reached out his hands to touch it. He applied the lightest possible touch, stroking the outermost edges of the strands with the tips of his fingers. Using both hands, he created a vibrant, colorful source of constant movement. I wanted Taylor to enter into more of an interaction with me, so I picked up the ball that changed colors when it was squeezed and held it in front of him. As soon as he shifted his attention to it, I squeezed the ball several times, creating the visual effect. Taylor took this ball and pressed it briefly to his lips. He went back to stroking the Koosh ball. Next, I held the stubby-surfaced ball in the palm of my hand in front of him. He again shifted his attention to the new object, but this time he was unwilling to touch it. He glanced at me, establishing fleeting eye contact. Then he pushed my hand away from him and resumed his light touching of the Koosh ball.

Now that Taylor had acknowledged my presence, we began our dialogue. It was only then that I started to use words. When you are working with children who have autism spectrum disorders and are functionally nonverbal, sensory toys provide the entry point for a genuine conversation. Talking at the beginning of the encounter communicates to the child that you are just another source of stressful verbal demands.

Their reaction to verbal demands is usually to retreat. Talking makes it more difficult for the child to relax and settle into a true conversation.

As Taylor continued to touch the sensory ball he had selected as his favorite, I introduced a new sensory toy—a plastic globe that created spinning lights when a small button was depressed on the handle. Once again, I held the toy in front of Taylor until he directed his attention to it. I depressed the button to start the spinning lights, then lifted my finger to turn off the lights. I did this several times, saying "On...off...on...off" to match the visual sequence. I handed the toy to Taylor, and he rotated it in his hands, examining the details of the globe and the handle. I had a matching plastic globe and began to make my globe turn on and off. Taylor watched me and soon began to push the button on his globe to make the lights spin. The Koosh ball was still on the table in front of him, but Taylor was focused on mastering the cause-and-effect relationship created by the button on the plastic globe.

Spinning Globe Wands

It can be helpful at times to have two identical objects to keep the conversation going without interruption.

By now Taylor was showing me that he could anticipate the flow of our conversation: I would introduce interesting toys and materials, and he would watch me and then explore the toys on his own. It was helpful to have two identical toys at times because it allowed us to continue our conversation without the interruption that occurs when a toy is taken from a child to show the child how to use it. When Taylor placed his face close to his globe, I did the same with mine. When he made a vocalization, I mirrored his comment. The experience of having another person mirror his actions helped Taylor include me in his exploration of the sensory toys and gave me insight into his worldview.

Taylor was showing us how quickly he learned cause-and-effect routines. He showed us that he was able to imitate when given a visual model and that he was able to understand and anticipate routines. His parents were in the room with him, along with three other adults gathered around the table. The presence of multiple adults in the evaluation session allowed for a comparison between how Taylor responded to the social aspects of the setting and how a neuro-typical child the same age would respond. In Taylor's case, he did not reference his parents or the team of evaluators during the session. Even when we voiced social praise and encouragement or tried to secure his attention by calling his name, Taylor did not respond. He was captured by the sensory toys and the experience of participating in the sensory conversation. He oriented his body toward me and established fleeting eye contact several times throughout the play session, because he was actively engaged in sharing a sensory experience with me. I was communicating with him in a way that made perfect sense to him, and he responded by staying with me throughout the session.

> *Having the primary evaluator seated to the child's left allows the child to work in a sequence from left to right as tasks are introduced.*

Once the routine of sensory play was established, it was time to introduce a few structured demands. Rather than remove Taylor's preferred toy, I introduced the structured task by placing the materials on the table in front of him. In Taylor's case, the first structured task was a sorting and stacking task consisting of a strip of wood embedded with five colored dowels of increasing size from left to right. The first dowel was red, with the number "1" painted on the wooden strip under the dowel. The remaining dowels were orange, yellow, green, and blue, with the corresponding numbers 2 through 5 painted under each colored dowel. To help Taylor shift his agenda from the colored Koosh ball to the sorting task, I held one of the colored rings in the palm of my hand until he looked at it. I gestured with the ring toward the dowel strip and said, "Put on." Then I held the ring close to him and he took it from me. He hesitated and then placed the ring on the correct dowel, matching the colors. Several times, Taylor placed the colored ring on the incorrect dowel. Each time, I took the ring off the dowel, placed it on the table in front of him, and said, "Fix it." He did. When he had placed all of the rings on the dowels, we all verbally praised him and I indicated the task was finished by saying "Finished." Next, I directed Taylor to take the entire wooden strip and place it in a basket on the table to his right.

As soon as he finished this task, I directed his attention back to a sensory toy. After the first several tasks, Taylor clearly sought out his favorite, the Koosh ball. I began introducing other sensory toys in between structured tasks, including several small animal toys that vibrated when a string was pulled. He was able to shift his attention away from the Koosh ball and enjoy the exploration of novel sensory toys. The pattern of shifting between developmental activities that were on the evaluator's agenda and activities that were on the child's sensory-seeking agenda allowed us to gain an authentic view of Taylor's learning style. He was less resistant to our demands because he anticipated the sequence of working with us followed by the opportunity to engage in a sensory, self-directed activity.

> *Once the child engages in a sensory conversation with the primary evaluator, add interactions with other team members.*

Once Taylor had established a conversation with me, it was time to include the other team members in the evaluation process. Sarah, the speech-language therapist, was seated to Taylor's right. We switched seats so she would be in the flow of Taylor's established conversational entry point. Children with significant autism oftentimes respond best to new people if they are introduced within a previously established routine. Sarah was able to gain important information about Taylor's language and communication skills by entering the conversation in this way. At the end of the evaluation session, we had a comparison of her direct interactions with Taylor and mine.

Sarah placed a puzzle in front of Taylor. The puzzle had six pictures inset into the wooden frame and each picture fit into a geometric shape. The picture of a clock was inset into the circle shape, a school bus into the rectangular shape, and so on. Geometric-shaped pieces in solid colors fit over the inset pictures. Sarah handed the shaped wooden pieces to Taylor one at a time. As Taylor placed each solid colored piece over the corresponding picture, Sarah named the picture.

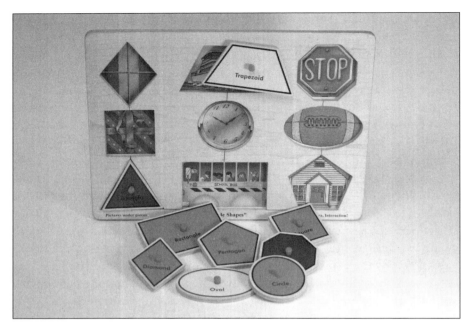

Shape Inset Puzzle

"It goes on the *school bus*," she said, as Taylor placed the yellow rectangular piece on top of the bus. She continued to label each picture as Taylor placed the puzzle pieces into the jig.

When he put the final shape in place, Sarah held out one hand and said, "Find the *school bus*."

Taylor briefly moved his hand over the board and handed Sarah the rectangular piece.

Sarah continued by asking, "Where's the *pizza*?"

Taylor handed her the triangular piece, which covered the picture of the pizza, and continued to correctly recall the picture under each shape when Sarah gave him the verbal prompt. In this way, Taylor was able to show us that his memory for visual details and his understanding of language when he was given visual prompts were well developed.

Taylor's parents were in the evaluation room, and they not only observed Taylor's responses to us and to our materials, but they also provided information about how their son responded to them under the circumstances of the play-based evaluation session. Once Taylor became engaged with the sensory toys and our conversational routine, he did not glance up to find his parents or include them in his play in any way. His parents told us after the session that Taylor's response to them in the room and his response to the materials represented his authentic pattern of behavior. They told us that they were surprised, however, at how long he sustained his attention to various tasks and how cooperative he had been in working with us. The sensory foundation provided by our neuro-atypical conversational approach with Taylor allowed us to get to know him in a genuine way in a relatively short period of time.

A CONVERSATION WITH A CHILD WITH PERVASIVE DEVELOPMENTAL DISORDER NOT OTHERWISE SPECIFIED (PDD-NOS)

Here's an example of a sensory-based conversation with a child with a PDD-NOS developmental profile. Emily was a beautiful 7-year-old girl with long, curly red hair. She was in the first grade when she was referred for an autism evaluation. When she was initially seen by the autism evaluation team, Emily had a diagnosis of a speech and language impairment. She had received early intervention and assistance in the area of speech and language development and had made great progress. Emily attended kindergarten, and with the support of the special education teacher and the teaching assistant, she was able to follow her daily routine and keep up with the class. For the most part, she preferred playing by herself, but she would often play beside her peers. Her preferred activity was staying in the dress-up center and acting out Disney Princess scenes in front of the mirror. When her teacher directed Emily to move to the next activity, she was usually able to do so after one or two prompts. Emily continued to receive speech and language therapy throughout her kindergarten year and her language skills showed gradual but consistent improvement.

When Emily started first grade, her underlying pattern of developmental differences became more pronounced. Her parents and teachers noticed that Emily asked questions about her schedule repeatedly and continued to ask questions even when she was given the answer. She showed a high level of anxiety during transition times and resisted moving from her preferred activities—using the computer and looking at books—to the activities being completed by the rest of the class. She seemed to be in her own world at times, talking to herself and acting out scenes from videotapes about Disney Princesses. When she talked to her peers, Emily oftentimes started the conversation by repeating a phrase from a Disney Princess video, such as "I just love happy endings!" from *Sleeping Beauty*, or "Now that's more like it!" from *Cinderella*, or "Bravo! That was wonderful!" from *Beauty and the Beast*. These phrases were delivered with an exclamatory intonation, and Emily did not vary the way she made her princess comments. As she spoke, she twirled in a circle or curtsied while holding the hem of her imaginary dress. She usually did not wait to see what response she would get from her peers, but danced off on her own before returning to make another statement.

On the day of the team evaluation, Martha, the speech pathologist on the team, and I went to Emily's first-grade classroom to get her. We were introduced to Emily by her teacher, and when we said hello, Emily blurted out a high-pitched "Hi!" while twisting her fingers together in front of her. She glanced fleetingly in our general direction but did not make eye contact or look at us. When Emily's teacher told her she would be going with us, Emily bolted for the door and began walking quickly down the hallway without us. We caught up with her and told her where we were going, but she did not slow her pace.

"I like Disney Princesses," I said, as I walked beside Emily.

"So do I!" she replied. I waited to see if she would elaborate, but she just kept walking. She began walking a little closer to me and stopped twisting her hands. She continued to clasp them by her fingertips in front of her, but visibly relaxed.

"The seaweed is always greener…" I half-sang the start of a song from *The Little Mermaid*.

"…in somebody else's lake!" Emily finished the line. "Did you know that Ariel is a beautiful princess, but Ursula is an evil octopus!"

"Who is more evil, Ursula or Maleficent?" I asked, offering her a comparison question. (Maleficent is a character from the *Sleeping Beauty* movie.)

"Don't talk about Maleficent! She is too scary! She turns into a dragon!" Emily started twisting her hands again.

"Okay. She is too scary! Who is the most beautiful, Ariel or Rose?"

"Ariel is the Little Mermaid and Rose is the Sleeping Beauty!"

"I know, I know, but who is the most beautiful princess?"

"Rose is very beautiful! But something bad happens. 'Before the sun sets on her sixteenth birthday, she shall prick her finger…and die!'" Emily quoted the prophetic curse from *Sleeping Beauty*.

"I like her fairy godmothers," I said.

"Their names are Flora, Fauna, and Merriweather!" replied Emily.

"Does Merriweather wear a pink dress or a blue dress?" I asked.

"Merriweather wears a blue dress."

I could tell that during our conversation Emily was picturing the characters from the Disney movie *Sleeping Beauty*. I thought of a scene from the movie involving the fairy godmothers and asked Emily about it.

"Do you remember when Merriweather and Flora had a fight over Rose's dress?" I asked.

"They used their wands and said, 'Make it pink! Make it blue!'" Emily quoted the line from the scene.

"When they had the fight with their wands, what happened to the dress, Emily?"

"It was pink *and* blue!" She smiled and tensed her body in response to thinking about the scene.

> By naming familiar characters from her favorite videos, we gave Emily the sensory entry point to have a genuine conversation with us.

By this time, we had entered the evaluation room and were seated at the table. Emily sat between Martha and me. She had her body turned toward me in anticipation of continuing our conversation about movie scenes she could picture in her head. It was time for Martha to become an active part of the conversational circle.

"Emily, my friend Miss Martha likes Disney Princesses too. Ask her about her favorite princess," I said.

Emily turned her entire torso in the chair to face Martha. "Do you like Ariel as your favorite princess?" she asked.

Martha was ready to jump in because she had done her princess homework.

"I like Ariel and Jasmine!" she told Emily in a mildly exclamatory tone that mirrored Emily's speech pattern.

"I like Ariel, too! Did you know that Jasmine is the princess in *Aladdin*!" Emily replied.

"But she'd better watch out for that bad guy! Oh no, I can't remember his name!" Martha responded.

"Jafar! She has to watch out for Jafar!" said Emily. "But Aladdin will help her!"

The unfolding conversation about Disney Princess movies allowed us to gain a rich, detailed understanding of how intensely captured Emily became by the visual images she carried in her head. The ease with which she fell into the conversation with us about a variety of princess movies and her recall of dialogue and scenes provided us with a keen understanding of how her internal agenda captured her attention.

> Mirroring Emily's exclamatory prosody resulted in a smooth conversational flow.

Once we had a qualitative experience of participating in a conversation with Emily that centered on her internal focus, we were ready to introduce more traditionally structured activities. We started by drawing Emily's attention to the water ring toss game that was on the table in front of her.

"Emily, let's play this game now!" Martha said.

"Okay!" Emily replied as she began to press the button on the front of the game. Colored rings began swirling in the water, floating down to land on the small spikes inside the game.

"Oh, however beautiful they are!" she said, sounding like a princess as she watched the movement of the rings.

She stopped talking as she focused on the visual input provided by the ring toss game. Many children with PDD-NOS have difficulty talking and exploring visually interesting toys simultaneously. This was the case with Emily.

Martha and I remained quiet. We were waiting to see if Emily would resume a conversation with us or reference us in any way. She did not. After a few minutes of watching Emily play, I said, "May I have a turn?"

Without looking at me or removing her gaze from the moving rings, Emily agreeably said, "Sure!" She pushed the ring toss game in my direction. Emily sat in the chair with her torso leaning forward so her tousled red hair partially covered her face.

I asked her how the toy worked.

"You push the button!"

"Should I push it fast or slow?"

"Push it fast!"

I quickly pushed the button multiple times. The rings did a wild dance in the water. Emily let out a short, delighted laugh and her eyes remained glued to the action going on in the ring toss game. She leaned a little farther forward and held her fingers together in front of her.

"This is so fun!" I exclaimed. "Whose turn is it next?"

"Mine!" said Emily, as she reached for the base of the ring toss game.

After a minute, Martha said, "Oh, that looks like fun!"

> *Prompt the child to take turns. Wait to see if the child is able to generalize the social rule and spontaneously offer a turn to one of the team members.*

Emily did not respond or offer Martha a turn.

"Emily, who did not get a turn yet?" I asked.

"Here, you take a turn," said Emily, as she pushed the base of the toy toward Martha. Her eyes remained focused on the rings. Martha took a long turn while Emily watched and waited. Emily was not able to spontaneously extend the social reciprocity of taking turns. This is often the case with children who have a PDD-NOS developmental profile. They are dependent on the social structure provided by adults to interpret and follow social cues.

It is important to note that Emily did not offer to talk about her obvious love of princesses until we provided the structure and prompts to do so. Emily had been in school programs since she was 3 years old and had learned to restrict her comments with adults. It was only when we invited her to talk about her interest that we were able to gain a picture of how profoundly involved her interior life was with her replaying of the content and images of her beloved movies.

Many young girls are enthralled with the Disney Princesses. In fact, parents can buy an astonishing number of videos about Disney Princesses for their children. Emily's conversation with us revealed her neuro-atypical interest in princesses when she focused on repeating dialogue and became distressed at the mention of one of the villains.

One other difference was Emily's preoccupation with a subject that is usually a fascination for preschool girls. By the time most girls are in first grade, their interests have matured beyond Disney Princesses. Emily's interest in dialogue and visual details, paired with the socially immature subject matter, showed a neuro-atypical pattern of interest often seen in children with a PDD-NOS developmental profile. By doing our homework and learning a few names and facts about Disney Princesses, we were able to enter Emily's interior world. It was a happy and fascinating place that competed with her ability to focus on activities and relationships in her school and home life. Our understanding of the degree to which Emily was pulled into her own agenda was an essential part of developing practical strategies to help her learn and participate socially in the first-grade world surrounding her.

Why did we look at Emily as a child with PDD-NOS and not Autistic Disorder or Asperger's Syndrome? In addition to the sensory-based diagnostic interview described in this section, we considered all of the information gathered during the autism evaluation process when making our diagnostic decision. We ruled out Autistic Disorder because Emily was able to initiate social conversations and use her language in more fluid and appropriate ways than a child with an Autistic Disorder profile. Moreover, she consistently initiated and responded to social prompts in a way that is more commonly associated with PDD-NOS than with Autistic Disorder. We ruled out Asperger's Syndrome because Emily lacked the developed language skills and use of language that characterize children with Asperger's Syndrome.

A VALUABLE ADDITION TO THE EVALUATION PROCESS

The examples described in this chapter show how an evaluation team can establish a neuro-atypical conversation with children on the autism spectrum. Children enjoy the process of exploring sensory-based toys and topics during the diagnostic interview session, and as a result, an authentic sample of their style of relating to the world emerges. Unlike more traditional clinical interviews, neuro-atypical conversations are interactive exchanges between the adults and children that revolve around sensory-based objects and topics of conversation. The characteristics of each of the three forms of autism spectrum disorders, as listed in the behavioral profiles described in chapter 1, can be quickly identified and linked to individual children when evaluation teams have neuro-atypical conversations with children as part of their evaluation process. The neuro-atypical conversation adds a valuable piece to the evaluation process.

Keep in mind that in addition to the information gained from the sensory-based diagnostic interview, the final diagnosis a team makes for a child includes information gathered from other facets of the evaluation process. Information gathered through the parent and teacher interviews, behavior checklists, observations in the school setting, and other standardized testing are also considered as an evaluation team determines a child's diagnosis. The sensory-based diagnostic interview provides a unique and detailed profile of the child's style of relating to the world that is difficult to draw out using the other parts of the diagnostic process.

Now that we've discussed neuro-atypical conversations with children on the autism spectrum, let's move on to talk about how to have authentic and meaningful conversations with their parents.

How does the sensory-based diagnostic interview change when an adolescent is evaluated?

In many ways, the sensory-based diagnostic interview follows the same pattern with adolescents as it does with younger children. When an adolescent is suspected of having Asperger's Syndrome or a high-functioning form of an autism spectrum disorder, it is helpful if the evaluators are prepared to discuss the adolescent's preferred topics by asking relevant questions and making comparison statements using facts and information about the topics. The sensory toys selected should be age-appropriate. Science toys and high-interest visual prompts, such as video game strategy guides or books, work well with adolescents. For adolescents who like to draw, encouraging them to draw a preferred picture also works well. Sensory stress balls can be introduced for children of any age.

When the adolescent is nonverbal or is functioning with significant autistic and developmental delays, the conversation will be most effective if evaluators limit their talking and introduce sensory-based toys and materials.

The Team Evaluation Process for the Sensory-Based Diagnostic Interview

What is the team evaluation process?

- It is an interactive exchange between the child and a team of evaluation specialists from various disciplines.
- It involves finding a sensory entry point so evaluators can actively engage in a play-based conversation with the child.
- It provides a qualitatively different experience from observing behavior in the traditional clinical sense.

How is it structured?

- Sensory toys, sensory-based conversational techniques, and direct interaction between the child and the evaluators form the conversation.
- One team member leads the conversation, but all team members participate at some point during the process.
- The session includes sensory play that follows the child's agenda as well as play that is structured by the evaluators.

What are the benefits of having a team?

- Having one child and multiple adults in the evaluation session provides a unique situation for interactions and play.
- The team process allows for an authentic sample of the way the child organizes and uses language, social, and sensory input that is not always apparent during standardized testing or during structured conversations or work sessions.
- Evaluation team members have access to a shared sample of interactions with the child to inform their diagnostic discussion.

CHAPTER 3

Conversations With Parents

The Parent Interview

The Conversational Approach to Interviewing Parents

What is the conversational approach to interviewing parents?

- It is a face-to-face conversation that allows parents to form an authentic connection with the evaluator prior to the team evaluation.
- The conversational format allows parents to tell stories that illustrate their present concerns about their child.
- Parents are encouraged to talk about what they like best about their child in addition to discussing challenging behaviors.

How does the evaluator structure the conversation?

- Questions provide the entry point for a conversational exchange between the parents and the evaluator.
- The face-to-face conversation allows the evaluator to ask follow-up questions to gather qualitative and descriptive information from parents about their child and their expectations regarding the evaluation process.
- The evaluator adapts his or her communication style to the style of the parents.

What are the benefits of the conversational approach?

- Parents gain a sense of being valuable participants in their child's evaluation process.
- Participating in the conversation helps parents deal with the emotional aspects of having a child with developmental differences.
- Information provided by the parents helps the evaluation team anticipate sensory toys to use and topics to address during the sensory-based diagnostic interview with the child.

PARENTS NEED TO TELL THEIR STORIES

"I wanted you to evaluate Mike because I wasn't happy with his first autism evaluation," said Mike's mother. She had asked her son's school district to provide a second opinion because she disagreed with the initial evaluation findings. We were meeting to have our first conversation regarding her concerns about Mike.

She held up Mike's evaluation report. "To be honest with you, I was really surprised to read the parent section of this report. Nobody interviewed me, and the comments attributed to me didn't sound like me. I have a friend in education and I asked her to read this report. She told me the parent section was based on the checklists I filled out for them. Once I understood that, I could see where they got their information. I was frustrated, though, because they didn't describe the Mike I live with. I think they missed the diagnosis."

I listened as Mike's mother told me her story.

She continued. "When you told me you needed to have a conversation with me before you evaluated my son, I was relieved. I wasn't going to agree to let you test him unless you wanted to talk with me first."

Mike's mother expressed a reaction many parents have when they are not included as an integral part of their child's evaluation process. Parents need to tell stories about their children. Evaluators benefit from listening to those stories.

With the conversational approach to the parent interview process, evaluators have an informal but structured conversation with the child's parents. Questions provide the entry point for a conversational exchange between the parents and the members of their child's evaluation team. The characteristics of the child's behavior unfold as the parents share stories about their child's interests, relationships with family members, and daily activities. A face-to-face conversation allows parents to express their worries and concerns while they form an authentic connection with the members of the evaluation team who are participating in the interview. Through stories, parents share what they like best about their child as well as discuss challenging behaviors. They gain a sense of being valuable participants in the evaluation of their child.

Conversations Versus Checklists

Let's stop for a moment and contrast two approaches to gathering information from a child's parents during an autism evaluation. When parents provide information about their child by responding to checklists or questionnaires consisting of lists of behaviors, the evaluators gain a list of behaviors. From this list, they can quantify the likelihood that the child's behaviors are linked to an autism spectrum disorder. However, the parents are often left feeling that the checklist items did not capture the essence of their child's unique qualities. Anxiety surfaces, as parents worry about whether the evaluation team reviewing the checklists will make a diagnosis that reflects a thorough understanding of their child.

When parents participate in a conversation with members of their child's evaluation team, they are able to tell stories that describe their child as a unique individual. They are encouraged to talk about their child's strengths and endearing qualities, and to tell the evaluation team the things they enjoy most about their child. The conversation helps parents deal with the emotional aspects of having a child with developmental differences through the process of discussing their concerns with trusted professionals. The foundation of trust formed between the parents and the evaluation team during the parent interview thus becomes a source of emotional support when parents are faced with hearing a difficult diagnosis at the end of the evaluation process.

Checklists provide important information as part of a best practices autism evaluation, but only if they are used to supplement the valuable information that unfolds during the conversation between the parents and the members of their child's evaluation team. When parents receive a checklist prior to participating in a personal interview, an opportunity to establish a context for completing the checklist is lost. Most checklists related to autism spectrum disorders include the words *autism* or *Asperger's Syndrome* in their titles. Handing out checklists prior to a personal interview signals to parents that the priority for information lies with quantitative lists rather than in the parents' more nuanced perspective on their child. This can be off-putting for some parents. It may also predispose or limit the conversation with parents. For these reasons, evaluators should consider having parents complete behavior checklists only after the parent interview has been conducted.

Asking parents to complete behavior checklists after the personal interview allows the evaluation team to establish a context for the checklists and to answer any questions that might arise. Now when the team member hands out the checklist, the parents have already established a sense of connection with the team member who conducted the interview. As a result, parents are more likely to perceive the information they provide on the checklists as a supplement to the rich and detailed information they provided in the personal interview. The conversation in the next section will give you an idea of how the parent interview unfolds using the conversational approach.

> ## *How does the conversational approach to interviewing parents differ from a traditional parent interview?*
>
> In the conversational approach, the emphasis is on providing a structure for parents to share their concerns and their stories about their child. I think of it as a highly specialized form of a conversation rather than as a formal interview. The questions provide the structure that allows parents to talk about their experiences with their child.
>
> In a more traditional clinical interview, parents respond to questions in a chronological order, starting with the child's developmental and medical history, and proceeding from there. Because the conversational approach to the parent interview is organized around the current concerns and preoccupations the parents have about their child, they experience the interview more as a conversation and less as a clinical interview. As a result, they tend to form more of a bond with the members of the evaluation team conducting the interview. The relaxed atmosphere created by the conversational approach allows the parents to share more detailed information about their child with the evaluation team.

AN INTERVIEW WITH JONATHON'S PARENTS

Here's an example of a parent interview using a conversational approach. It is based on an interview with Jonathon's parents. Jonathon, a 10-year-old boy who was in his first semester of fourth grade, was referred for an autism evaluation by his parents and teachers. Although he had some unusual behaviors and difficulty making friends, up until the fourth grade he was able to complete his assignments successfully. It is not uncommon for very bright children to have their initial referral for an autism evaluation occur when they enter the upper elementary grades. At the time of this referral, Jonathon's increased struggles with the fourth-grade-level critical thinking and writing tasks, combined with his obvious distress regarding the more complex social relationships among his preadolescent classmates, created enough concern for a formal evaluation to be requested. The goal of the autism evaluation was to determine whether Jonathon's social, organizational, and writing challenges were due to an underlying pervasive developmental disorder on the autism spectrum. Neither Linda, the speech therapist on the team, nor I had interviewed Jonathon prior to this parent interview session, but we had both observed him at school and were familiar with the details of his referral.

Jonathon was a tall boy with a slight build and long legs. He walked with his torso and head positioned in front of his lower body. He often had a slight smile on his face and appeared to be absorbed in a conversation with himself. When we observed him at school, Jonathon initiated social interactions with his classmates by standing in front of them and making a dramatic statement in a somewhat loud and stilted voice. Instead of waiting for their response, he turned on his heel and walked away, with his head and torso leading the way. In the lunchroom, he sat at the end of the table and perched on the stool, with his feet on the seat. He appeared to be unaware of the social conversations taking place around him, but would occasionally make a statement to no one in particular.

Linda and I met with Jonathon's parents at his school. We arranged to meet in the conference room where we would not be interrupted during our conversation. After introducing ourselves, we invited Jonathon's parents to sit next to each other at the table. Linda and I took care to seat ourselves in proximity to the parents in a manner that best facilitated a close, intimate conversation, as opposed to a formal meeting. The seating arrangement was important because it allowed for an easy conversational flow between the parents and us—the professionals conducting the interview. After exchanging a few pleasantries, we were ready to settle into our conversation about Jonathon.

"What are your main concerns about Jonathon right now?" I asked. I wanted the parents to begin the process by telling us about their immediate concerns for their son.

> *Start with a question about the present instead of asking about the child's early development. This helps parents relax and talk about their immediate concerns.*

His father jumped right in, and it was clear from his comments that he had given this a great deal of thought. "He's really been struggling socially this year. Jonathon's always been happy to go his own way, but this year he's starting to notice his differences. The work is getting harder for him, especially the language arts papers that require critical thinking on his part. He gets really frustrated and has been asking us why his brain doesn't work right."

Jonathon's mother added, "I would say my biggest concern for Jonathon is his social development. He's not as mature as some of the kids in his class and he's been having trouble handling it when they tease him. Sometimes he overreacts to their comments. Last week his teacher told me he shouted at his group during a science project and told them they were all fired. Then when they laughed, he became upset. He's been coming home in a more agitated frame of mind lately and it's been harder for him to handle doing his homework. He's been spending more time in his room reading and acting out movie scenes. We don't want him to start developing a negative self-image, but we don't know what we need to do to help him at this point."

"So you're most concerned about helping Jonathon with his social skills and with some of his academic work—and you're worried about some of the comments he's been making about seeing himself as different from his peers," I said.

"That's right," replied Jonathon's father. "He's always been a happy kid, eager to go to school and full of energy at home. Lately he's seemed a little more preoccupied and gets more easily frustrated when we ask him to do things around the house. He's been telling us he wants to stay home and work on his acting. What he really wants to do is to stay home, watch movies, and avoid the social stress of school. He even asked his mother last week if she would teach him at home."

"Of course that would seem like a great solution to Jonathon, but we want him to learn how to cope with the social world," his mother said. "He has so much potential in so many areas. We want him to get the help he needs to cope with the demands of school. We're kind of worried about how he's going to do when he moves from the relative security of the elementary campus to the middle school next year. Jonathon is so naive and trusting, and he doesn't know how to read people's intentions. We don't want him to be a target for teasing or for being bullied."

"That's one reason we asked for this evaluation," his father interjected. "So we could figure out what exactly is going on with him and find ways to help and support him."

"Has Jonathon had any testing done before to look at his developmental differences?" I took this opportunity to ask about previous testing and the results.

"No formal testing," said his father. "He has a cousin with Asperger's Syndrome—my sister's son—and we wondered whether Jonathon might not have the same sort of problem. When his teacher mentioned it this year, we felt it was time to look at this possibility more formally."

To let the parents know how much we appreciated their decision to pursue the autism evaluation for their son, I said, "We're glad you decided to have the evaluation done and we're looking forward to working with Jonathon."

"We are too," said his mother.

> Having a face-to-face conversation opened the door for both parents to share personal and detailed information about their child.

"Let's talk a bit about Jonathon at home. He has an older brother, right?" It was time to gather specific home information. We started by confirming that Jonathon had an older brother, a fact we had gathered from our review of his school records prior to the parent interview.

"Yes, Mark," his mother stated. "Mark is in the sixth grade and he is a great big brother. He's very patient, so the two of them get along pretty well most of the time. When Jonathon gets caught up in acting out a movie scene or telling us a long story, Mark is a good listener. Mark is a really social guy and is always having friends over to the house—very different from Jonathon because he's much more of a loner. Even so, Jonathon likes to hang out with Mark and his friends when they play video games. He likes to tell them strategies they could use to beat various game levels and his advice is usually pretty good. When Mark doesn't want Jonathon around, he and his friends just go outside to shoot baskets. Jonathon doesn't like to go outside and generally doesn't follow them out of the house."

"I've tried to get him to shoot baskets, but Jonathon would rather stay inside and act out a scene from the movie *Air Bud*," his father commented with a sigh.

"Tell us what activities Jonathon likes to do at home," I asked.

His mother began to talk about Jonathon's interest in movies. "If he could spend all day watching movies and then acting out his favorite scenes, he would. Jonathon has always loved watching videos and movies. When he was a toddler, he watched each of his favorite videos so many times that he memorized the dialogue and the actions of the characters. He has a fantastic memory for dialogue. He basically learned how to read by having us read his favorite story books over and over while he memorized the text and somehow associated the words on the page with the words he had memorized. Remember that?" Jonathon's mother addressed her comment to her husband. This natural conversational flow signaled to us that Jonathon's parents were comfortable with the interview process. They were able to concentrate on discussing their son in a relaxed and candid way.

"It was pretty amazing," her husband replied. "Mark is bright, but he doesn't have Jonathon's knack for recalling details."

Jonathon's mother said, "When Jonathon's not watching movies, he likes to go on the Internet and memorize facts and movie trivia. One of his favorite sites is IMDB—the Internet Movie Database. He loves to tell us the blow-by-blow details once he's gathered new movie trivia. We've worked hard to teach him to have conversations about something other than movies, but he forgets sometimes at home and dives into talking about the latest movie. He likes to tell us the rating level and why the movie was given a PG-13 or an R rating." It was clear from his mother's description that Jonathon had a longstanding special interest in movies.

"One afternoon I was tired, and I turned on the television while I put my feet up," she went on. "There was some movie on and when Jonathon walked in the room he glanced at the TV for a second and then told me I shouldn't be watching an R-rated movie when children under the age of 17 were present. Not much gets by him." His mother told this story with a bemused look on her face.

"So rules are important to Jonathon?" I asked, as a follow-up to his mother's story.

She replied, "It actually causes problems for him at home and at school. We have to be careful what we tell him because he is very literal in his interpretation of things and holds us to exactly what we say. There is no nuance for Jonathon, just black or white."

His father weighed in. "It takes a lot of explaining to get him to calm down once he perceives us as breaking a rule or not following through on something we said we'd do but didn't do because our plans changed."

"It sounds like changes in his routine are difficult for him," I commented.

"He does pretty well if we let him know beforehand about upcoming changes. Verbal reminders really help him, so we have to make a point to remember to let him know about things in advance," said his mother. "The problem is, if we place too much emphasis on alerting him to a change in his expected routine, he can become fixated on thinking about it and it upsets him that way."

"Describe to us what Jonathon does when he gets agitated or upset," I asked.

"It was much more of a problem when he was younger because it took him a long time to calm down. He had trouble expressing himself when he got upset. Now he's learned to use his words and to go to his room to regroup. Of course that only works in certain situations," his mother said.

"It's been a couple of years now since we've had to leave an event and take him home because he was too upset to stay," recalled his father. "What I notice more now that he's older is that Jonathon has trouble letting go of something that's bothering him. He brings things up weeks later and wants to rehash the situation all over again."

After discussing Jonathon's emotions and behavior for a few more minutes, we returned to asking about his preferred interests. We wanted to make sure we learned as much as we could about his preferred topics before we had our conversation with Jonathon so we could direct the conversation to his areas of interest.

"Lately he's become interested in television situation comedies from the '50s and '60s—*The Honeymooners* and *The Dick Van Dyke Show*," his father said.

Linda, the speech therapist, had been writing down all of the information provided by Jonathon's parents during the interview. She made a note about Jonathon's interest in the television programs that were from an era far removed from his own.

> *Write down all the details shared by the parents. Recording the specific details sends a signal to the parents that you are really listening and helps you prepare for your interview with the child. Later, when the parents see your summary report, they will appreciate reading the accurate details from your conversation with them.*

"We signed him up to participate in several community theater productions as a way to channel his interest into something productive. He loves trying out for plays and is pretty good at it. He's had bit parts in several plays so far—he just finished being one of the lost boys in *Peter Pan*. The hard part for Jonathon is handling the social aspects of being in the group at the theater center. He wants to tell the director what to do and how to structure the scenes. That doesn't always go over very well," his father commented. Then, smiling, he added, "But I've found that the community theater actors and directors can be an eccentric group of people, so they're quite accepting of Jonathon."

"He also goes to Cub Scouts with his dad, but that has been a little harder for him," his mother added. "Jonathon likes the activities but doesn't like the more loosely structured social time."

His father sighed, conveying how hard it has been to try to help Jonathon follow the social flow in various settings. "Yes, he's very serious about scouting. He read the manual and wants to earn enough badges to become an Eagle Scout. During the meetings he relates to the other boys by telling them what they should be doing. He recites the Scout's Code of Honor sometimes. I've tried to help him understand how to relax and have fun, but it's hard for him. When he tries to relate to the other boys, he usually gets into a character and approaches the boys in character, quoting dialogue."

"It's been really hard to get Jonathon to understand how to relate to his peers," his mother said. "Adults love talking to him because he's interesting and entertaining. Little kids like him because he can literally become one of their favorite video characters. His classmates don't understand why a smart kid like Jonathon can't get it together and just talk with them."

His father commented, "Now that he's getting older, he's noticing that he is not in sync with his peers and it's beginning to bother him. Lately he's been telling his peers that they're fired or that he's going to let them know who's the boss." His father's comments highlighted how Jonathon's unusual and repetitive use of phrases was out of step with his peers.

Jonathon's mother started to laugh at the memory of hearing her son use his well-worn phrases. Her smile moved into a struggle with tears as she put her concerns into words.

"It sounds funny when he says stuff like that, but it's upsetting to see that he really doesn't get it. Sometimes when I see how other kids react to the things Jonathon says, my heart aches for him." She wiped tears from the corner of one eye as her husband patted her arm.

"In a way, it's more painful for us than for him, though. A lot of times Jonathon just doesn't understand how the things he says are out of step with how other kids talk," said his father, making an observation that described his son and comforted his wife at the same time.

"That's true," his mother said. "I just worry about how he'll handle it with his classmates when the social gap gets bigger in middle school. He's so content most of the time that I'd hate to see his confidence in himself shaken."

"You really understand him and support him," I said. As Jonathon's parents shared their emotions, they also showed us how resilient they were as a couple and as parents.

> *Jonathon's parents were able to share some of their feelings of grief about their son's social challenges through the process of participating in our conversation.*

With the conversational flow well established, Jonathon's parents went on to tell us about their son's behavior and interests in great detail. We explored the types of situations that distressed Jonathon as well as how his parents reacted to him when he became upset. We also asked about his sleeping and eating patterns, his response to pain, his response to changes in his routine, whether he had any unusual fears, and if he was taking any medications on a routine basis.

After our detailed discussion about their current concerns, we asked Jonathon's parents about his developmental history. Talking about their son's developmental history after they had already discussed their most pressing concerns helped them form a genuine bond with us.

Throughout the conversation, we made sure that we asked specific questions about Jonathon's behavior and development in the three key areas of language and communication, social relationships and emotional responses, and sensory use and interests. In this way, we introduced the focus on the three key areas of development associated with autism spectrum disorders that we would revisit with the parents during the conversation to discuss Jonathon's diagnosis after his completed evaluation.

We concluded the interview by asking a few additional key questions.

"If you had to pick three words to describe Jonathon, what would they be?" I asked.

His parents simultaneously raised their eyebrows and smiled.

"Creative," said his father.

"Happy," added his mother.

"And very bright," his father said, while his mother nodded in agreement.

"What do you like best about Jonathon?" I continued.

"His creativity and his gentle spirit. He is the kindest person you'll ever meet. He has such positive energy and he makes us laugh all the time with his ability to get into character. We just want to help him figure out how to read the social landscape as well as he mimics the actors in his favorite films," his mother said, in a voice filled with emotion.

"He's so capable in terms of his academic work," added his father. "But it's really difficult to get him to shift his attention to his schoolwork—especially when he has to organize his thoughts and write a paper. That's something we need some help with—finding ways to keep him focused on his paper writing instead of resisting the process so vigorously."

> *Encouraging Jonathon's parents to talk about his positive attributes ended the conversation on a positive note.*

Now that we'd had a thorough, detailed conversation about their son, I asked his parents what their goal was in requesting the evaluation. "What would you like to get out of this evaluation process?"

"To learn whether it makes sense to talk about him as a person with Asperger's Syndrome," his father remarked.

"And to learn what we need to do—at home and at school—to help him close the social gap as much as possible. We want to find other ways—we know there must be some ways—to help him become less frustrated with his work when he has to organize his thoughts and get his ideas down on paper," his mother said.

"You mentioned that Jonathon has a cousin with Asperger's Syndrome. Have you done any reading about Asperger's Syndrome and autism spectrum disorders?" I asked.

"Both of us have done some reading and we've talked about what we've read together. It's a little overwhelming when you start looking into the whole autism area. Mainly we've looked at some Web sites about Asperger's Syndrome," said his father.

> *Asking parents what they've learned so far about autism spectrum disorders helps you discover where they are in the process of understanding their child's suspected developmental differences. This information helps guide the conversation with parents when you discuss the child's diagnosis after the evaluation.*

"As you've been reading and talking, do you see some of those characteristics in Jonathon?" I asked.

His father paused for a moment, then said, "If he has it, I think he's only got a bit of it. That's comparing him to the people described in the reading I've done and knowing his cousin. To me, Jonathon is a lot like I was growing up."

"I definitely see the characteristics in Jonathon. But I spend the most time with him," his mother said.

As we concluded our conversation, we told Jonathon's parents how much we had enjoyed talking with them. We also reiterated that we were looking forward to having the opportunity to get to know their son during our upcoming conversation with him. We asked Jonathon's parents if they had any additional questions about the evaluation process, or if there was anything else they felt we needed to know about their son before our scheduled meeting with him.

Jonathon's parents took a moment to reflect on our conversation before they replied.

"No, I think you covered a lot of ground with us today," concluded his father. "We look forward to learning what you think about Jonathon after you meet with him."

FEATURES OF THE PARENT INTERVIEW PROCESS USING THE CONVERSATIONAL APPROACH

Before we had our conversation with Jonathon's parents, we discussed which team member would conduct the interview. Since we were able to include two team members in the interview session, Linda, the speech therapist, recorded all of the parents' comments while I assumed primary responsibility for the conversation with them. When only one team member is available to conduct the interview, that person can take notes while he or she talks, but it is preferable to have a second person available to transcribe the conversation. We reserved a private room at the school and placed a sign on the door to minimize interruptions during our conversation with the parents. Before the interview, we reviewed Jonathon's referral and background information to familiarize ourselves with his developmental history and other recorded information.

During the interview, we made sure to create a seating arrangement that promoted, rather than detracted from, establishing a conversational atmosphere. For example, we invited the parents to sit next to each other. When parents sit opposite each other, or to the left and right of the team member who is conducting the interview, it is difficult for the interviewer to maintain eye contact with both parents and talk with them at the same time. We also made sure to sit in close proximity to the parents, to create an environment that was more intimate and less formal. The goal is to establish a comfortable atmosphere, so that parents have a structured and conversational way to participate in the interview.

Although we had a list of specific questions we wanted to ask, we posed them in a conversational style. As evaluators, we spent most of our time listening to Jonathon's parents. One question led to the next in a fluid, natural style. We paid careful attention to how the parents comfortably expressed themselves, and we mirrored their conversational style by pacing our speech and adjusting our vocabulary and body language to match theirs. We used questions to structure the conversation, but we focused on listening to the details shared by Jonathon's parents. We encouraged Jonathon's parents to tell stories about him, and we wrote down the details of their stories.

The parent interview using the conversational approach took a little over an hour to complete. By the end of the conversation, Jonathon's parents had the opportunity to share many details about their son and left feeling a positive connection with their son's evaluation team. Their confidence in the team was bolstered because they experienced a professional interview that put them at ease by encouraging them to share their thoughts and feelings about their son. Sharing stories about Jonathon will help his parents as they move through the grief process of accepting that their child has developmental differences.

After we completed our conversation with Jonathon's parents, we expressed genuine appreciation to them for taking the time to talk with us about their child. Once the parent interview was over, we shared the detailed information with the other members of our evaluation team. We were able to do this because Linda had written down all of the information shared by Jonathon's parents during the interview as it unfolded. Since Jonathon was being evaluated as a student with possible Asperger's Syndrome, we completed the parent interview portion of the Parent and Teacher Interview protocol from the *Monteiro Interview Guidelines for Diagnosing Asperger's Syndrome* (MIGDAS; Monteiro, 2008). The MIGDAS Parent and Teacher Interview protocol contains detailed questions to ask parents and teachers during an interview using the conversational approach and provides space to write the comments made by parents and teachers after each question. We made sure that our questions covered the three key areas in the descriptive triangle (language and communication, social relationships and emotional responses, and sensory use and interests). A list of key topics to cover in a parent interview for children across the autism spectrum is provided in Table 4.

Although it is always preferable to have a face-to-face conversation with parents during the evaluation, there may be times when circumstances do not allow for it. At these times, evaluators should find alternative ways of completing the parent interview, such as over the telephone. My experience has been that completing the parent interview over the telephone works best if the interviewer arranges a specific time to call and complete the interview. When a specified time is agreed upon, parents are more likely to be able to focus on the conversation rather than trying to answer questions on the spur of the moment. Sometimes parents even set up conference calls so both parents can participate in the conversation. The important thing to remember is that an in-depth parent interview should always be a part of the evaluation process.

Now that we've discussed how to conduct a parent interview using the conversational approach, let's move on to discuss how to use the conversational approach to interview the child's teacher.

Table 4
Key Topics to Cover During the Parent Interview

- Start with questions about current concerns.

- Ask questions about each of the three key areas in the visual triangle (language and communication, social relationships and emotional responses, sensory use and interests).

- Ask follow-up questions to prompt parents to share detailed stories and information.

- Include questions about positive attributes (what the parents like best about their child, words they would use to describe their child).

- Find out what the parents have read or learned so far about autism spectrum disorders.

- Ask parents what their expectations are for the evaluation process.

- Consider giving parents behavior checklists to complete after, rather than before, the parent interview.

Guidelines for Conducting the Parent Interview Using the Conversational Approach

Before the parent interview...

- Decide which team member will be conducting the interview. Whenever possible, include a second team member to sit in on the conversation and make detailed notes.
- Review the child's referral and background information.
- Find a private room in which to have a conversation with the parents.

During the parent interview...

- Establish a comfortable atmosphere so that the parents have a structured, conversational way to participate in their child's evaluation process. Mirror their conversational style.
- Use questions to structure the conversation around the three key areas affected by autism spectrum disorders, but focus on listening to details and encouraging parents to tell stories about their child and describe their child's special interests. Write down the details of their stories.
- Ask parents directly what they hope to gain from the evaluation process. Ask them what they have learned so far about autism spectrum disorders.

After the parent interview...

- Express genuine appreciation to the parents for taking time to talk with you in detail about their child. Provide the parents with the behavior checklists that need to be completed for the evaluation.
- Remember that the positive bond the parents form with the evaluation team facilitates the process of discussing the child's diagnosis after the evaluation is completed.
- Share the detailed information with the rest of the evaluation team. Make sure information regarding the child's preferred topics and activities is reviewed so these interests and activities can be included in the sensory-based diagnostic interview.

CHAPTER 4

Conversations With Teachers

The Teacher Interview

The Conversational Approach to Interviewing Teachers

What is the conversational approach to interviewing teachers?

- It is a face-to-face conversation that provides teachers with an opportunity to discuss valuable observations and concerns.
- The conversational format encourages teachers to tell stories that illustrate their present concerns about the child.
- Teachers are guided to reflect on the child's behavioral profile in the three key areas of language and communication, social relationships and emotional responses, and sensory use and interests.

How does the evaluator structure the conversation?

- Whenever possible, the teacher conversation occurs after members of the evaluation team have observed the child in the classroom setting and before the sensory-based diagnostic interview.
- The interview is structured to help teachers discuss their concerns in a time-efficient manner. Often, the conversation involves the teacher and one member of the evaluation team.
- Teachers are given behavior checklists to complete at the end of the conversation.

What are the benefits of the conversational approach?

- Teachers gain a sense of being valuable participant's in the child's evaluation process.
- Information provided by teachers helps the evaluation team anticipate toys to use and topics to address during the sensory-based diagnostic interview with the child.
- The groundwork is laid for a productive follow-up meeting to discuss the evaluation results and make educational recommendations.

TEACHERS NEED TO SHARE THEIR CONCERNS

"I'm glad you met with me to talk about Peter before his evaluation," Peter's teacher said at the end of our conversational interview. "I wanted to make sure you knew where I was coming from with my concerns about him and now I know you understand. I'll work on these checklists and get them back to you by tomorrow afternoon."

"Thank you for taking the time to meet with me. Your insight into Peter and all of the information you provided will help us get the best possible picture of him when we complete our diagnostic interview with him," I said, expressing genuine appreciation for her time and involvement in the interview process. "Since you told me that he is fascinated by science fiction and fantasy role-playing computer games, I know I need to brush up on my facts and information about those areas."

"Don't worry too much about that. Peter will be happy to fill you in and correct you if you get any of your facts wrong. You know, I hadn't thought about his distracted behaviors in class being driven by his sensory needs until we talked today. When you asked if he was distracted by his own agenda and thoughts, and if he ever focused on visual details that other students ignore, you were describing Peter. He has trouble shifting his attention from what he's looking at to what I want him to do. That's why he seems to do better following my directions when I go over to him and show him exactly what I want him to do. Between his attention to visual details and his preoccupation with the details about role-playing games, it's hard for Peter to stay on track in class."

Peter's teacher reacted to the conversational nature of the teacher interview with appreciation that she was getting an opportunity to express her concerns and observations prior to the autism evaluation of her student. She made several new connections about how Peter learned as she answered the specific interview questions, and she shared unique details about Peter's passionate interest in science fiction and computer role-playing games. The positive reaction Peter's teacher expressed reflects what most teachers feel when they are included as an integral part of the evaluation process.

In the conversational approach used in the teacher interview, a member of the evaluation team schedules a time for an in-depth interview with the child's teacher. The face-to-face conversation provides teachers with an opportunity to discuss valuable observations and concerns, while the interview questions provide the structure needed to create an efficient interview process. Just as the parent interview focuses on present concerns, the teacher interview works best if the questions provide teachers with the necessary structure to discuss their present concerns about the student. Teachers are also guided to reflect on the child's behavioral profile in the three key areas of language and communication, social relationships and emotional responses, and sensory use and interests.

Teachers are typically very busy and their free time during the school day is limited. My experience has been that teachers respond best to the interview if I have specific questions prepared to ask them. General questions such as "How is the student doing in class?" will yield less helpful information than questions that ask the teacher to describe how the student acts or responds in specific situations. When focused questions are asked, the interview process takes less than an hour to complete, usually only a half hour.

Whenever possible, the teacher interview should occur after members of the evaluation team have observed the child in the classroom setting. If members of the evaluation team have observed the child, common ground is established for the conversation between a team member and the teacher. Teachers gain a sense of being valuable participants in the evaluation process, and the information provided by the teacher helps the evaluation team anticipate the toys to use and the topics to address during the sensory-based diagnostic interview. In addition, the teacher interview lays the groundwork for a productive follow-up meeting to discuss the evaluation results and make educational recommendations for the student.

An ideal time to give behavior checklists to teachers is at the end of the teacher interview. The conversation establishes a context for the checklists because the teacher has just discussed his or her observations of the student and is thinking about the student's behavioral profile. The personal connection established between the teacher and the evaluation team member conducting the interview provides additional motivation to complete the checklists and promptly return them. The conversation in the next section will give you an idea of how the teacher interview unfolds using the conversational approach.

Is it okay to bypass the teacher interview and only ask the teacher to fill out behavior checklists?

The teacher interview allows teachers to participate in the evaluation process by sharing their personal viewpoint. The nuanced responses teachers provide in an interview cannot be translated into the responses they provide when they complete a behavior checklist. My experience has been that when I give teachers behavior checklists to complete after they have participated in the interview process, they are more likely to understand the scope of what they are being asked to do and they complete the checklists with more care and attention to detail. Teachers have valuable information about the students they teach and like to be asked their opinions. They are more likely to feel that they are an integral part of the evaluation process if they are asked to participate in a personal interview in addition to filling out checklists.

AN INTERVIEW WITH EVAN'S TEACHER

Here's an example of a teacher interview using the conversational approach. It is based on my interview with a third-grade teacher, Mrs. Loomis. Evan, an 8-year-old boy in his first semester of third grade, was referred for an autism evaluation by Mrs. Loomis. Although Evan was already identified as a student with learning differences in the area of written expression skills, Mrs. Loomis made the referral to formally address some behavioral differences seen in Evan that were not typical of other students with that specific learning difficulty. At the time of the referral, Evan was receiving extra support in class to help with his writing assignments.

I met with Evan's teacher to complete the teacher interview after I'd had an opportunity to observe Evan in the classroom that morning. Pam, the educational diagnostician on our team, had observed Evan on a previous day. I had observed Evan in the classroom, and Pam had observed him in the lunchroom and hallways, and during recess. Mrs. Loomis and I met for the interview during her 30-minute planning period.

> *Whenever possible, conduct a classroom observation before meeting with the child's teacher. Try to schedule the teacher interview during a convenient time during the school day. Plan approximately 30 minutes for your conversation with the teacher.*

I started the conversation with Mrs. Loomis by expressing my appreciation for her giving me her valuable time. "Thanks for taking time during your planning period to meet with me. Since you know Evan well, I really wanted to have an opportunity to get your input before we meet with him."

"No problem. Evan is a puzzle and I'm glad he's being evaluated this year," said Mrs. Loomis. "He's been struggling and we need to get him more help."

"I'm glad I had a chance to observe him during your math lesson this morning. Pam also had a chance to observe him during lunch and recess yesterday. Would you say his behavior was typical today?"

"Very much so. You probably noticed how caught up he became in drawing pictures of bugs. He is fascinated by insects, reptiles, and other animals and knows a surprising amount of information about them. It's hard for him to follow the lesson unless I stand next to him and redirect his attention."

Mrs. Loomis confirmed what Pam and I had noted when we observed Evan. He drew pictures of bugs on his notebook during most of the lesson. Pam reported that during recess, Evan spent his time squatting in front of anthills and picking up insects with leaves.

"So, getting Evan to focus on his work is one of your concerns right now," I said, commenting on Mrs. Loomis's observation. "Tell me what other concerns you have about Evan."

> Early in the conversation, ask what concerns the teacher has about the child.

She replied, "There are several things that concern me. He seems to be in his own world a lot of the time and it's hard for him to stay focused on what we're doing. He is capable of doing most of the work but doesn't get started unless I prompt or remind him. He's quite disorganized with his materials and can't find his books and papers a lot of the time. He constantly checks insect or animal books out of the library and tries to read them when he's supposed to be doing his work."

"I'm also worried about how he is with his classmates," she continued. "Evan hasn't developed any friendships this year and he rarely talks with the other kids. I have a good group this year and they're kind to him, but they notice he's different socially."

"Can we talk more about Evan's interest in insects and other animals?" I asked, prompting the teacher to elaborate on Evan's area of special interest.

> Ask follow-up questions to encourage the teacher to share details about the child's areas of interest.

"Don't forget reptiles," Mrs. Loomis smiled, as she started to talk about Evan's intense focus on his special topic. "Evan can tell you lots of facts about reptiles as well. He knows how many species of snakes and lizards there are and can describe them in detail. He has his favorite insects and likes to talk about the loudest and biggest insects in the world. Lately, he's been interested in pouched animals and has been collecting facts about Australia."

As Mrs. Loomis shared information about Evan's entomological interests, I made a note of the details to help prepare for our interview with Evan.

"So is Evan also interested in geography?" I asked.

"You know, I've noticed in the past couple of weeks that he started telling me where various reptiles, insects, and mammals live in the world when he tells me facts about them. He pays attention during our geography lessons and contributes to the discussion by sharing interesting facts," said Mrs. Loomis.

"It sounds like Evan likes to talk with you about his interests. Tell me what your conversations are like," I said.

"You said talk *with* me. Evan actually tends to talk *at* me. He is definitely one-sided in his conversations with me. When he comes up to tell me something, I've learned to ask him, 'Evan, is what you're about to tell me related to what we're discussing right now?', and that seems to help him shift to what he needs to be focused on."

I urged Mrs. Loomis to tell me more about Evan's use of language. "Talk a little more about Evan's communication style."

Mrs. Loomis gathered her thoughts for a moment before she replied. "It's as though he doesn't vary the way he talks. Everything he says is delivered in the same measured, precise, and formal way. He sounds like he's giving a lecture instead of having a conversation."

"So his delivery of information sounds more formal than other children in your class?" I asked.

"Yes," Mrs. Loomis continued. "Evan seems to jump right in to tell me facts about his areas of interest. It's hard for him to participate in a casual conversation with me or with his classmates."

"What about relationships with his peers?" I asked. "You mentioned that Evan rarely talks to the other students and that he hasn't developed any friendships."

> *Remember to ask questions about the child's language, social, and sensory behaviors.*

Mrs. Loomis replied, "That's a big area of concern I have for him. He seems to be pretty oblivious to even basic social skills with the other kids. You probably noticed today that when I gave the class 5 minutes of free time, most of the children spent that time visiting with each other. Evan seems to be out of step with the social flow most of the time. Sometimes he forgets to line up or to put his things away, and he doesn't seem to look around him to follow the lead of the other students. There is one girl in my class who looks after Evan and sees to it that he stays with the group. The problem is, none of the other students are interested in hearing Evan talk about bugs or reptiles. And Evan has a hard time figuring out how to talk about anything else."

"You mentioned that a girl in the class sometimes looks after Evan and that you frequently have to stand beside Evan to prompt him to refocus on the task at hand. Tell me how Evan handles transitions during the day and how he responds to changes in his routines," I asked.

"I'm glad you asked me about that," replied Mrs. Loomis. "He gets upset whenever we change our expected routine. We had a fire drill the other day and it really rattled him. He didn't want to go outside because it was about to rain. The noise really upset him as well. He curled up in a ball in the back of the room by the bookshelf and it took me 10 minutes to get him to calm down enough to leave the building. Usually I try to remember to tell him in advance when a fire drill is coming, but sometimes we don't have any warning."

"Do noises in general seem to bother or distract him?" I asked.

"It's interesting. When he becomes engrossed in a book or a drawing, Evan's capacity to block out sounds is amazing. I think that's part of why he gets upset at times when we have changes in our routine and he has to shift gears and follow the flow. At other times, he seems to become preoccupied with sounds that no one else pays attention to. Like the other day, he was listening to some birds chirping outside and couldn't seem to shift his attention away from listening to that distant distraction." Mrs. Loomis looked off in the distance as she recalled this information about her student.

"Tell me about Evan's physical movements in comparison to the other students in your class. Is he physically coordinated? Does he sit in his chair like other kids? Does he participate in P.E. and recess?" I asked, prompting her to tell me about Evan's body awareness and his movements and mannerisms.

"Part of what makes Evan seem like he's in his own world a lot of the time is how he seems to glide when he walks. He never varies his pace, which can be hard when the rest of the class comes in off the playground and he lingers. When he sees a bug or an anthill on the playground, he squats in front of it and tries to get as close to it as possible. He sort of prances when he runs. He sits in his chair like other students but tends to keep his face close to the paper when he draws or writes. You'd have to ask the P.E. teacher how he is in that class," said Mrs. Loomis.

"You mentioned that Evan tends to keep his face close to the paper when he writes or draws. Tell me about his written work," I asked.

> Ask specific questions about academic skills and challenges.

"Well, you know he has a learning disability in the area of written expression. He loves to draw but gets really frustrated when he has to write. He tells me that he doesn't know what to write and that the assignment is too hard and too long, no matter what assignment we're working on. He does better when I give him written prompts to choose from during writing assignments. His journal entries usually have lots of drawings and some sentences about bugs or reptiles. His handwriting is hard to read and I know he gets frustrated with it. We're working with him to teach him how to keyboard so he can start typing his papers on the computer," Mrs. Loomis said, describing Evan's writing challenges.

"In terms of academics, tell us about Evan's abilities. It sounds like written work is an area of significant challenge for him. What are his strengths?" I asked. (Because Mrs. Loomis knows that I am taking notes for the autism evaluation team, I sometimes use "us," as in "tell us.")

"He's a great reader and his recall of facts and details is exceptional. His math skills are strong and I'd place him in the top third of the class in math." Mrs. Loomis paused to reflect for a moment. "In addition to his writing challenges, Evan has difficulty sometimes picking up on the motivation of characters and the themes in fiction books we cover in class."

"That's good to know," I said, as I wrote this information down on my interview form. "I want to go back for a minute and ask you to talk about Evan's emotions. You described how upset he became during the fire drill. Does Evan become upset very often? Does he express emotions in class?"

"A lot of the time Evan has a little smile on his face, but it's a private smile. He doesn't look at other people very often. He is one of the gentlest children I've ever taught and he has a sweet, cooperative nature. He worries about the welfare of insects and gets upset when kids step on or kick ant piles. I wouldn't be surprised if he grows up to be an entomologist someday. The funny thing is, he seems to show more emotion toward insects than toward his classmates." Mrs. Loomis reflected on how Evan expressed emotions. "As far as how often he gets upset, it hasn't really been a problem. Usually I can talk with him and give him a few minutes to adjust and he does fine."

"So your concerns about Evan's behavior in school are..." I prompted Mrs. Loomis to sum up her concerns in this area.

"Getting organized. Being more independent. Following the flow of the classroom. Learning to be social with his classmates," Mrs. Loomis replied.

> *Toward the end of the conversation, ask a question to help the teacher summarize his or her concerns.*

"What do you hope to get out of this evaluation process?" I asked.

"That's a good question." She gathered her thoughts for a moment before she continued. "I started this referral to the autism team because I was worried about Evan's ability to manage in school as he gets older. I've been teaching for a long time, and Evan is a unique child. If he doesn't have some form of autism, maybe your evaluation will help us understand what makes him so different. He is so smart, but it's hard for him to focus on the things I want him to learn. He has such a hard time understanding how to be social with the other kids that I worry about how he'll do as he becomes older. He is an innocent and naive child who doesn't seem to have the awareness he needs to deal with other kids his age." Mrs. Loomis paused before saying, "Also, I hope your evaluation gives me ideas on how to help Evan get better organized and to focus on what is going on in the classroom instead of focusing so much on his interests. I would like to see him get extra help in the social skills area as well."

"Have you taught students with a diagnosis of Autistic Disorder, Asperger's Syndrome, or Pervasive Developmental Disorder Not Otherwise Specified (PDD-NOS) in the past?" I asked, in part to gain an understanding of how much experience Mrs. Loomis had in dealing with students on the autism spectrum.

Mrs. Loomis shared her background with me. "Last year I had a student who had pretty severe autism. He spent part of the day in my room, but he had a teaching assistant with him. I went to a workshop last summer about Asperger's Syndrome, and looking back, I've probably taught several undiagnosed students in the past. When I was getting to know Evan at the beginning of the year, I pulled out my notes from the summer workshop and many of the things described in the workshop seemed to apply to him. That's when I made the referral for testing. Evan's parents were supportive of the referral after I talked with them. I talked to his mom last week, and even though she's nervous about this whole process, she told me she really would like to understand what makes Evan tick."

> Express genuine appreciation for the teacher's time and input.
> Discuss behavior checklists at the end of the conversation.

"We're glad you made the referral, Mrs. Loomis, and we look forward to getting to know Evan. I know your planning period is about over, and again, I appreciate your taking time to talk about Evan. Your comments were insightful and helpful. It's obvious that you care about your students and want the best for Evan. Is there anything else you'd like to talk about before we conclude?" I asked.

"I don't think so. I think we covered all of the things that I'm concerned about," Mrs. Loomis replied.

"In that case, thanks again for meeting with me. I have some checklists I'd like to ask you to complete and get back to me," I said. Now that our conversation was ending, I gave Mrs. Loomis several checklists to complete as part of the evaluation process.

Mrs. Loomis reviewed the details of how to complete the checklists with me. "I'm glad we met to talk about Evan today. I look forward to learning what your team comes up with after you finish your evaluation. Do you know when we'll meet again?"

I reviewed the evaluation process with her. In this case, Evan's parents wanted Mrs. Loomis to be included in the parent meeting when we discussed the results of Evan's evaluation, so she would be present when we talked about specific instructional recommendations.

FEATURES OF THE TEACHER INTERVIEW PROCESS USING THE CONVERSATIONAL APPROACH

Before the interview with Evan's teacher, the members of the evaluation team reviewed the referral and background information to familiarize ourselves with the details of Evan's school situation. Both Pam, the educational diagnostician, and I scheduled times to observe Evan; we planned to visit on different days and at different times to make sure we saw Evan in as many different situations as possible. Since I was able to visit the school and observe Evan prior to his teacher's planning period, we decided that I would schedule the teacher interview and meet with Mrs. Loomis during her planning period. I arranged for us to meet in a conference room in the school office area so we could have a private conversation.

During the interview, although I had a list of specific questions I wanted to ask, I did so in a conversational style. I wanted to make sure we talked about Evan's behaviors in the key areas of language and communication, social relationships and emotional responses, and sensory use and interests. Evan's teacher was able to provide important information about Evan's current areas of interest so we could prepare to talk about and share toys and materials that tapped into his preferred topics during the sensory-based diagnostic interview. For questions, I used the teacher portion of the Parent and Teacher Interview protocol from the *Monteiro Interview Guidelines for Diagnosing Asperger's Syndrome* (MIGDAS; Monteiro, 2008). The interview protocol helped me structure the conversation and provided me with a place to write Mrs. Loomis's responses. A list of key topics to cover in a teacher interview with children across the autism spectrum is presented in Table 5.

Table 5
Key Topics to Cover During the Teacher Interview

- Start with questions about current concerns.

- Ask questions about each of the three key areas in the visual triangle (language and communication, social relationships and emotional responses, sensory use and interests).

- Ask follow-up questions to prompt teachers to share detailed stories and information.

- Include questions about positive attributes (what the teachers like best about the student, areas of academic ability).

- Find out what the teachers have read or learned so far about autism spectrum disorders.

- Ask teachers what their expectations are for the evaluation process.

- Consider giving teachers behavior checklists to complete after, rather than before, the teacher interview.

I ended our conversation by introducing the behavior checklists and asking Mrs. Loomis to complete them and return them to the team. Like most teachers who have a student being evaluated for possible autism, Mrs. Loomis wanted to know when we would be getting back with her to discuss our findings. As a team, we planned to have a brief meeting with Mrs. Loomis immediately before we met with Evan's parents. Briefly discussing the results of the evaluation with the child's teacher before meeting with the parents sets the stage for good communication and allows time to address any differences in opinion that might arise. When appropriate, inviting the teacher to sit in on the follow-up meeting with the child's parents helps the parents experience support from an important person in their child's daily life. Issues related to discussing a child's diagnosis with parents and teachers are covered in chapters 6 and 7.

After the teacher interview, I made sure Evan's teacher knew how much we valued and appreciated her time and input. The positive bond we established laid the groundwork for discussing Evan's diagnosis at the end of the evaluation process and paved the way for Evan's teacher to be receptive to the instructional recommendations our team would be proposing. I shared the detailed information from the teacher interview with the rest of the evaluation team so we could prepare for our diagnostic conversation with Evan.

As with the parent interview, you may find there are times when setting up a face-to-face teacher interview is not possible, and an alternative way of completing the teacher interview is needed. Sometimes teachers are willing to participate in a scheduled phone interview after school hours. Teachers can write their answers to interview questions as well. If time constraints place the evaluation team in a position where it will work best to obtain the detailed information from the teacher by having the teacher write his or her responses instead of participating in a personal interview, make sure you have a brief follow-up conversation to review the written responses. The follow-up conversation provides an ideal time to present the teacher with checklists to fill out.

Now that we've talked about how to complete the child, parent, and teacher interviews using the conversational approach, let's talk about the conversation that takes place among team members as they work collaboratively to make a diagnosis.

Guidelines for Conducting the Teacher Interview Using the Conversational Approach

Before the teacher interview...

- Decide which team member will conduct the interview. Whenever possible, complete a classroom observation of the child prior to the teacher interview.
- Review the referral and background information so you are familiar with the teacher's general concerns and the student's specific problem areas.
- Find a private room in which to have the conversation with the teacher. Whenever possible, schedule the interview for a planning period or another time that does not take away from instruction.

During the teacher interview...

- Start by asking about areas of concern. Prompt the teacher to provide details about the student's specific interests and behaviors.
- Use the questions to structure the conversation so the teacher efficiently discusses his or her concerns about the student in each of the three key areas related to autism spectrum disorders.
- Ask the teacher what he or she hopes to gain from the evaluation process. Take the time to answer any additional questions, including how the follow-up with the teacher will take place.

After the teacher interview...

- Express genuine appreciation to the teacher for taking the time to talk with you in detail about the student being evaluated. Give the teacher behavior checklists to complete.
- Remember that the positive bond a teacher forms with the evaluation team facilitates the process of discussing the child's diagnosis and increases the teacher's receptivity to the educational recommendations made by the evaluation team.
- Share the detailed information with the rest of the evaluation team. Make sure information regarding the child's preferred topics and activities is reviewed so these interests and activities can be included in the sensory-based diagnostic interview.

CHAPTER 5

Collaborative Team Conversations

From Interview to Diagnosis

Collaborative Team Conversations and the Sensory-Based Diagnostic Interview

Before the sensory-based diagnostic interview with the child, team members should...

- Share information from a variety of sources in a conversational exchange.
- Develop a qualitative rather than a quantitative vocabulary to discuss the child's behavioral profile.
- Use the information discussed to plan the most effective entry point for the neuro-atypical conversation with the child.

During the sensory-based diagnostic interview, team members should...

- Adopt a combination of interactive and observational styles, and draw out the behavioral profile of the child in the three key areas by interacting with the child using the sensory materials in a dynamic way.
- Minimize talking among themselves about the child and the child's behaviors.
- Understand that seeing a child with a team of evaluators provides an opportunity to compare the child's communication, social, and sensory behaviors to neuro-typical peers in a similar situation.

After the sensory-based diagnostic interview, team members should...

- Immediately discuss their observations from the neuro-atypical conversation with the child and review all information gathered during the evaluation process.
- Organize their discussion of the child's behavioral profile in each of the three key areas.
- Find the most compelling way to describe the child's behavioral profile and agree on a specific diagnosis.

A TEAM CONVERSATION ABOUT BRIAN

Preparing for the Sensory-Based Diagnostic Interview

"We're going to bring Brian in here shortly, but first we have plenty of time to go over his information and get organized," said Paula, the efficient psychometrician on our team. It was Paula's responsibility to coordinate the schedule of events involved in Brian's evaluation process, and she had completed his intellectual and achievement testing several weeks prior to this meeting.

> One member of the team assumes responsibility for coordinating all aspects of the evaluation process. In this case, it was Paula, the psychometrician.

Our team met in preparation for the last part of the evaluation process for Brian, an 11-year-old fifth-grade student with a previous diagnosis of speech and language delays. Beatrice, the speech therapist on our team, had completed standardized speech and language testing with Brian the week before our scheduled team evaluation.

"Paula and I met with his parents yesterday for the parent interview," Beatrice added. "It went really well. They are eager to meet with us after we work with Brian as a team.

"They told us he loves to play video games and to draw video game characters. So, Marilyn, do you know anything about the *Mario* video games?" Beatrice asked, wanting to make sure I was ready to start a conversation with Brian about his preferred topics.

"That's a popular set of game characters for children on the spectrum and for children in general," I replied. "Mario the plumber, his brother Luigi, and Yoshi are a few of the main characters." We grinned at each other. Beatrice frequently enjoyed quizzing me about the topics of interest to the children we evaluated together. Fortunately, this time I knew a few names to rattle off for her.

It was my job on the team to be the primary interviewer during our conversation with Brian. In addition to being able to talk about his areas of interest, I would be responsible for introducing the sensory-based toys and materials and structuring the conversation when we met with Brian as a team. It also would be my job to lead the discussion with Brian's parents when we delivered the diagnosis in our follow-up meeting with them.

> Often the team leader is the psychologist, but any member of the team can be designated as the leader. The leader is responsible for sharing the evaluation results with the parents and may or may not assume the role of the primary interviewer during the sensory-based diagnostic interview.

"What else interests Brian?" I asked.

Paula reviewed her notes from the parent interview. "Cartoons," she said. "He loves to watch them and to draw the characters. He also likes watching movies and enjoys watching the credits and the special features on DVDs. His parents told us that Brian watches the same movies repeatedly and prefers to have the closed caption script on the screen."

Beatrice added, "We talked with the parents about how the closed captioning probably helps Brian process the language because he can see it and read the text each time he watches the movie. On standardized testing, his language scores were low, given his average intelligence."

Paula said, "Take a look at his intellectual and achievement scores. His intelligence scores were average to high average, and he has strong basic reading and math skills. His language skills all came out low or low average, though. Oral expression, listening comprehension, reading comprehension, and written expression are all difficult for him." We all took some time to review and discuss the quantitative results of the standardized testing.

"He's been receiving speech and language therapy once a week since kindergarten. His therapist told us Brian has made gains in his ability to communicate, but speaking in social situations is still difficult for him. She told us he is quiet most of the time. His teacher told us the same thing about Brian in the classroom," Paula said, referring to the notes taken during her teacher interview and her conversation with the speech therapist.

She continued, "His teacher told us that Brian learns new information quickly, but he gets frustrated in class. She said he likes to keep his desk completely clear of materials except a sharpened pencil, the subject book, and the notebook he needs for a given assignment. She said he gets quite preoccupied with keeping his pencil sharpened and keeping the area surrounding his desk free of clutter. He gets upset when his classmates leave their backpacks or materials on the floor near his desk, and he yells at them when he thinks their things are in his space. At recess he will shoot baskets but becomes agitated when the other boys crowd around him. They tease him sometimes because Brian predictably makes an angry face and yells at them."

"At home, he plays with his younger brother at times. His parents described a similar pattern of getting upset when his brother gets in his space," Beatrice added. "They reported that Brian doesn't have any friends, and they see a definite difference between Brian's social skills and his brother's skills. They're not sure how much of this can be explained by Brian's language challenges. His mother told us she's done some reading on autism spectrum disorders and sees some characteristics in him. His lack of social skills was one of his parents' main concerns. The other was helping him manage his fears and his emotional reaction to changes in his routine."

> *The conversation among team members focused on describing the qualitative behavioral profile that emerged from the parent and teacher interviews and the classroom observations. Quantitative data were reviewed, but the emphasis was on discussing qualitative details that revealed Brian's unique behavioral profile.*

Paula jumped back into the conversation as she scanned her parent interview notes. "Brian's parents told us he doesn't want to ride his bicycle because he is afraid he'll fall down. He won't play soccer anymore because he was hit by a ball and doesn't want to get hit again. Overall, they described Brian as being extremely cautious. Noises bother him and he keeps his fingers in his ears when the family is out in public or in crowded places. He won't see movies in the theater because of the noise level. He cries easily and even small changes in his routine set him off."

"That reminds me," Beatrice interjected. "Didn't his teacher also tell you that he cries when his work isn't perfect?"

"That's right. He also erases his work repeatedly in an attempt to make everything perfect. She told us that when she gives directions to the whole class, she breaks down the directions into small steps for him. She also mentioned that she helped Brian set up an organizational binder. That's cut down on his crying in the past couple of months," Paula said.

"And we had his parents and teacher fill out the GADS," added Paula, as she handed me a copy of the *Gilliam Asperger's Disorder Scale* (GADS; Gilliam, 2001) checklist so I could see the items rated as *frequently observed* and *sometimes observed* by his parents and teacher.

"The teacher's probability score is quite a bit lower than the parents' score, but both rated a number of behaviors suggestive of developmental differences on the autism spectrum," I commented, as I reviewed the results of the checklist.

Paula remarked, "His teacher mentioned that she isn't sure what exactly is going on with Brian and getting in the way of his learning. She sees the language and communication difficulties and doesn't know if they are the reason he cries, gets angry with his classmates, and is sensitive to noises. It's going to be important that we meet with her individually and go over our findings in detail before we meet with her and his parents together."

"That's good to know. Let's make sure we allow plenty of time to meet with her before Brian's parents come in for the follow-up meeting," I said. I was grateful that Paula was so thorough in her conversations with the teacher and parents.

"Before we get Brian, let's talk a little about him in the context of the three key areas of the triangle. What did you notice when you observed him in the classroom?" I asked.

> *Paula and Beatrice described their observations of Brian in the classroom. They organized their observations and talked about Brian in the key areas of communication, social, and sensory behaviors.*

Beatrice focused on describing her observations of Brian's language and communication skills. "Brian rarely talked during the time I was in the classroom. He never spoke to his peers but did glance up and frown at one boy walking past his desk. When his teacher asked him a direct question, it took Brian almost a minute to answer. He used a very quiet voice."

Paula said, "I visited the classroom on a day they had a school assembly, so their schedule was thrown off. Brian followed his teacher around the room and kept telling her, 'Speech is at one thirty today, not at eleven o'clock,' until she physically led him back to his desk and told him to focus on his work. Socially, Brian kept to himself during my observation. In the lunchroom, he sat at the end of a table with his body turned away from the group. He didn't speak to any of the other children at the table. When they talked and laughed, he glanced in their direction once but didn't change the expression on his face. When he was in line waiting to use the bathroom, he yelled 'Stop it!' to the boy next to him when the boy was laughing and pushing another classmate next to Brian. After he yelled, he didn't look at the boy to see his reaction. Several boys in the line mimicked Brian, but he didn't seem to react to that."

Paula continued, "Also, he put his fingers in his ears when the noise volume in the lunchroom escalated. I noticed he ate only a few bites of his lunch. His teacher said Brian rarely eats his lunch, and he seems to be bothered by the noise level. She told us she's noticed that he puts his fingers in his ears a lot."

"Are we about ready to bring Brian in here?" Beatrice asked. "His teacher and his mother both told him that some ladies would be meeting with him at school today. Of course he's already worked with Paula and me. It will be interesting to see if he remembers us."

"It sounds like he might be somewhat hesitant to talk with us at first," I said. "Let's start out with an emphasis on exploring the sensory toys and minimize questions and talking. Didn't you say he likes to draw?"

"That's right, he does. His parents said he's really good at it, too," Paula said.

"Then let's have him draw some pictures for us early on in the session," I said.

As I made this suggestion, Paula already had blank sheets of paper and a colored pencil laid out on the table.

> Our team conversation helped us to discover the entry point for our upcoming conversation with Brian. We agreed that starting with an emphasis on play and limiting our use of language would help Brian relax and show us his authentic behavioral profile.

"Let's walk down to his classroom together to get him," I suggested. "Who wants to go with me?"

"Why don't you go, Beatrice. You worked with him last week. I'll stay here and get settled in at the table to take notes," said Paula. She expressed her preference to take more of an observational than a dynamic role in the upcoming conversation with Brian.

As we prepared to go to Brian's classroom, I organized some of the sensory toys and materials on the floor beside my chair. We would invite Brian to sit in a chair at the rectangular table, and I would sit to his left. Beatrice was planning to sit beside me and Paula would sit to Brian's right. I placed a magnetic sculpture with multiple pieces consisting of small rods and metal acrobats that stuck to an oval magnetic base on the table in front of what would be Brian's chair before I joined Beatrice at the door. We were ready to have our neuro-atypical conversation with Brian.

A TEAM CONVERSATION WITH BRIAN

Conducting the Sensory-Based Diagnostic Interview

Since Beatrice had already met Brian, she and I went to the classroom to get him for the interview session. When his teacher called Brian to the door, Beatrice leaned down to greet him.

"Hi, Brian," Beatrice said quietly, as she looked at him. Brian glanced at her briefly and then stood with his gaze averted to the side. She waited a moment before she continued. "It's nice to see you again." Brian maintained his silent focus on something in the distance. He had a solemn expression on his face. Again she paused before adding, "Do you remember working with me?"

After a moment, Brian nodded his head to indicate that he remembered meeting Beatrice.

"This is my friend, Dr. Monteiro," Beatrice said, as she gestured toward me. "She's going to go with us to the room where we were last week."

I waited until Brian glanced in my direction and waved my hand in an arc to greet him. He moved his right hand slightly but did not complete a gesture of greeting. Beatrice led the way and we entered the room to join Paula. Brian walked in silence beside us.

"Brian, this is my friend, Mrs. Peterson," Beatrice said, as she stretched her arm toward Paula, who was seated at the table. "Go ahead and sit next to her."

Brian glanced briefly at Paula, but his gaze settled on the magnetic sculpture on the table as he slipped into the chair in front of him. He began configuring the magnets into a pyramid of acrobats. A minute passed. He maintained a serious expression on his face as he focused his attention on the magnets and his construction.

Paula contemplated his sculpture in silence along with me and Beatrice. "That looks great," she said, pointing to his creation. She leaned toward him and placed her elbows on the table as she spoke.

Brian stiffened his posture and a look of anxiety settled on his face. Paula and I exchanged a glance as we both registered Brian's reaction to her physical proximity to him. Paula eased back in her chair, but Brian remained in a hyperalert state.

> *We minimized our talking at the start of the conversation and allowed pauses after each statement or question to give Brian ample time to process the verbal information. We also avoided talking about Brian and his responses in front of him.*

Now that we knew Brian was highly reactive to his perception of other people entering his personal space, we were able to plan accordingly for the rest of the session. Because he was so reactive to seemingly minor physical approaches, I decided to move the conversation along by inviting Brian to participate in one of his well-loved and familiar activities instead of introducing more novel sensory-based toys and materials. I gently slid a piece of blank paper in front of Brian along with the colored pencil. I had a pencil in my hand as well.

"I wish I could draw Mario," I sighed in a quiet voice. I paused a moment before continuing. Brian maintained his stiff posture but responded to the mention of the name of a familiar computer game character. "Okay if I draw something, Brian?" I suspended my hand with the pencil over the blank page as I waited for his acknowledgment and reaction to my request.

Although Brian did not speak, his facial expression and body posture relaxed slightly, indicating his interest in this new activity. I drew an oval on the page and colored in several circles within the oval. Then I drew a second one. By the time I'd colored in the second "egg," I could tell that Brian recognized my drawing as a depiction of the "eggs" that are associated with a character in several *Mario* games.

"Whose eggs are these?" I asked.

"Yoshi," Brian replied without hesitation.

"Can you draw Yoshi?" I asked.

> Shifting to a familiar, preferred activity helped Brian relax and abandon his anxiety about the novel situation. The use of a visual prompt helped him access his language and engage in conversation with me.

Brian picked up the colored pencil and hunched his entire body over the page. As he focused on completing his drawing, he quickly became absorbed in this process and appeared less aware of his surroundings. In a surprisingly short period of time, Brian created a highly detailed and instantly recognizable rendition of the Yoshi character. He sat back as he took in the details of his picture. He did not look at or reference me, Paula, or Beatrice, but sat still as he continued to examine his drawing.

"Hey, that looks just like Yoshi," I said. "But where is Mario?"

In a seamless motion, Brian once again hunched over the page and drew an astonishingly accurate picture of the plumber, including his moustache and overalls.

As Brian completed his second drawing, it was apparent that he was engaged in a neuro-atypical conversation with me. His body posture relaxed and the quality of his movements indicated that he was receptive to this social exchange and wanted it to continue. However, like most children with a pervasive developmental disorder, he was dependent on me to keep the interaction structured and move the process forward.

Another neuro-atypical characteristic of my conversation with Brian was his intense focus on the visual details of the activity paired with his lack of apparent interest in or ability to include the other adults in the room in this exchange. Even when Paula and Beatrice complimented Brian on his artwork, he did not reference them. When I referenced them and they added comments, Brian remained passive and waited until he received another prompt to draw additional pictures.

After Brian drew pictures of his favorite cartoon characters, I brought out several spinning toys that lit up when a button was pushed. Two of the toys were globes with LED lights that created changing, multicolored patterns. Another was a "light chaser" toy with a handle and droopy plastic stems that lit up and spun when the handle was squeezed. Yet another was a long pole with a ball attached to the end. Pushing a button on the handle caused the ball to light up in a colorful strobe effect. Brian explored the light properties of each of the toys and selected the one he liked the best to use more extensively. He picked up one of the globes and proceeded to intently focus on the light display while he involuntarily tensed his body and pushed his elbows into his sides.

"Oohh, that looks like fun," Beatrice said to Brian. "Can I have one?" She reached her arm across the table.

"Sure," Brian replied, as he randomly grabbed one of the remaining toys and handed it to her. He briefly established eye contact with Beatrice and watched as she activated her toy.

Beatrice waved her light chaser in the air, creating a pattern that resembled an atom in motion. She leaned her arm toward Brian so their two lit objects could collide. Brian allowed her to tap his globe and imitated her actions several times before he resumed his solitary play. When I picked up the second globe and entered into the game, Brian participated by tapping his globe against our toys for several exchanges. When we paused, he didn't invite us back into a light fight.

> We interacted with Brian with the light toys to gain an understanding of his social and sensory responses during a physical game that required little language. Compared to other 11-year-old boys, Brian's exploration of the light toys was driven by sensory rather than social dynamics.

"Wait a minute. Who else needs a light?" I asked, prompting Brian to notice that Paula was not yet equipped to wave a light wand in the air.

Brian pushed the remaining strobe light in Paula's direction. After she waved and tapped it for a minute, she introduced a new idea. "Let's trade," she offered.

"Sure," he said, as he handed her his globe in exchange for the strobe wand. After a moment, he reached out to have her return his preferred globe. When she protested, he looked at the remaining light toys and approached me because I had the remaining globe.

"How about you have this one?" he offered. "Is it time for math? Is it eleven thirty?" Brian's anxiety surfaced as he asked repeatedly about his interrupted school routine. "Math is at eleven thirty today," he reiterated.

> Although Brian appeared to prompt a social exchange with Paula, he did so only to obtain his preferred toy again. His use of social gestures to obtain access to a preferred sensory object is characteristic of children with high-functioning Autistic Disorder.

Brian had already shown us how well he could draw when he was able to focus on his preferred areas of video and cartoon characters. We wanted to see what his artwork was like when we asked him to draw more conventional pictures.

I put another piece of paper in front of him. "Brian, will you draw a picture of yourself for us?" I asked.

Brian picked up his pencil and looked at the blank sheet of paper for almost a minute. He placed his pencil close to the paper but did not begin his drawing. Finally he drew a rudimentary circle with dots for eyes, a line for the mouth, and a stick figure.

"How 'bout this picture?" he asked, as he began drawing a detailed rendition of Timmy Turner, a cartoon character. Brian's reluctance to draw a picture of himself and his quick redirection to drawing a preferred picture is a pattern that is often seen in children with autism spectrum disorders.

We continued with our team conversation by introducing a variety of toys and activities. Our play with Brian was a combination of interactional exchanges with him and observations as he explored some of the materials on his own terms. In the end, we were able to have a shared experience with Brian and obtain a detailed sample of his behavioral profile in the areas of communication, social, and sensory skills and behaviors.

> **How important is it for evaluators to know details about the child's areas of interest?**
>
> Probably more important than knowing a lot about the child's preferred topics is for members of the evaluation team to know *enough* about the topics to drop some names and ask a few comparison questions. What you're trying to do with the introduction of a preferred topic is to create a prompt for the child to show you how captured he or she becomes by the topic. Children who have autism spectrum disorders display a quality of becoming caught up in reliving the visual aspects of the topic. That quality can be clearly detected by the evaluators when they introduce topics of interest during the sensory-based diagnostic interview.
>
> Members of the autism evaluation team typically enjoy gathering specific facts and information about the child's preferred topics in preparation for the interview. What is important to convey to the child is that you have a genuine interest in listening to information about his or her preferred topics. That interest is conveyed to children on the spectrum by stating facts and information about their topics of interest.

A TEAM CONVERSATION ABOUT BRIAN

Reaching Consensus on Brian's Diagnosis

"What a great artist," said Beatrice. "He has an amazing visual memory for details."

"Drawing pictures was definitely his entry point for our conversation," Paula said. "I wanted to see if he would acknowledge me and respond to me in a social way when he was building his magnetic sculpture beside me, especially because I spent so much time with him a few weeks ago doing his intellectual and achievement testing. When he became anxious and reacted so strongly to the combination of my social comments and physical proximity, I backed off. Our plan to use his love of drawing to help ease him into the conversation turned out to be the way to go."

> *Our collaborative team conversation took place immediately following our interview with Brian.*

"I'm glad you complimented him at the beginning of the session and leaned in to share his space at the table, Paula. It helped us see how tremendously anxious he becomes when social and language demands are placed on him," I commented.

"Probing for a social entry point gave us a lot of good information," Paula said. "But his response to your neuro-atypical entry point was dramatically different. When you mentioned Mario out of the blue and drew the eggs, he was instantly transported to a pleasant and familiar experience."

"That was definitely my experience with him. Brian really didn't need a context other than the verbal and visual cues that triggered his preferred interest in the video and cartoon characters," I said.

"There seemed to be a sensory aspect to his drawing—both in terms of the content and his intense focus on the visual details, didn't you think?" asked Beatrice.

"Oh, most definitely," I responded. "Wasn't it interesting that he had such difficulty responding to the request to draw a picture of himself? The contrast between his detailed drawings of the Mario characters and his self-portrait was dramatic."

"We've seen that before with other artistic children with autism spectrum disorders," Beatrice commented. "His difficulty in drawing a socially based picture fits with his overall social challenges. Brian's play in general throughout the session was sensory-seeking instead of social."

"What was your social experience with him, Beatrice, when you asked him to give you a light chaser?" Paula asked.

"Brian looked at me and watched what I did with the toy, but he wasn't able to extend our social contact. Even though he said 'sure' and looked at me, he wasn't able to reciprocate or sustain his use of social gestures in the way most children do during that type of social exchange," Beatrice commented. "When I waved my light chaser around and tapped his, I had a sense that he enjoyed the interactive play, but he didn't seem to know what to do to keep it going. He was dependent on me to structure the social aspects of our play."

"That was my sense as well," I affirmed. "It was apparent that Brian enjoyed the social aspects of sharing the interest in his drawings, but he was dependent on me to structure the interaction.

> *Discussing our observations in a collaborative conversation allowed Brian's distinctive behavioral profile to emerge. Input from each team member was respected and valued.*

"Throughout the session, Brian reacted to us with a pattern of social developmental differences. I'm thinking about how Brian's response to the 'light fight' compared to other 11-year-old boys," I said. I wanted our team to reflect on some of the differences in development Brian showed us during our conversation.

Paula said, "He showed us some definite differences. Most boys would have asked us where we got the toys and might have asked questions about the choice of activity. They also would have introduced variations in the fight, and in general they would have participated in a highly interactive way. Think about how Joseph responded to us a couple of weeks ago." She referenced a 10-year-old boy the team had evaluated several weeks earlier. The team had ruled out a diagnosis of autism spectrum disorder for that child due to his social use of language and the social-exchange quality of his play.

"I thought Brian showed us a pattern of language, social, and sensory developmental differences. His use of language definitely showed a pattern of differences in addition to his delays," added Beatrice. "There was the delayed processing time and the use of single words and short phrases instead of more complex, age-appropriate language skills. And Brian also used his language in a neuro-atypical way."

"Like when he asked the same question over and over about what time his math class started," Paula reflected.

> *Our discussion was organized around the visual framework of the three key areas of language and communication, social relationships and emotional responses, and sensory use and interests. We focused on qualitative descriptions of Brian's behavior.*

"Brian has considerable anxiety that is triggered by language and social demands," I remarked. "Throughout the session, his spontaneous comments revolved around either labeling objects and events in his immediate visual environment or asking repetitive questions about the time for his next activity. My sense was that having his routine disrupted was very stressful for Brian."

"His response to us was typical of what his teacher and parents have seen as well," Beatrice added.

"So let's go over his behavioral profile in detail," I suggested. It was time for us to organize our observations in the visual framework of the triangle of developmental differences. Throughout our conversation,

Paula had written down each of our observations, using the visual framework for the three key areas of language and communication, social relationships and emotional responses, and sensory use and interests, to create Brian's unique behavioral profile. Brian's resulting behavioral profile is shown in Figure 7.

> *The creation of Brian's visual triangle allowed his distinctive diagnostic profile to emerge. Organizing our observations using the visual framework helped us reach a consensus on his diagnosis.*

As we discussed his behaviors and organized our observations around the visual framework of the triangle, Brian's diagnostic profile clearly emerged. We had taken into account all of our sources of information to help us determine the most compelling way to talk about his learning challenges.

"Talking about Brian as a child with an autism spectrum disorder really makes sense," Beatrice remarked, as we gathered around the triangle depicting his individual behavioral profile.

"I agree," I said. "His language delays are only part of the picture. He also showed us a pattern of differences in how he related to us and in his sensory-driven interests and use of the toys. At the same time, he clearly enjoyed the shared play with the light toys, but only momentarily. And in the classroom, although he does some social initiating with his peers, for the most part he is not social with them."

> *In determining Brian's diagnosis, we reviewed the sensory-based diagnostic interview, as well as multiple sources of collateral information (e.g., results of standardized testing, information from parent and teacher interviews). We also completed a* Childhood Autism Rating Scale *form and reviewed relevant diagnostic criteria.*

"Overall, do you think his pattern of mild but significant developmental differences is a better fit with the profile of high-functioning Autistic Disorder or Pervasive Developmental Disorder Not Otherwise Specified?"

"High-functioning Autistic Disorder really describes him," Paula reflected. "Even though he responded briefly to our social play, he

FIGURE 7
Brian's Autistic Disorder Behavioral Profile

AUTISTIC DISORDER

MILD — SIGNIFICANT

Language and *Communication*

- Rarely speaks
- Speaks in a whisper or low volume
- Needs extra time to process language
- Language skills less developed than nonverbal reasoning skills
- Asked perseverative questions about his schedule and routine
- Organized language best when he had visual contextual cues
- Rarely initiates and has difficulty sustaining social conversations
- Nonverbal language, such as eye contact and changes in facial expression, was limited
- Able to use and respond somewhat to both verbal and nonverbal cues and requests

Sensory Use and *Interests*

- Highly sensitive to changes in his routine
- Strong memory for visual details
- Sensory-seeking drive to his play
- Sensitive to physical boundaries
- Seeks out repetitive play, but can be redirected
- Unusual movements include body tensing, face close to paper when drawing
- Interests focus on drawing video game and cartoon characters; restricted range of interests for his age

Social Relationships and *Emotional Responses*

- Neutral expression most of the time
- Anxious about social exchanges
- When relaxed, is somewhat responsive to people
- Social interactions with peers are difficult
- Anxious about changes in his routine
- Responsive to structured social play, but unable to initiate and sustain social exchanges

showed us a consistent pattern of sensory-driven behavior. He explored the toys in a sensory-seeking way, and he showed sensory sensitivity to sounds and to our physical presence. The sensory aspect to his way of reacting to the world is best described by Autistic Disorder rather than by PDD-NOS."

Beatrice added her observations. "He has the uneven pattern of development, with his nonverbal reasoning skills in the average to above average range and his language skills considerably less developed. The level of anxiety he experiences when he is placed in unstructured situations that require language and social behaviors is also typical of children with Autistic Disorder. Changes in his routine are highly stressful for him."

I added my thoughts to the discussion. "Let's not forget his sensory drive to focus on his preferred activities, including drawing cartoon figures and watching movie credits. He has a preoccupation with his internal agenda that became apparent during the diagnostic interview. It was difficult for him to shift to our agenda and to respond to our prompts with the interactive play. He was dependent on us to structure the social play. That's also typical of children with Autistic Disorder.

"With a diagnosis of PDD-NOS, we would have seen less perseverative and restricted use of language," I continued. "The way Brian repeated his questions and the rote and scripted quality of his speech were typical of what we see in children with Autistic Disorder. Children with PDD-NOS show a broader ability to use language to initiate social exchanges. If Brian had shown us more of a pattern of initiating social interactions, both in our session and in the classroom, he would have shown us the pattern of behavior that is more typical of children with PDD-NOS."

"Brian was captured by the visual details inherent in his drawings, and it was difficult for him to redirect his attention to include us when we introduced alternate activities," Beatrice said. "Also, he showed us the intense, repetitive body movements and mannerisms that the toys elicit in children with classic autism. Even though the duration of his repetitive movements was brief, the intensity with which he became captured by the visual details of the materials and the intensity of his body tensing fit with the pattern of Autistic Disorder more than with PDD-NOS. He showed us the pattern of mild but significant developmental differences we see in children with high-functioning Autistic Disorder."

> **What is the difference between a quantitative and a qualitative vocabulary?**
>
> The distinction between a *quantitative* and a *qualitative* vocabulary is important. The diagnostic process involved in determining whether a child has an autism spectrum disorder involves gathering information, both quantitative (numerical) and qualitative (descriptive). Ultimately, it is clinical judgment, informed by both quantitative and qualitative information, that guides an evaluation team to make the actual diagnosis for an individual child. In my experience, when evaluators focus on their *quantitative* vocabulary, they talk only about the child's scores on various standardized measures. The tendency during a quantitative discussion is to reduce the scope of the discussion about the child to numbers that are linked to generic behavioral descriptions.
>
> When evaluation teams focus their discussion on quantitative results, it becomes difficult to develop a comprehensive and qualitative description of the child. The visual framework described in this book provides an organizational tool that guides evaluation teams to discuss the child's qualitative behavioral profile instead of the sum of numerical results. A *qualitative* vocabulary refers to a discussion of the child's words and actions, as the evaluation team systematically reviews the three key areas of the child's communication, social, and sensory responses.
>
> When evaluation teams use a qualitative vocabulary, along with the structure provided by the visual framework, they can develop a detailed description of the child's behavioral profile. That description can then be supported by the quantitative results and applied to a diagnosis as a natural step in the diagnostic process. This process considerably enhances the team's ability to reach accurate and complete diagnostic conclusions.

Linking Brian's Diagnosis to His Educational Plan

"Let's talk about ways to support Brian's language and communication differences," I said. "His teacher has done a great job of including some organizational and visual supports already."

"The organizational notebook she set up for him is good because it's a place where he can put his pending assignments and his finished work. Brian also needs a written schedule, though, so he can see what is coming next and feel in control by crossing off each event as he goes through his day," Paula added. "The visual schedule will help him with his difficulty during transition times because he'll be able to reference it each time a transition time comes up. Having him check off activities as he completes them will help him get a better sense of closure so he can move from one activity to the next."

> We organized our discussion of suggested educational supports for Brian around the three key areas of language and communication, social relationships and emotional responses, and sensory use and interests.

"Definitely. In addition to his schedule and the checklist, it might also be a good idea to set up a 'pending' file in the classroom to help Brian become less upset when it's time to change activities and he isn't finished yet," I suggested.

"Clearly, he does best when he has visual organization paired with predictable routines," Beatrice commented. "I noticed that his teacher uses a lot of verbal direction and redirection instead of step-by-step visual directions. Adding visual checklists with directions on them would give her another way to help Brian organize his behavior and stay focused on his work."

"I agree. The more Brian can rely on visual cues and supports, the less anxious he will become. Also, the visual backup will help him process spoken language better. When we talk with his teacher, we can make the link between Brian's use of closed caption wording when he watches his movies and the use of written instructions in the classroom," I said, recalling relevant information from the parent interview.

> Discussing Brian's educational needs in the area of language and communication after his evaluation helped us make practical links between his learning style and the types of classroom interventions that would benefit him.

"That's a good way to talk about why Brian needs visual supports," added Beatrice. "We may also want to talk about ways to help Brian access the language he needs to work on written assignments. He would benefit from access to word banks, visual worksheets that outline the steps involved in writing assignments, and even giving him some selections to choose from when he is asked to tell the main idea from a passage he's read.

"Of course, it's also going to be important for us to continue to systematically build his language skills through therapy and applied practice," Beatrice reflected.

"I think we also need to emphasize the need for Brian to link the use of his visual supports to a daily check-in time with a mentor adult. That could be either his classroom teacher or a special education teacher," I recommended.

"The daily check-in sheet creates a way for Brian to visually go through the steps involved in monitoring his work and his behavior. It also gives him predictable language prompts to help him express himself."

"Brian's language challenges and his preoccupation with his interests make his social relationships with his classmates difficult," Beatrice added. "He yells at them or ignores them. I would like to see him get some coaching and direct teaching to learn the words and actions he needs to use in social situations. He needs to have the replacement words and actions visually laid out for him, not just told to him."

"That's right. A visual discrimination sheet that shows what he 'used to do' and contrasts it with what he does 'now' would be really helpful for him," I said. "Getting back to the idea of his use of closed captions and his love of drawing, Brian would respond well to the use of social scripts and comic strip depictions of what to say and do in various everyday situations."

"Including his social scripts in his organizational notebook would give him a place to keep them and would help his teachers remind him to use his scripts in social situations," added Paula.

"Brian's anxiety is linked to social and language demands as well as with times when he has to shift from his agenda to the agenda of others. The use of social scripts and adding a systematic way for him to rate how he is doing throughout the day would give him a greater sense of predictability and control," Beatrice stated.

"Speaking of helping him manage his anxiety," Paula said, "let's make sure we talk about his need for systematic sensory breaks during the day. He needs to be able to anticipate specific times when he will be able to unplug from demands for a short period of time to draw or move so he can successfully regroup. We should suggest collaborating with the occupational therapist and his teacher to set up sensory breaks."

"The breaks need to be associated with Brian's use of his self-monitoring system so he can start to regulate his own needs throughout the school day," Beatrice added.

"Self-regulation is so important for Brian," I remarked. "He'll become more aware of his needs once the visual supports are put into place, along with having the system tied to a mentor adult.

"You mentioned creating opportunities for Brian to draw during the day," I continued. "We should also look into ways to create opportunities for Brian to develop his natural artistic talent. He may be able to work with the art teacher to develop more technical skills or be coached to enter some art competitions."

"I could see that being a positive thing for him," Paula added. "Let's be sure to talk about that with his teacher and his parents. They'll need to work together closely to make sure his visual supports are in place across settings.

"Okay," Paula continued. "As we were talking, I wrote out our suggestions for Brian's educational supports. Let's go over them and see if there's anything else we want to add."

Throughout our conversation, Paula had written our suggestions around a triangle, creating an outline of our ideas for Brian's individualized educational supports. Figure 8 depicts the visual profile of suggested educational supports for Brian.

FIGURE 8
Suggested Educational Supports for Brian

Language and *Communication*

- Does best with visual organization and predictable routines
- Organizational notebook system will help him manage his anxiety and should include:
  - Daily check-in sheet
  - Section for assignments and homework
  - List of adults and a help plan
  - Self-rating scale
- In class, consider using step-by-step visual directions
- Language supports may include word banks, identifying main ideas from a selection, and a visual framework for written assignments
- Consider using a "pending" file as a physical transition routine when tasks are not finished
- Continue to systematically build language skills through therapy and applied practice

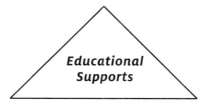

Sensory Use and Interests

- Allow times during the day for art breaks
- Develop sensory routines
- Link the use of sensory routines with self-monitoring routines ("How am I doing?")
- Develop art talent into possible vocational skill
- Take preoccupation with drawing cartoons and develop it into functional skill set

Social Relationships and Emotional Responses

- Develop language and social skills with visual scripts and guided practice with peers
- Develop adaptive words and actions to replace yelling at peers

We had used the visual framework to gather information, have our conversation with Brian, and organize our observations. During our next step we literally wrote our diagnostic conclusions around the triangle and linked those conclusions to suggestions for his educational program. Now we were ready to have our diagnostic conversations with Brian's parents and teacher.

AN EXAMPLE OF A DIFFERENTIAL DIAGNOSIS

A Team Conversation With Felix

Now that we've listened to one team's conversation with Brian, let's compare Brian to Felix, another child with speech and language delays. Before I describe the diagnostic conversation the evaluation team had with Felix, I'll provide some background information. On this evaluation team, I worked with Pam, a speech therapist, and Marco, a school psychologist.

Felix was a 6-year-old boy who was referred for an autism evaluation by his kindergarten teacher. His mother told the evaluation team that Felix was seen by a neurologist when he was a toddler. The parents were told at that time that their son had autism and would not be able to make friends or communicate as he got older. Despite this prediction, Felix acquired basic language skills as he participated in a preschool program for children with disabilities. At the time of our evaluation, he was receiving speech therapy twice a week and was enrolled in a regular education kindergarten program.

Felix's mother told the team that her son was withdrawn as a young child and didn't begin talking until after his third birthday. Although he was now able to talk and communicate, his mother noted that Felix became shy and anxious when he had to respond to questions or hold conversations with people outside of his immediate family. When he did talk, he tended to whisper and became visibly distraught when he was encouraged to speak louder.

Felix's mother told the team that at home Felix was affectionate and liked to play rough and tumble games with his father. He only recently started to enjoy cartoons and television shows. She mentioned that he liked watching cartoons about Clifford the Big Red Dog. The family had a dog named Clifford. His mother shared that Felix had a behavior pattern of finding important papers to tear up when he was left alone. She indicated that he seemed to select items to rip up that would capture the attention of his parents. Other than his anxiety surrounding talking, Felix's mother reported that her son slept well at night, ate a variety of foods, and was not particularly bothered by noises or crowds.

Felix's mother remarked that since he had started attending

kindergarten, he had been talking more. At home she noticed that Felix was beginning to ask questions and offer comments when he was with other members of his family.

Felix's teacher told the team that in the classroom Felix refused to participate in group activities regardless of the encouragement or consequences she provided. He would only speak in a whisper and only when he was in a small group or alone with her. She reported that when she asked him questions, he responded by repeatedly wringing his hands together.

In terms of Felix's social skills, his teacher noted that Felix had recently found a buddy in the class and the two boys consistently played together at recess and sought each other out in class. Regarding Felix's academic work, she stated that Felix learned new concepts and information quickly when he could see the steps involved, especially if she used a picture or diagram to explain the new information. Cognitive testing had revealed a significant gap between Felix's verbal abilities and his nonverbal reasoning skills. Although his verbal abilities fell in the low average to borderline range for his age, his nonverbal reasoning skills were measured to be well in the average range.

Both Pam, the speech therapist, and Marco, the school psychologist, had observed Felix in his classroom in the weeks prior to our evaluation session. They noticed that Felix rarely spoke, and when he did, he made brief statements and spoke in a whisper. During group lessons, they observed that Felix frequently wandered around the perimeter of the room instead of remaining seated with the group. They noticed that during his wandering, Felix periodically looked at his teacher and his classmates and watched their actions and activities. On the playground, he was observed playing chase and hugging another boy. Felix approached the boy to play and the other boy appeared to seek out Felix as well.

"Hi, Felix," Marco said, as he leaned over to be at eye level with him. His teacher had just introduced Marco and me as people who would be working with him this morning.

Felix looked at each of us as he studied our faces and took in the situation.

"Hey, are you ready to come with us and play some games?" Marco asked, as he continued to lean over close to Felix.

Looking at both of us again, Felix nodded his head.

"Okay, then. Let's go down to Mrs. Campbell's room. Do you remember where that is?" Marco built on the affirmative nod received from Felix. Felix nodded again and the three of us walked down the hall to the speech room.

"Good job, Felix!" Marco paused before speaking again, giving Felix time to process his comments. "You sure know your way around the school."

As we entered the interview room, Marco said, "Hey, check out this cool toy." He pointed to the table where a water ring toss game was positioned in front of a chair. Pam was seated at the table next to the toy. She smiled at Felix and he shyly smiled back.

"Hi, Felix. Remember me? Mrs. Campbell?" Pam patted the chair next to her as she spoke. Again Felix nodded, to acknowledge his recollection of meeting Pam before. He glanced over at Marco and me once more before he sat in front of the ring toss game. Felix looked at Pam as he reached for the toy and hesitated before he grasped hold of it.

"Go ahead. Show us how many rings you can get on there," Pam said, urging Felix to get started with his exploration of the toy.

As Felix began to push the button that made the rings swirl in the water and fall toward the pegs, Marco sat down beside him and I sat next to Marco. As several of the rings landed on the pegs, Felix looked up at Marco and me and smiled. He turned his head toward Pam and smiled at her as well.

"Way to go, Felix!" Marco said, raising his hand for a "high-five" gesture. Felix quickly slapped his hand and the smile spread to his eyes. Clearly, he was enjoying himself.

"Try again," Pam said.

As Felix started pushing the button with abandon, causing the rings to circle rapidly and glide toward the pegs, Marco leaned over the table and placed his face on the opposite side of the transparent toy. As he did so, Felix immediately shifted his visual attention away from the toy and grinned back at Marco. Marco sat back in his chair and said, "Man, that looks like fun."

Felix pushed the toy toward Marco and looked at him, clearly indicating that it was Marco's turn.

> *Marco and Pam purposefully set up the entry point for the conversation with Felix to emphasize play rather than spoken conversation.*

"My turn?" Marco asked. Felix nodded vigorously. Marco took the toy and frowned at it. "So tell me what I do to make this work."

Felix pointed to the button.

"So what do I do?" Marco persisted.

"Push it," Felix said. He had finally spoken. Marco pushed the toy gently away from him with both hands and then stopped. He waited and we were all silent.

"Push the *button*," Felix clarified. Marco immediately pushed the button in rapid succession and we all laughed and congratulated him. Felix looked pleased that his advice was so well received. We were delighted to hear him speak.

After a few turns for all of us, Marco introduced several plastic insects that crawled after they were wound using a knob on the side of each toy. He held a green and an orange caterpillar in the palm of his hand and offered them to Felix.

"Do you want the green one or the orange one?" Marco asked Felix.

Felix alternated between looking at the caterpillars and looking at Marco. "Orange one," he said.

Pam stepped in with a language prompt. "Felix, use a sentence."

Felix paused for a moment, and said, "I want the orange one."

"Wind it up," Marco urged, as he held the green one. When Felix started to wind up his caterpillar, Marco did the same. After Felix watched the caterpillars crawl across the table, making a mechanical noise as they inched their way forward, he handed the green one back to Marco and said, "Let's have a race."

Pam placed a pencil on the table and said, "Start here."

Felix stood up in excitement. He wound his caterpillar and looked at Marco and then at Pam, anticipating the signal to start the race.

After two races, Pam said, "What about me?"

I chimed in as well. "I want to play, too."

"Oh, sure," Felix said. He looked around at the toys on the floor next to Marco and selected a windup crab for Pam and a fish with a pull string for me.

"Okay. Okay. Ready, set, go!" Felix was getting as wound up as the toys as he enjoyed the game. A couple of times when his caterpillar was in last place, he pushed it forward with his finger. Each time he "cheated" in this way, he giggled and looked at Marco, Pam, or me to see our reactions.

The game drew to a close as Marco held out a plastic storage bag and asked Felix to help him put all the toys back in the bag. Marco then handed a pencil to Felix and slid a blank piece of paper in front of him.

"Let's draw some pictures," he suggested.

> Marco's open-ended suggestion for Felix to draw pictures provided an opportunity to learn whether he would focus on a preferred topic or draw something with a social reference point. His mother had mentioned that Marco enjoyed watching a cartoon about Clifford, a big red dog.

"Okay." Felix shifted his attention from the game to the paper-and-pencil task with ease. "What do you want me to draw?" he asked.

"Draw anything you want," Marco said.

"Hmmm. Maybe…maybe I'll draw…maybe…my dog!" Felix perked up as he made his decision. He industriously began drawing his picture. His tongue protruded slightly from the right corner of his mouth as he concentrated on the task.

"Tell us about your dog," said Pam, prompting Felix to talk while he worked.

Felix had to finish his drawing before he was able to respond to her question. "My dog is called Clifford," he grinned. "My Clifford is big, but he is not red!" Felix was referring to the children's stories about a big red dog named Clifford.

"That's a great picture, Felix," Marco said. This drew Felix's attention immediately back to his drawing. He studied it briefly and then continued to draw. Felix drew a doghouse and then added a stick figure representing himself. He added his mother and father and baby sister to the picture. Then he added their house, a tree, and some grass. He finished his picture by adding some clouds with a flourish.

> *Social praise and attention were meaningful to Felix. He was motivated to expand on his drawing after we showed an interest in it and praised his hard work.*

We continued our session with Felix using a combination of interactive activities and observations of his behavior. Each time we pulled back and assumed a passive role in the session, Felix pulled us back into an interactional exchange by asking questions, handing us toys, and looking in the bag for additional games to play. When it was time to go back to class, he asked us when we would be coming back. He gave each of us a spontaneous hug and skipped down the hallway several times as we made the trek to his classroom. When he entered his classroom, he sighed audibly and visibly tensed his body. His shoulders slumped and he assumed a posture of defeat. As he took his place on the carpet with the rest of his class, he threw a glance of longing over his shoulder at us and waved goodbye.

A Diagnosis for Felix

"Wow, what a great kid," Marco commented, after we took Felix back to the classroom. "Did you see the look on his face when we left him in his classroom?"

"He looked like he'd rather continue to play with us, that's for sure," Pam said.

I added my observations. "His entry point with us—his way of connecting with us—throughout the interview was driven by social relationships and emotional responses. It was dramatically apparent from the beginning of the session that Felix is a child for whom social and emotional connections are more of a driving force than the sensory agenda that captures children on the autism spectrum."

"I agree," said Marco. "Even though Felix didn't say a word for the longest time at the start of the session, he consistently showed us in nonverbal ways that he wanted to have a social connection with each of us. He used eye contact and smiles and facial expressions. His body posture and gestures all signaled that he wanted to establish a social connection."

Pam said, "He was so responsive to social praise and attention. It was apparent that it motivated him to have us compliment him and pay attention to him."

"Let's talk about his behavioral profile in the three key areas," I said. "What did you notice about his language and communication?"

> *After the sensory-based diagnostic interview with Felix, we discussed his behavioral profile in each of the three key areas.*

"He was definitely reluctant to speak at first," Marco commented. "But from the very start of the session, he used nonverbal communication functions to make a social link with us. One distinctive quality of his use of nonverbal language functions was his consistent attention to our responses. When he pointed to something, he paid attention to our responses. He also used a wide range of natural facial expressions to convey information—something we don't see in children with autism spectrum disorders."

"I completely agree," I added. "Felix consistently initiated social communication with us and was not dependent on us to prompt him to do so. What did you think about his expressive language skills, Pam?"

"Clearly expressive language is difficult for him," Pam replied. "The pattern of his language use is something I see a lot with children who have a significant language learning difference. He was reluctant to speak at first and preferred using phrases instead of sentences. And yet when I prompted him to extend his utterances, he was able to use full sentences."

"And he spontaneously asked a full question when I suggested that we draw some pictures," Marco recalled.

Pam looked at her notes where she had scripted a language sample for Felix during the interview session. "That's right. He asked, 'What do you want me to draw?'"

Scanning her notes, she continued. "It was hard for him to express his thoughts in any detail and it was apparent that his expressive language challenges limit his ability to communicate. Did you notice how much trouble he had responding to and using language when he was drawing or playing with some of the toys that required manipulation and focus?"

"Definitely," I said. "It makes sense why he has so much trouble staying focused and engaged in the language-driven environment of the classroom."

"Let's talk more about his social relationships and emotional responses," Marco said. "His play with us had a quality of social connection rather than a sensory drive. Felix liked organizing and having races with us and giggled whenever he 'cheated' by pushing his toy to the finish line ahead of ours."

"And his drawing was all about social relationships," Pam added. "At first, I thought we might see a restricted range of interests when he talked about drawing Clifford the dog. But when he continued to add his family and to use the drawing to share social information with us, clearly he showed us a neuro-typical response to social relationships."

I added my observations. "Felix's expressive language challenges definitely limit his ability to talk with his peers, but he has established a genuine connection with one other boy in his class. He also watches what the other kids are doing a lot of the time. The challenge for Felix is not so much a lack of understanding of social relationships, but how to work around his communication deficits."

"I agree," Marco said.

"What about his sensory use and interests?" Pam asked.

"His response to the toys was primarily social," Marco responded. "He moved from toy to toy with ease and was more interested in the toys when he was able to participate in a social exchange as part of his exploration."

"Unlike children with autism spectrum disorders, Felix introduced variations into his play," I added. "He watched what we did and participated in the exploration of the toys in an interactive and reciprocal way."

Pam said, "And even though he got pretty wound up with the races with the wind-up toys, he didn't use any repetitive or involuntary sensory responses to the sensory input. He jumped up and down a few times, but in an excited way rather than in the repetitive or self-involved sensory pattern we see with children on the autism spectrum."

As we discussed Felix's behavioral profile, Pam wrote our comments

> *Felix's behavioral profile lacked the pattern of developmental differences that characterize children with autism spectrum disorders. His responses during the sensory-based diagnostic interview helped us make a differential diagnosis and rule out the presence of an autism spectrum disorder.*

around the visual triangle. Felix's behavioral profile is depicted in Figure 9.

"So what is the most compelling way to understand Felix's learning challenges?" I asked. "His significant learning differences account for his social and language challenges better than a diagnosis of a broader pervasive developmental disorder on the autism spectrum."

FIGURE 9
Felix's Language Learning Differences Behavioral Profile

Language and Communication

- Reticent to speak
- Speaks in short phrases, but occasionally uses full sentences and questions
- Intonation and inflection vary and match the content of his speech
- Needs extra time to process language
- Language skills less developed than nonverbal reasoning skills
- Organized language best when he had visual contextual cues
- Initiates and participates in social conversations, but language use is limited
- Nonverbal language, such as eye contact and changes in facial expression, extensively and appropriately used
- Able to use and respond consistently and appropriately to both verbal and nonverbal cues and requests

Differences in Development

Sensory Use and Interests

- Flexible about changes in his routine
- Strong memory for visual details
- Social rather than sensory-seeking drive to his play
- Showed a range of age-appropriate interests
- Seeks out social play, but can be redirected
- No repetitive use of unusual body movements
- Drawings and play with the examiners focused on social content

Social Relationships and Emotional Responses

- Used varied and appropriate facial expressions
- Responded positively to social exchanges
- When relaxed, is consistently responsive to people
- Social interactions with peers is limited, but has established genuine friendship with a peer
- Responsive to social praise and attention
- Responsive to structured social play
- Able to initiate and sustain social exchanges

"I agree," said Marco. "Felix has a clear social drive, and social relationships are important to him. He did not show us the neuro-atypical pattern of seeking out repetitive sensory input that is a key difference for children with autism spectrum disorders."

"He obviously enjoyed the social aspects of exploring the toys," added Pam.

"At the same time, like most children with significant language challenges, Felix relies on visual cues in the classroom to guide him through the school day," I said. "In terms of educational supports, he would really benefit from more visual aids to understand directions in the classroom."

"And he will continue to need speech and language therapy to develop his expressive language skills," Pam said.

"Adding some social language practice to his speech and language sessions would help him expand his use of words with his classmates," added Marco.

As we discussed educational supports for Felix, we wrote our suggestions beside the visual triangle. Felix's educational supports are depicted in Figure 10.

FIGURE 10
Suggested Educational Supports for Felix

Language *and* Communication

- In class, consider using step-by-step visual directions
- Language supports may include word banks, identifying main ideas from a selection, and a visual framework for written assignments
- Continue to systematically build language skills through therapy and applied practice
- Add social language practice to speech and language therapy sessions

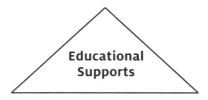

Sensory Use
and
Interests

- Provide visual supports to supplement verbal directions
- Provide age-appropriate physical breaks and play routines

Social Relationships
and
Emotional Responses

- Develop language and social skills with visual scripts and guided practice with peers

"Since he and his classmate have already developed a genuine connection, it would be helpful to provide Felix with some social language practice to expand his social language repertoire when he plays with his friend," Marco said. "Adding some social language practice would help him branch out to form successful relationships with other classmates as well."

"Academically, Felix is a capable child, but he has difficulty processing the language during class instruction," I added. "He would benefit from having instructions visually laid out for him."

"The more he can follow visual directions, the better able he is going to be to stay focused on the lessons taking place in the classroom," Marco said.

Our sensory-based diagnostic interview with Felix allowed us to gain a perspective on his communication, social, and sensory behavioral profile. We were able to compare his responses to us and the sensory toys with the responses seen in other children in a similar situation. Felix's pattern of responses helped us to rule out the diagnosis of an autism spectrum disorder and to describe his learning challenges in practical and compelling terms.

THE COLLABORATIVE TEAM PROCESS

The collaborative team conversation process helps evaluation team members discuss the child's behavioral profile and reach a consensus regarding the most compelling diagnosis for that child. The most compelling diagnosis is the one that best describes that child's specific challenges. Team members will feel most assured about their diagnosis when they can talk about it in this way. Once the evaluation team completes the collaborative team process, they are ready to discuss the diagnosis with the child's parents and teacher.

Now that we've talked about the conversations that take place among team members as they work collaboratively to reach a diagnosis, let's talk about the process involved when the evaluation team discusses the diagnosis with a child's parents and teacher.

How difficult is it to form an autism evaluation team, and how do newly formed teams learn to work together?

The biggest challenge in forming an autism evaluation team is making the commitment to do so. As the incidence rate of autism spectrum disorders continues to rise, there is a pressing need for experienced evaluation specialists to accurately make these complex diagnostic determinations. Assembling an autism evaluation team is the best way to obtain a comprehensive diagnostic profile of a child suspected of having an autism spectrum disorder.

The commitment to form an autism evaluation team starts with administrative support. In other words, to form a team that consists of professionals from various disciplines (e.g., psychology, speech and language pathology, occupational therapy) in a school district or clinic, there must be administrative support to allocate time in each person's schedule to participate in team evaluation activities and to provide training relevant to diagnosing autism spectrum disorders.

Teams that work together consistently are most likely to become accurate and efficient in addressing complex diagnostic questions. Once the team is formed, it helps if the members discuss the process they want to use as a team and decide what role each member will play in the process. The best teams are ones that combine predictable structure with built-in flexibility. Usually on an autism evaluation team, there are members who especially enjoy interacting with children, and others who like talking with parents and teachers, or taking notes and making observations. It is important to discuss what role each team member feels is a good fit with his or her skills, training, and personality. Even though there may be a specific role each team member finds to be the most comfortable, the best teams are ones on which all the members are trained to complete all the parts of the evaluation process: parent and teacher interviews, leading the sensory-based diagnostic interview, recording observational information and data, and so on.

Collaborative Team Conversations: Discussing the Diagnosis

What is the collaborative team conversation to discuss the child's diagnosis?

- It is a discussion that takes place immediately following the interview with the child.
- Team members review all of the information gathered during the evaluation process.
- The discussion of the child's behavioral profile using qualitative language allows team members to identify the child's distinctive behavioral profile.

How is it structured?

- Although one team member leads the discussion, all members participate in the collaborative conversation and each member's input is respected and valued.
- The discussion is organized around the visual framework of the three key areas of the child's language, social, and sensory behavioral profile.
- The creation of a visual triangle for the child that lists specific behaviors in each of the key areas channels the discussion among team members to focus on the behaviors that are characteristic of autism spectrum disorders.

What are the benefits?

- Team members must come to a consensus on the diagnosis before discussing the diagnosis with parents and teachers.
- Differential diagnoses unfold clearly when the multidisciplinary team discusses the child's unique behavioral profile in detail.
- The team discusses the link between the child's diagnosis and suggestions for the child's educational program.

CHAPTER 6

Conversations With Parents

The Diagnostic Feedback Conversation

The Diagnostic Feedback Conversation

What is the diagnostic feedback conversation?

- It is a continuation of the conversation between the parents and the evaluation team that started during the parent interview.
- It is an informal but structured meeting to discuss the child's diagnosis.
- Teachers and others may be included in this conversation, but the focus is on the conversation between the parents and the evaluators.

How is it structured?

- The conversation begins with the evaluators sharing stories and details about the child that convey their genuine appreciation and understanding of the child to the parents.
- Evaluators utilize the descriptive triangle to provide parents with a visual framework for understanding their child's pattern of developmental differences, using nontechnical but specific language.
- The conversation ends with a focus on practical strategies to address the child's developmental differences in the three key areas.

What are the benefits?

- The conversation focuses first on describing the behavioral profile of the child, and then on discussing the formal diagnosis. Parents appreciate this attention to their child's unique qualities.
- The conversation allows time for parents to absorb difficult news and process their grief over receiving the diagnosis.
- The conversation includes a discussion of the child's positive qualities and links them to practical teaching strategies.

PREPARING FOR THE
DIAGNOSTIC FEEDBACK CONVERSATION WITH PARENTS

Before I talk with parents about their child and the diagnosis of an autism spectrum disorder, I prepare myself by thinking about how exceptionally stressful it is for parents to hear such a difficult and lifelong diagnosis. Most of the time, parents already have an idea that something is different in their child's development, but they just don't have a clear understanding of what those differences mean and how to make sense out of them. The process of revisiting hopes and expectations for a child and replacing them with a revised worldview to accommodate their child's neurological differences is a hard path for parents. We need to be sensitive to parents and aware of where they are in the acceptance process as we discuss their child and the child's diagnosis.

What exactly is the diagnostic feedback conversation? It is an informal but structured meeting to discuss the outcome of the evaluation process. Think of it as a continuation of the conversation you started with the parents during the parent interview. One member of the evaluation team, often the psychologist, takes the lead in the conversation, but the meeting works best if all members of the evaluation team are present. When possible, request permission from the child's parents to include the child's teacher, speech therapist, and even the school principal in the conversation. This collaborative meeting among the parents, evaluation team, and school staff directly connected to the child helps parents experience a sense of support and community as they receive their child's diagnosis. If the parents allow school staff to be included in the conversation, make sure the staff understand the diagnosis by discussing your findings with them prior to their participation. Some parents prefer to have the diagnostic feedback conversation with only the evaluation team present. Be sure to discuss these options with parents and address confidentiality concerns relevant to the setting in which the evaluation is conducted, as you plan and structure the diagnostic feedback conversation.

Although parents and teachers of children diagnosed with autism spectrum disorders will eventually participate in a formal, legal meeting to determine educational goals and objectives (referred to as an IEP, or individualized education plan, meeting), I recommend having a separate diagnostic feedback session, before the IEP meeting, to discuss the results of the evaluation with parents and school staff. The less formal collaborative meeting to discuss the outcome of the autism team evaluation allows parents to focus on the description of their child and the meaning of the diagnosis without the added pressure of reviewing a written report, along with specific goals and objectives based on the diagnostic information.

During an IEP meeting, the many legal procedures in place take away from the process of discussing a child's diagnosis in informal terms. My experience has been that even though school staff are very busy, they welcome the opportunity to sit in on the diagnostic feedback session with a child's parents and the autism evaluation team. After participating in the meeting, school staff have a better understanding of the child's unique behavioral profile and also have a bond with the child's parents. When the parents and school staff reconvene later at a formal IEP meeting, they are better prepared to review the details of the child's educational eligibility and instructional goals because they previously shared the experience of hearing about the child's behavioral profile from the evaluation team.

The structure of the diagnostic feedback conversation is important because parents need to experience an atmosphere of support and trust as they prepare to absorb the diagnostic news about their child. Evaluators can establish such an atmosphere by sharing stories about the child that convey their genuine appreciation and understanding of the child to the parents. Parents appreciate this attention to their child's unique qualities. Additionally, using a conversational style makes it easier to focus on a child's strengths and positive qualities rather than on his or her deficits and the diagnostic label. An atmosphere of support and trust will occur naturally when evaluators use nontechnical but specific language to describe the child's behavior and diagnosis.

Before the diagnostic feedback conversation begins, evaluation team members should discuss the entry point for talking to the parents. How prepared do the parents seem to be to hear and accept a diagnosis for their child? How much have they read and what is their level of understanding about autism spectrum disorders? Discussing these types of questions assists the team in tailoring the tone of this important conversation.

When the diagnosis is presented in a conversational format, parents have time to absorb key information about their child's developmental differences. They are able to process some of the emotions that arise as they take in the information about their child's neurological differences. When the diagnosis is discussed with parents in a conversational manner, parents are able to move through the nonfinite, or ambiguous, grief process in a natural and productive way.

DELIVERING THE DIAGNOSIS

The diagnostic feedback conversation works best if evaluators describe the unique behavioral profile of the child before delivering the diagnosis. Sometimes parents are anxious about the feedback and want to know the diagnosis right away. When parents are anxious to hear a "yes" or "no" regarding whether their child has a behavioral profile consistent with an

> ### *What is the nonfinite grief process?*
>
> Nonfinite grief is a psychological term that refers to the dual processes of confronting the fear response triggered by a threat to an individual's well-being and eventually accepting that threat. When parents receive a diagnosis of an autism spectrum disorder for their child, the diagnosis represents an unclear, or ambiguous, threat to the parents' well-being. As parents grapple with what the diagnosis actually means in relation to their child, their view of the child, and their family life as it relates to having a child with a diagnosis of a lifelong developmental difference, they confront profound feelings of grief and loss. The threat to their anticipation of their child's "normal" development and progression through predictable life stages becomes palpable when a diagnosis is given. With their child's diagnosis of an autism spectrum disorder, parents are faced with the need to revisit their expectations. At the same time, the threat that arises from such a diagnosis is unclear, in the sense that it is impossible to predict the precise ways in which the diagnosis will affect the child's life.
>
> When parents ask questions such as "Will my child learn how to drive? Get married? Go to college?", they are expressing some of the deep fears and concerns that arise as the unclear threat of the diagnosis sinks in. Having an awareness of this grief process is critical for autism evaluation teams. This awareness allows the evaluation team members to deliver the information about the child and the child's diagnosis in compassionate and personal terms. Remember that the delivery of the diagnosis is part of a process the parents are going through. When you make time during the conversation to allow parents to absorb what you are saying and ask the questions that come to mind, you are helping them move through their personal nonfinite grief process about their child.

autism spectrum disorder, I like to start the diagnostic feedback session by confirming that the team either saw or did not see "differences in development" when working with the child. I have found that it works best, however, to follow the format of discussing the differences in each of the three areas of the descriptive triangle prior to discussing the specific diagnostic label. Mentioning at the start of the session that the team saw differences in the child's development (or, conversely, did not see differences) reduces the parents' anxiety, allowing them to settle in and listen to the specifics as the team describes the child's behavioral profile. Even parents who have already received a medical diagnosis report that the process of hearing specifics about their child's behavior and having those specifics organized into the descriptive triangle categories is profoundly helpful.

While talking with the parents about their child, evaluators should draw the triangle representing the three areas of developmental differences that make up autism spectrum disorders. This provides a visual framework to help explain the child's behavioral profile. Taking the time to draw the descriptive triangle gives both the evaluator and the parents a chance to focus their thoughts on the child's behavioral profile. The diagnostic picture literally unfolds as the conversation progresses. As the three key areas are discussed, parents develop an understanding of what it means to have a child diagnosed with an autism spectrum disorder. When the diagnostic term *Autistic Disorder, Pervasive Developmental Disorder,* or *Asperger's Syndrome* is finally mentioned, parents are better prepared to deal with it because the visual framework has helped them to make the link between their child's behavioral profile and the diagnosis.

I recommend drawing the descriptive triangle as opposed to giving parents a preprinted copy of it or providing a copy of the child's individual descriptive triangle with all of the child's behavioral characteristics listed under each heading. A preprinted triangle detracts from the personal nature of the diagnostic feedback conversation, and seeing all of the child's characteristics at once can be distracting and overwhelming to parents. In addition to providing a visual focal point during the diagnostic feedback conversation, the triangle drawing gives the parents something tangible to take with them at the end of the conversation. This personalized drawing helps them continue the process of absorbing the implications of the diagnosis after they leave and incorporating this new information into their view of their child.

Sometimes the diagnostic feedback conversation is focused on a diagnosis other than an autism spectrum disorder. If the team is ruling out a diagnosis of an autism spectrum disorder, usually they have decided that the child's behavioral profile and educational challenges are best described by a different diagnostic category, such as a specific learning disability, an emotional disturbance, an attention-deficit disorder, or an underlying genetic disorder or other medical condition. Sometimes there are several factors in play that do not include an autism spectrum disorder. In these cases, I recommend discussing the specific diagnoses and listing them on a sheet for the parents, rather than drawing the descriptive triangle. It is confusing for parents to see the autism triangle but hear that their child does not fit the profile. In your discussion with the parents when you rule out an autism spectrum disorder, it is important to highlight the social, communication, and sensory learning patterns seen in their child that are not typically seen in children with autism spectrum disorders. This discussion usually leads to an understanding on the part of the parents that a diagnosis other than an autism spectrum disorder is the most compelling way to understand their child's learning challenges.

The ultimate goal of the diagnostic feedback conversation is to forge a genuine and meaningful bond between the parents, the child's evaluation team, and the child's school team. The bond is forged when parents, evaluators, and teachers share the complex grief process as they share stories and information about the child's specific pattern of developmental differences. Rather than emphasizing a diagnostic label, the diagnostic feedback conversation emphasizes an understanding and appreciation of the child as a unique and special individual.

A SAMPLE DIAGNOSTIC FEEDBACK CONVERSATION

Here is an example of a diagnostic feedback conversation with the parents of Eric, an intelligent, talkative 4-year-old boy with a perpetual, subtle smile on his face. Eric was referred for an autism evaluation after his parents enrolled him in a private preschool and he had difficulty following his preschool routine. Two weeks prior to this diagnostic feedback conversation with his parents, Eric was seen by me and two additional members of the autism evaluation team: Donna, the educational diagnostician, and Mona, the speech therapist. Eric's parents had observed the team evaluation and were returning to meet with the team for the diagnostic feedback conversation.

We invited Mrs. Rodriguez, the teacher for preschool children with autism spectrum disorders in Eric's school district, to sit in on the diagnostic feedback session. We had talked with Mrs. Rodriguez prior to this meeting to explain our diagnosis and prepare her for her participation in the meeting with Eric's parents.

Is it common for parents to observe their child's autism evaluation?

As a general rule, parents of school-aged children do not sit in on the sensory-based diagnostic interview session. It's more common for parents of younger children to sit in on the session than parents of older children. Some teams have an evaluation setting with a one-way mirror that allows parents to watch the evaluation from a separate room. In general, when parents have a clear understanding of the evaluation process, they are better equipped to accept the diagnostic outcome.

With younger children, having the parents in the evaluation room provides diagnostic information. The team can compare the child's response to the parents and contrast that response with the expected response seen in neuro-typical children of the same age in similar circumstances. Evaluation teams need to have the flexibility to make decisions about what role the parents play in the evaluation setting based on the individual circumstances each child presents.

To help us organize our thoughts before the conversation with Eric's parents, we created an individualized triangle that listed Eric's observed behaviors under the three triangle headings. Eric's individualized triangle is depicted in Figure 11. Although we used the individualized triangle to organize

FIGURE 11
Eric's Autistic Disorder Behavioral Profile

HIGH-FUNCTIONING AUTISTIC DISORDER

MILD — SIGNIFICANT

Language and *Communication*

- Beginning to use words and short phrases
- Uses language primarily to label visual objects in his immediate environment
- Labeling is the key way he uses language and organizes information
- Speaks with a lilting, exclamatory cadence
- Repeated dialogue from favorite videos *(Wallace and Gromit)*
- Organizes language best when he has visual contextual cues
- Had difficulty orienting to a speaker and answering questions
- Did not direct his statements or questions to a listener
- Nonverbal language, such as eye contact and changes in facial expression, was limited
- Production of language better developed than his ability to respond to verbal requests

Differences in Development

Sensory Use and *Interests*

- Organizes information visually
- Strong intrinsic interest in learning
- Play was sensory-seeking (visual, tactile) rather than socially driven
- Startled by sounds unless he controlled the source
- Strong memory for visual details
- Seeks out repetitive play, but can be redirected
- Unusual movements include close visual inspection of objects, lining things up, body tensing
- Most cooperative with tasks that used manipulative materials and provided visual contextual cues (puzzles, magnets, taking apart kinetic flashlight)

Social Relationships and *Emotional Responses*

- Positive bond with parents
- Appealing spontaneous smile and laugh, but did not share them in a social way
- Generally happy, self-contained demeanor unless stressed
- Preferred to play on his own agenda
- Resisted shared play
- Neutral expression most of the time
- Rigid about fishing game
- Anxious about social exchanges
- Did not use eye contact to give or receive social information

our thoughts prior to the diagnostic feedback conversation with his parents, during the actual conversation we drew the generic triangle. The use of the generic triangle helped us lay out Eric's individualized behavioral profile in a sequential and conversational way. His parents were able to listen to and absorb each piece of information as the conversation unfolded rather than trying to focus on the whole picture at once.

It was time to have our conversation with the parents to share the results of our evaluation.

"We really enjoyed the opportunity to work with Eric. He was as delightful as you described him to be," I said, as we began the diagnostic feedback conversation. Eric's parents were seated in the conference room with the evaluation team and Mrs. Rodriguez. As with the parent interview, care was taken to establish a seating arrangement that best facilitated a close, intimate conversation, as opposed to a formal meeting.

The strained smile on Eric's mother's face visibly relaxed as she absorbed my introductory comments. His father appeared serious but relaxed, with one hand resting lightly on his wife's forearm.

"We were glad you were able to sit in during Eric's evaluation time with us. He really seemed to enjoy himself, didn't he?" I said, referring to the fact that his parents had been present for the sensory-based diagnostic interview several weeks earlier.

"When he got home that day, he asked for some of those toys," said Eric's mother, smiling. "He really got excited playing with the robot arm and those light-up toys. He was having the time of his life when you let him turn off the lights so he could see all the colors spinning on those toys."

> Set a comfortable tone for this difficult conversation by showing a genuine appreciation of the child. Start the conversation by sharing stories.

His father joined the conversation and shared his thoughts. "I was happy to see him relax with all of you. He played a lot, yeah, but I was proud of the way he settled down and worked when you gave him the puzzles and books."

"He *did* work hard. Did he do anything in particular that surprised you?" I asked.

"I didn't know he knew the names of so many kinds of fish and sea creatures. We knew he knew his dinosaurs because he names them all the time at home, but I was surprised at how much language he used with you. Surprised and excited," he said.

"Yes, it was exciting when he labeled the squid and the seahorse. I liked it when he imitated me and made his lower lip stick out like the grouper fish," I said. We spent a few relaxed and pleasant moments recalling parts of the evaluation session.

Eric's parents responded to us in a genuine, connected way. We had established a conversational tone that conveyed an authentic understanding of, and interest in, their son.

It was time to talk about Eric's behavioral profile and then his diagnosis.

"Let's talk a little about what we learned about Eric during this process," I said, as I drew a triangle on a sheet of paper on the table in front of Eric's parents. "When we played with Eric, we were looking at whether he showed us a pattern of differences in his development compared to other 4-year-olds."

I wrote the words *Differences in Development* inside the triangle like this:

"The three areas we looked at were, how he used his language and communication," I said, as I paused and wrote the words *Language and Communication* above the top of the triangle like this:

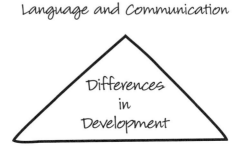

"How he acted with us socially and expressed his emotions." I continued talking as I wrote the words *Social Relationships and Emotional Responses* under the right side of the triangle like this:

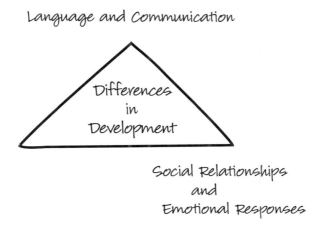

"And we looked at how he used his senses—how he looked at things, touched things, reacted to sounds—and how that affected his play and interests." I wrote the words *Sensory Use and Interests* under the left side of the triangle like this:

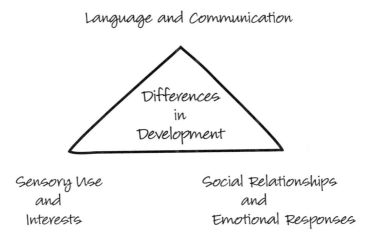

Eric's parents leaned forward and listened intently as they focused on the diagram and words.

> We drew the generic triangle for Eric's parents during our conversation with them to discuss the diagnosis. The triangle created a framework for our dialogue.

"Let's talk about Eric's language and communication first. He is really beginning to use a lot of language, and as you heard, he talked almost constantly during our play session together," I said. I paused as his parents nodded their agreement.

"He talked with all of you like he does at home," his mother added.

"That's good to know. He really seemed comfortable with us and didn't hold back," I replied. "What we noticed about Eric's talking was that most of what he said revolved around his labeling things in his immediate surroundings. When he wasn't labeling the objects he was looking at, he was repeating short segments of dialogue from his favorite videos. During our session, he labeled the colors of the lights and stacking rings, and named the animals in the zoo book. He named the letters of the alphabet and the numbers in the number puzzle. He even named a few things that surprised you, as you mentioned a few minutes ago."

"Right, the sea creatures. I hadn't really noticed it in quite that way before, but Eric *is* always labeling and naming things," his mother said.

"He has a solid vocabulary for labeling things he sees, and it's expanding daily. It's a key way that he uses language and organizes information," I said.

> We discussed Eric's language and communication profile first. We used qualitative descriptions of his behavior that highlighted his developmental differences as well as his strengths.

"The difference in Eric's use of language that we saw was his almost exclusive focus on labeling things and on repeating seemingly random dialogue from his favorite movies. Even when he asked questions, he was using the question to set up an opportunity to provide the answer. And the answer was always labeling something he was looking at or remembered."

I continued, "The social use of language seems more difficult for him. Eric didn't use his language to gain our attention or to invite us to share in his play. When he asked us questions, he didn't direct the question to anyone in particular or look at anyone to make sure someone was listening."

Eric's father responded. "That's right. We've talked about how Eric usually asks questions that he already knows the answers to, and how it feels like he's really talking more for his own benefit than really talking with us. In fact, we've wondered why he's having trouble understanding how to have a conversation because he talks all the time. He can have a conversation with himself when he's repeating a scene from a video, but he can't answer our questions."

I replied, "We noticed that as well when he was with us. That challenge in understanding the social aspects of language is a key difference in how Eric is developing his language skills.

"Another difference in his language development that we noticed is his way of speaking. What I mean by that is, Eric seems to use the same tone of voice and lilting pattern when he talks. He uses a high-pitched voice and has an excited, or exclamatory, way of ending every sentence."

His mother agreed. "We've noticed that. Sometimes he repeats something he's heard before. He tends to use the same phrases when he gets excited or frustrated, and he says them the same way every time," she said.

"That's right," I said. "You pointed out that he was repeating phrases from the *Wallace and Gromit* videos when he said 'Cheese, Gromit, cheese!' and 'Anti-pesto, you're here!'"

"For some reason he's become fascinated with *Wallace and Gromit*," his father commented. "He sounds just like the man when he says one of the lines. What is that line exactly?" He turned to his wife to see if she recalled the phrase.

"The one about cheese. He sounds just like the British character when he says it, too." Eric's mother looked thoughtful for a moment before her face registered her recollection of the phrase.

"'Oh I *do* like a bit of gorgon*zow*la!'" she exclaimed, drawing out a British accent as she mimicked her son's use of the character's trademark phrase.

We complimented her on being such a good mimic and for paying such close attention to Eric's interests and his use of language. Then we continued on a more serious note.

> *Stop and listen throughout the conversational exchange. Allow time for parents to absorb information and make important connections.*

"There were a few other differences we noticed in Eric's use of language and communication," I continued. "It was more difficult for him to respond to our questions and comments than it was for him to generate language on his own agenda. In other words, *processing* the language of others was more challenging for Eric than *producing* language himself." Again, I paused to give his parents some time to absorb what I was saying about their son's use of language.

"You know, you're right about that. It's hard to get his attention when we say things to him," his mother said, agreeing with our observation about Eric's pattern of processing the language of others.

"Exactly," I continued. "It wasn't so much that we got a sense that Eric didn't understand what we were saying. We felt that he had the skills to understand the language. It was really a matter of his difficulty in attaching functional meaning to the words. We noticed that Eric was able to understand our requests most successfully when our words were paired with visual contextual cues. If he could see what we were talking about, he was more likely to tune into our language and respond to us."

"That's so true. We know Eric understands what we say to him. It's just hard to predict when he's going to tune in to what we say. Looking back, it makes a lot of sense that when Eric tunes in to what we're saying, it's usually when we give him some 'visual cues' as you called them," his father reflected. His mother nodded in agreement.

"So do you feel we have a good picture of Eric's language and communication?" I asked.

"Most definitely. Yes. You're describing him," his mother and father said, echoing each other's comments.

"Now that we've talked about some of the key differences in the way Eric is developing his use of language and communication, let's talk about how he acts socially with others and how he manages his emotions," I said. I underlined *Language and Communication* in the diagram as I said those words, then underlined the words *Social Relationships and Emotional Responses* as I began to discuss Eric's behavioral profile in the second of the three key areas.

"One of the first things we noticed about Eric is the strong and comfortable bond he shares with each of you. He's obviously very attached to you and you treat him in a loving, accepting, and caring way," I said.

Eric's mother responded in a voice filled with emotion. "He's our baby. We love him." Tears welled up in her eyes and her husband squeezed one of her hands as she pressed her other hand to one eye.

We sat quietly for a moment to make time for the emotions that were a natural part of this conversation about their child.

> *Allow time for emotions to surface. Respect how difficult this process is for parents.*

"That's not to say that he isn't quite the little toot sometimes," his father gently quipped as he squeezed his wife's hand and released it.

"That's for sure. Like when he gets up in the middle of the night and turns on the DVD so he can watch one of his movies," his mother said as she smiled.

"A happy boy, but not a sleepy boy," I commented and smiled.

"That's one thing we are grateful for," his father said. "Eric is a good-natured and generally happy child. We're thankful for that."

"We definitely saw that happy, agreeable nature during our time with him," I said, before beginning to discuss Eric's social and emotional differences.

"When we played with Eric, one of the things we were doing was comparing his response to us and to you with the response of other 4-year-olds." I looked at his parents while they nodded, indicating they were listening intently.

"Eric was interested in most of our toys and materials, which was great," I continued. "But it was hard for him to include us in his play and exploration of the toys. The differences we saw in his social relationships centered on his drive to follow his own agenda. What I mean by that is that Eric didn't seem to be interested in including us in his play. He didn't initiate, or start, social exchanges with us. We had to intrude on his play and work our way into his agenda before he acknowledged us."

I remembered a part of the evaluation session that would give his parents an example of what I meant by "his own agenda."

"Remember when Eric was enjoying the fishing puzzle, labeling the names of all of the fish and sea creatures? He loved using the magnetic fishing pole to 'catch' the fish and lift them out of the puzzle, and even agreed to put the pieces into the plastic bag when I held it in front of him," I said.

"When I pretended to have the bag talk and say 'Feed me—I'm hungry', Eric followed my directions but didn't respond with the type of smile most 4-year-old children show when a bag starts asking to be fed," I continued. "Once the routine was established, though, he wanted to put every fish in the bag. When I changed the routine and had the bag spit out a fish, Eric responded by becoming somewhat agitated. He wanted to keep doing the static routine of placing each fish in the bag. When I gave him a choice by asking 'Eat it or spit it out?', he chose 'Eat it' every time. It was difficult for him to allow me to participate in his play and to introduce variations in established routines."

"That describes him when you say he's on his own agenda," his mother said. "He doesn't seem to want or need other people to play with him. In fact, as you saw, he gets frustrated with you if you try to play with him and make suggestions about what to do with toys or activities."

"Yes, that's exactly it," I agreed. "Eric has less of a need to use eye contact to give or receive social information. He did not look at us very often, and when he did it was mostly to check in to see what was coming next. When Eric asked us questions or handed us toys when we asked for them, it was difficult for him to use his eye contact in a social way as part of the interaction with us."

> By using descriptive language, we created a shared vocabulary to discuss Eric's behavioral profile.

"He doesn't look at us very much either," his father mused. "Except when he thinks he's in trouble or he wants something badly and needs our help to get it."

"Eric has a great smile and laugh, but it was hard for him to share them with us in a social way. He is more self-contained than many children his age," I said.

"You're right. Sometimes we ask him, 'Eric, what are you laughing about?' He seems like he's getting a real kick out of something and we want him to let us in on the joke," his mother commented.

"Most of the time, Eric seemed to have the same, almost neutral, expression on his face," I said. "When he opened the folding mirror we gave him and I asked him to make various expressions, Eric's change in expression was very subtle. He didn't glance over at us to see our reaction to his 'happy', 'sad', and 'mad' faces when we prompted him to make faces for us. He showed more of an interest in tilting the mirror at an angle to see the reflection of the dinosaur toys on the table."

"Now that you mention it, Eric does seem to have the same expression on his face most of the time," his mother remarked.

"Contented but self-contained," I said.

"Contented but self-contained," his parents both agreed.

"Eric did not seem to be very interested in or motivated by our social praise and attention when we played together. Have you noticed that as well?" I asked.

"Every once in a while he wants to show us what he's done and seems happy with our attention. But most of the time he'd rather be on his own and doesn't pay much attention to us or his sister," his mother noted. "I think we told you earlier that Eric doesn't go up to other kids either or want to play with them. How he acted with you is also how he acts with other children."

"So the social and emotional differences we're talking about are things you see in Eric as well," I commented.

"Oh yes, you're describing our boy," his father said.

> From time to time, stop and ask directly if the parents agree with your observations about their child.

"A real strength for Eric is his interest in a wide range of toys and materials and in learning. In addition to his love of dinosaurs, zoo animals, and books, he seems to have a real passion for figuring out how things work," I said, to highlight Eric's solid cognitive development.

"You mean like when he took your flashlight apart in record time?" His father laughed, as he recalled Eric's interest in a hand-operated flashlight Eric had dismantled as part of his exploration of the testing materials.

"Exactly," I replied.

"So now that we've talked about Eric's language and social development, let's talk about his sensory use and interests," I said, as I underlined the words *Sensory Use and Interests* on the triangle. "Eric showed us a pattern of mild but significant differences in the way he explored the sensory properties of the toys and in the way he explored his areas of interest."

I continued speaking as his parents looked at me expectantly. "When we talked about his language and communication, we talked about how Eric organizes his language around visual information. We noticed that he really is a visual learner in the sense that he pays very close attention to visual details." I paused to give his parents time to take in what I was saying.

His mother asked, "Like when he lies down next to his line of dinosaurs and looks at them, or gets close to the TV screen when his favorite video scenes come up?"

"Yes. We noticed that Eric organized his exploration of the world around him in a sensory-seeking way. In other words, he explored the toys and materials to receive sensory feedback. He explored the way things looked, felt, and sounded. His play was driven by this sensory-seeking pattern rather than by a need for social contact with other people." I paused as Eric's parents thought about what I'd said.

"At the same time that he sought out sensory input by lining up toys and matching them, and by pressing some of the sensory balls to his lips, he also showed us some definite areas of sensory sensitivity," I continued. "Remember how startled he was by the Thunder Tube and the sliding tubes that made the squawking sound?"

"Oh, yes," both parents said, as they nodded in agreement.

"But once he grabbed hold of them, he kept making the noises until you took them away from him. We see that pattern with Eric with lots of objects that make unexpected noises. They make him nervous unless he can control them," said his mother.

> *In the area of sensory use and interests, we highlighted Eric's sensory-seeking behavior patterns as well as his sensory sensitivities.*

"For Eric, his way of organizing his behavior in relation to the world around him is driven by a combination of his sensory-seeking needs and his sensory sensitivities," I said, as I directed his parents' attention back to the drawing of the triangle. "Let's look at these three areas again. When you think about Eric, it seems as though his entry point into the world—the way he organizes his behavior and makes sense out of what is going on around him—centers on his sensory use and interests." I circled those words on the diagram.

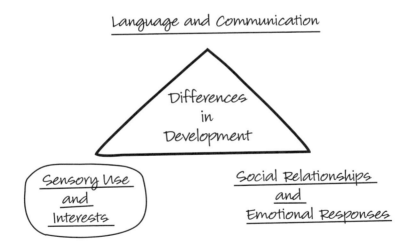

"Now think about his sister and how she relates to the world. Of course, she enjoys toys and playing on her own sometimes, but the way she organizes her behavior and makes sense out of the world—her entry point—is a combination of using her language and relating socially to others."

His mother replied, "I never thought about it that way before, but that is exactly what is different about Eric. His whole world is about how things look and feel to him. It motivates his play and it accounts for most of the times when he gets really upset. You really got to the core of what makes him tick."

She looked at her husband and said, "This makes so much sense to me."

"It's a good way to explain him," Eric's father agreed.

"If we understand his worldview and how he organizes his behavior to make sense of the world," I continued, "then we can make sure we teach him in ways that take his learning style into account."

> The shared language and the visual framework of the triangle helped us build an understanding with Eric's parents of his developmental differences in the three key areas relevant to an autism diagnosis. This structure helped prepare Eric's parents to understand what an autism diagnosis meant specifically in relation to Eric.

I drew an arrow on the left side of the triangle from the heading *Sensory Use and Interests* to *Language and Communication*. Then I said, "Eric already uses his expanding vocabulary to label many objects in his world. If we use his natural need for visual organization and for pairing language with visual information, we can teach him how to use his language in a more social way. And the way we teach him social skills and social language skills will make intuitive sense to him because we will be teaching him by starting at his natural entry point for understanding the world." I drew an arrow between the words *Sensory Use and Interests* and *Social Relationships and Emotional Responses*.

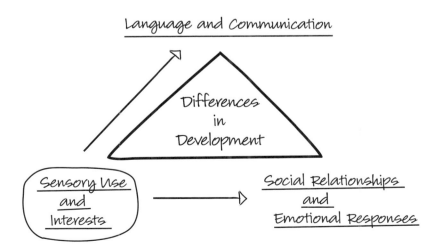

"Wow," his father said. "This makes so much sense. The way you're talking about him puts all of his differences and quirkiness into a perspective that explains him."

"And you got all of that from playing with him." His mother slowly shook her head as she reflected on this framework for understanding her son's worldview. "That's Eric. You are describing Eric."

"We're so glad. We really enjoyed getting to know him. Understanding how he puts things together is the key to understanding how to teach him so he can grow and develop to the best of his abilities," I said.

Now that we'd discussed Eric's behavioral profile, it was time to discuss the diagnosis. "As you know, one of the things we were looking at during this evaluation process was whether Eric has an autism spectrum disorder." I wrote the words *Autism Spectrum Disorders* at the top of the sheet with the drawing of the triangle like this:

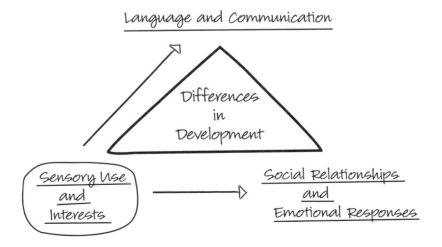

"When we see the pattern of differences in development in these three key areas that we saw with Eric, what we're describing is the learning pattern associated with an autism spectrum disorder."

I paused for a moment before adding, "Eric's pattern of developmental differences is a pattern we see in children who have high-functioning Autistic Disorder. He is smart and able to learn, but he learns differently."

> We discussed the diagnostic label after a thorough discussion of Eric's unique behavioral profile.

I wrote the words *High-Functioning Autistic Disorder* directly above the triangle and beneath the words *Autism Spectrum Disorders*, denoting Eric's diagnosis on the spectrum.

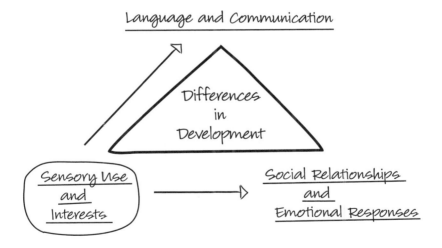

Eric's parents nodded their heads in agreement as they solemnly looked at the words on the page. They looked at me, inviting me to continue. I drew a line across the page with a notch on each end. "As you know, autism covers a wide range of developmental differences and ability levels. We looked at how much Eric's autism interferes with his ability to learn. Autism can interfere with a child's ability to learn anywhere from a mild to a significant degree." I wrote the word *Mild* at the left end of the line and the word *Significant* at the right end. "For Eric, his autism interferes with his ability to learn to a mild but significant degree." I paused before I continued to elaborate on Eric's diagnosis.

"We've been talking about how Eric organizes his world and learns differently, but at the same time, he is learning new things every day. We're saying that his autism affects him in a mild but significant way because it's critical that people understand his developmental differences so they teach him in ways that make sense to him."

I wrote the words *but significant* next to the word *Mild* and drew a circle on the line above the words to indicate the area on the spectrum where Eric was functioning.

"Does this fit with the way you see your son?" I asked.

"Oh, yes," his mother said. "It's hard to hear that word, but the way you explained how he learns makes so much sense."

"It's difficult to hear the word *autism*," I agreed. "But all it means is that Eric is learning with this pattern of developmental differences."

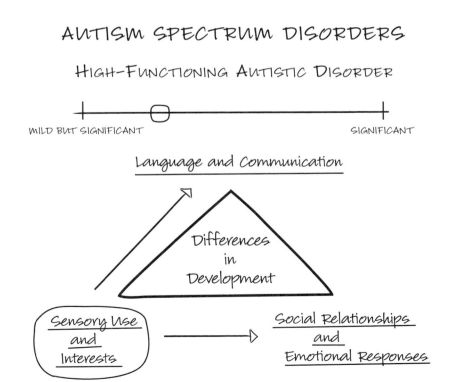

Eric's father had been quietly contemplating the diagram while he absorbed the information about his son. "Thank you for explaining this. It makes sense of what we knew about Eric but couldn't exactly describe."

"You mentioned that his autism is at the mild end," he continued. "Does that mean as he gets older he might get it together and not have it anymore?"

"That's a good question," I said. "I wish I could tell you that we were seeing a few differences that would go away or resolve on their own as Eric gets older. While there is no doubt that Eric will continue to learn, develop, and blossom as he gets older, what we're saying is that his pattern of development, of learning, of organizing information in the world—his worldview—shows a pattern of developmental differences that are characteristic of young children with high-functioning Autistic Disorder. We see this style of learning as a lifelong pattern for Eric. We don't know why he has this pattern of learning, but we know it is a brain difference that is more common in boys than in girls."

I drew their attention back to the words *Mild but significant* on the sheet in front of us. "Eric is going to grow and develop and change as he matures. He has loving parents who understand him and love him and accept him for who he is instead of trying to make him be someone he's not. You're giving him a gift of security that no one else can give him."

Eric's mother reached out and held her husband's hand. Her eyes welled with tears as she nodded in acceptance of my comments. "That's so true. Thank you for saying that," she murmured.

> We acknowledged how difficult it was for Eric's parents to hear Eric's diagnosis. Although we were clear in our delivery of his diagnosis, we emphasized Eric's strengths whenever possible. We overtly recognized the positive bond between Eric and his parents.

"Eric is a happy, secure child who is going home with you today the same child he was before you learned of this diagnosis. It's harder for you, his parents, because you have this news to absorb and process," I said, acknowledging their grief process.

"I see his differences," his father said. "I worry if he's going to be able to drive a car, or go to college, or get married and hold down a job. I guess you can't tell me if he'll be able to do all of that when he grows up." He looked at me with apparent sadness.

I acknowledged his sadness and apprehension about the future for his son. "Eric is so young. It's difficult to predict how any 4-year-old's life will unfold. The important thing to think about with Eric is that he is a happy, healthy child who is capable of learning and developing the skills he needs to get ready for kindergarten."

Continuing, I clarified, "When I said his high-functioning Autistic Disorder affects him in a mild but significant way, I was talking about his ability to learn and to use what he's taught. Eric has lots of capacity for learning. Understanding his autism learning style will help us make sure we use the teaching tools and methods that will make the most sense to him." As I reiterated Eric's capacity for learning while confirming the diagnosis, his parents both looked at me with acceptance in their eyes.

> *We were prepared to discuss questions about the future. While remaining clear about the diagnosis, we encouraged his parents to focus on Eric's strengths and immediate potential instead of worrying about his adult life.*

"Thank you," his father said with deep feeling. He took in the presence of the rest of the evaluation team for the first time since our diagnostic feedback conversation began. "All of you have been so helpful. Thank you for your help with Eric."

"Of course," Donna, the educational diagnostician, said. "Thank you for letting us work with Eric."

"He's a delightful boy," Mona, the speech therapist, said. "I was excited to see his language potential."

Mrs. Rodriguez, Eric's future preschool teacher, joined the conversation. "Thank you for including me in this meeting. I learned a lot about Eric and this will help me plan for him as he starts in the class. I look forward to working with Eric."

"Great, so do we," Eric's mother replied.

I said, "Now that we've talked about Eric's autism learning profile, let's talk about the types of visual supports Mrs. Rodriguez might use with Eric in the classroom to help him with his language and communication."

> *Once the diagnosis was made, we focused on linking Eric's learning style in the three key areas to general strategies designed to teach him in a successful way.*

Eric's parents leaned forward as they listened. "Because his language flows best when he has visual contextual cues, he'll respond well to the visual structure used in the preschool classroom," I continued. "He'll have a visual schedule with pictures and words describing each activity throughout the day. Eric will learn to use his visual schedule to anticipate his daily routine and regroup at the end of each activity while preparing to participate in the next activity. We find that children like your son really like the structure provided by having their own individual visual schedule."

"That's right," added Mrs. Rodriguez. "The children use their visual schedules. Many of them start talking more when they have the visual prompts."

"That sounds good," his father said.

Mrs. Rodriguez continued. "After he gets settled in and we see what type of visual schedule works best for him, his speech therapist and I will be glad to get together with you and brainstorm on how to set up a similar type of visual schedule at home if you'd like."

"That would be great," his mother agreed. "Anything you suggest that will help us help him is welcome."

Mrs. Rodriguez smiled at Eric's parents. "I'm looking forward to meeting your son and having him join our class. After this meeting, if you'd like to come down to my room for a minute to visit, I'll show you some of the visual schedules we're using with other children."

"We'd like that," his parents responded in unison.

I reentered the conversation. "Let's talk briefly about a few social supports Eric will have at school. Socially, he will have lots of routines during the day. Right now, he isn't using his language to talk about himself or his experiences in a social narrative. We'd like to suggest that you make some photo books about Eric that show him in social situations during the day. Under each photo it helps to write a short sentence in the first person, as if Eric is speaking. Using personal narrative photo books helps young children like Eric develop a better sense of themselves and teaches them about social relationships."

"He'll like those books, I think," said his mother. She then asked, "Would you like some pictures from home?"

"Definitely," Mrs. Rodriguez confirmed. "In fact, we can get together and I'll show you how to make some photo narrative books for home."

"Good. I know his sister will enjoy reading the books with him as much as we will," his mother said, conveying her excitement about using some of the strategies being suggested in the meeting.

"That's one way Mrs. Rodriguez and her team will work on his social language in school," I said. "They'll also use what we know about his sensory entry point to organize some of their teaching materials to capture Eric's interest and attention. We know Eric learns best when he can manipulate objects, so we'll encourage the use of manipulative materials when teaching him skills and concepts."

His parents nodded and I continued, "To help him begin to tolerate learning on the classroom agenda, we recommend the use of a mini-schedule to help Eric understand that *first* he'll be working with his teacher doing what she directs him to do and *then* he'll be able to do something on his own."

Mrs. Rodriguez added, "Many of the children in my class learn best when they can manipulate objects and when they have a visual way to understand what is expected of them. Eric will be able to look around the room during his work times and see his classmates doing similar routines. I find that the children respond best when I show them what is coming next instead of just telling them."

"That might help at home," his mother said. "Maybe we should start showing him what to expect instead of just telling him."

"Coming to school and having to follow our agenda is going to be somewhat stressful for Eric," Mona continued, while Mrs. Rodriguez nodded in agreement. "Even though for the most part I think he'll really enjoy his preschool routine, he'll probably still need some times during the day when he can unplug and follow his own agenda. We'll want to make sure we have some sensory routines or regrouping breaks in place for him to use throughout the day. Our occupational therapist will work with us to come up with some specific suggestions. Of course, we'll want to share those with you so you can use them at home if you'd like."

"This is so helpful," his mother stated. "I feel like you understand Eric and now we have a way to understand him, too. I think he'll respond well to the suggestions you're talking about. Thank you for all your help."

"So what happens next?" Eric's father signaled that he was ready for the meeting to end.

"Now that we've had a chance to talk with you, we'll write our report. The report will cover the details of what we talked about today: Eric's pattern of development in the three key areas, his diagnosis, and the suggestions for teaching him as he starts in the preschool program and prepares for kindergarten. Then we'll have a formal, legal meeting to put his goals and objectives into place," I said.

I closed with a few additional comments. "I know we've talked about a lot of things today and covered a lot of ground. Thank you for sharing your son with us. He was delightful and we all enjoyed meeting him and getting to know him."

His mother added, "Thank you for taking the time to get to know our Eric so well."

As we ended the meeting, I said, "This is a process, so remember that there will be many other opportunities for us to talk about Eric and your concerns about him. There will also be opportunities for you to meet and talk with other parents who have children on the autism spectrum. Was this helpful today?"

"Yes, very much so," his mother said. She smiled as his father picked up the paper depicting the triangle.

"Is this for us?" he asked.

"Of course. And remember, you'll be getting a typed report in a few weeks," I said.

"Great." Eric's father held out the triangle drawing. "This was very helpful, and we'll want to share this with Eric's grandparents so they can understand what is going on with him."

> We gave Eric's parents the hand-drawn triangle. The tangible, visual framework was both comforting and informative. Because it was drawn during the delivery of the diagnosis of their child, it was more personal than a typewritten or photocopied page.

We all stood up, and Eric's parents expressed good-byes and shook hands with everyone. They then left the room with Mrs. Rodriguez to take a look at Eric's future classroom. The members of the team spent a final few minutes reflecting on our experience of the conversation.

"What lovely parents," I commented, as I looked back on our exchanges with them. "So supportive of each other. I know this was very difficult for them to hear. Even though they knew Eric has differences, receiving a definite diagnosis is always hard."

"They stayed with you every step of the way," Donna remarked. "You did a great job walking them through how Eric's behavioral profile fits the visual triangle of differences in development before you talked about autism. I think they were much better prepared to hear that difficult diagnosis because they followed and understood your explanation of Eric's developmental differences."

"Thank you, Donna. This was a difficult conversation. Their sadness was palpable as we shared stories about Eric. At the same time, although they are definitely grieving, they have a foundation of resiliency that allowed them to take in the diagnosis and then to focus on our description of some of the school strategies," I said. I turned to Mona to give her feedback.

"Mona, I'm glad that you and Mrs. Rodriguez talked with Eric's parents about some of the key teaching strategies he will need. They left here with an understanding of the general strategies his teacher will be using to instruct him and linking those strategies to the three key areas of the triangle. His mother definitely left here with a sense of the practical things she can do to promote Eric's social development."

> We left time for the evaluation team to reflect on the conversation and discuss additional educational suggestions.

"Thanks, I thought it went really well," Mona agreed. "Eric's going to do so well with the other children in Mrs. Rodriguez's class."

I asked, "Are there any other suggestions you want to discuss and add to his report?"

Donna answered, "In addition to his visual schedule and social narrative photo books, we probably need to emphasize that Eric needs plenty of opportunities for guided play with his peers. I think he will respond well to the use of step-by-step visual narratives about how to approach and play with a peer."

"He likes music and responds well to music routines, so we'll talk about that in our report. We'll also develop the idea of using sensory regrouping breaks," I said.

Once we finished talking about instructional strategies, we spent a few minutes discussing which team members would be responsible for writing parts of the narrative report.

Donna said to me, "I'll give you my notes so you can write the *Behavioral Observations and Results* and *Summary and Recommendations* sections of the report. Mona and I will write the *Background Information* section, since we interviewed the parents and observed Eric in his private preschool class. Once your parts are written, I'll integrate them into the rest of the report and we'll be ready to sign it and send a copy to his parents and teacher."

Now that we'd had our diagnostic feedback conversation with Eric's parents, it was time for us to prepare our written conversation by writing Eric's narrative evaluation report. The process of writing a narrative report is detailed in the next chapter.

What if the parents disagree with the team's diagnosis?

Sometimes the child's parents do not accept the diagnostic outcome of the evaluation process. Evaluation teams are encouraged to understand that they do not have control over whether their diagnostic impressions are accepted by others; they can only control the degree to which their evaluation represents a comprehensive and best practices evaluation of the child. Sometimes parents and the evaluators have to "agree to disagree." My experience has been that when autism evaluation teams follow the model outlined in this book, even when parents start out with skepticism about the likelihood that their child either has or does not have an autism spectrum disorder, by the time they have participated in the entire process, consensus is reached between the child's parents and the evaluation team.

When should a child's diagnosis be shared with him or her, and how should it be discussed?

In my experience, the diagnostic feedback conversation works best when parents are the focus of the discussion. Once the child's parents receive the diagnosis for their child and have had an opportunity to come to terms with what the diagnosis means to them and their understanding of their child, it can be very helpful to guide the parents through the process of preparing to discuss the diagnosis with their child. When a diagnosis is shared with a child, the conversation with the child will work best if it occurs after the initial diagnostic feedback conversation with the child's parents.

The decision over whether to share the child's diagnosis with him or her is up to the child's parents. How and when the diagnosis is shared with a child or adolescent really is a personal decision parents need to make. In general, parents are the best source for discussing the diagnosis with their child. Parents gain confidence in how to approach this topic with their child by discussing the diagnosis with the team. Sometimes parents prefer including the professional when discussing the diagnosis with their child for the first time. The important thing evaluation teams can do for parents is to raise the question and provide a place for parents to discuss their thoughts and feelings about sharing the information with their child.

It is often a good idea to begin thinking about the best way to approach the child's diagnosis with him or her when the child begins to make comments indicating that he or she has noticed differences between his or her abilities and those of peers. When children on the spectrum make comments such as "My brain isn't working right," it suggests that they have begun to notice their developmental differences.

When children are very young, the diagnostic label generally does not help them understand their differences. Teaching children that everyone learns differently lays the groundwork for later discussions about autism spectrum disorders. Talking about the child's differences can be very helpful. Developmentally, questions about noticing differences typically emerge during early adolescence. That is often a good time to discuss the child's diagnosis.

Parents need to be the ones making the decision about when and how to discuss the child's diagnosis with him or her. Encourage parents to meet with a local professional familiar with autism spectrum disorders as they face this family milestone. Providing basic facts and reading material about autism spectrum disorders and discussing people who have the diagnosis and have led successful lives is a good way to approach this topic with young people.

Keep in mind that when the diagnosis is introduced properly, the adolescent's understanding of the diagnosis leads to a significant reduction in his or her overall anxiety level regarding perceived social struggles. Understanding the diagnosis will also help the young person develop adaptive self-advocacy skills.

Facilitating the Diagnostic Feedback Conversation

Before the diagnostic feedback conversation...

- Discuss the entry point for talking to the parents based on their readiness to hear a diagnosis and their knowledge of autism spectrum disorders.
- Review the child's behavioral profile organized into the three key areas of the visual triangle.
- Remember how stressful this process is for parents.

During the diagnostic feedback conversation...

- Establish an atmosphere of comfort and trust. Create a seating arrangement that facilitates a close, intimate conversation with the parents, and begin the conversation by sharing stories that express a genuine appreciation of their child.
- Pace the delivery of the information about the child's behavioral profile to allow ample time for the parents to process the emotional effect of the information as you go through the three key areas of the visual framework. Gain consensus throughout the conversation by asking the parents if your observations seem to describe their child.
- Provide information about the types of support services that will help to address the child's developmental differences.

After the diagnostic feedback conversation...

- End the session by genuinely thanking the parents for the opportunity to get to know their child.
- After the parents leave, spend a few minutes processing your impressions of their response to the diagnosis so the appropriate follow-up support can be discussed.
- Review the responsibilities of each team member in relation to writing the narrative evaluation report.

CHAPTER 7

Written Conversations

Constructing a Narrative Report

Written Conversations: The Narrative Report

What is the narrative report?

- The narrative report is the written conversation about the child.
- It includes information gathered by the evaluation team during the parent, teacher, and child (sensory-based) interviews.
- It emphasizes using qualitative descriptions of the child's behavioral profile and linking those descriptions to the diagnosis.

How is it structured?

- Narrative language is used in the three sections of the report: Background Information, Behavioral Observations and Results, and Summary and Recommendations.
- The visual framework is used to organize and describe the child's behavioral profile in the three key areas of language and communication, social relationships and emotional responses, and sensory use and interests.
- The child's behavioral profile is linked to practical suggestions for educational planning.

What are the benefits?

- The narrative style provides parents and teachers with a written report that describes the individual child in accessible language. A compelling link is established between the description of the child's behavioral profile and the diagnostic label.
- Because parents read the report after the diagnostic feedback conversation with the team, they are better prepared to see the diagnosis in print.
- The report provides parents and teachers with a common language and an understanding of the child's pattern of developmental differences as they plan the child's educational program.

THE NARRATIVE REPORT: A PARENT'S REACTION

"I just wanted to call and tell you how helpful it was to have your report when we met with Helena's school team." Helena's mother was calling to let me know the family had moved to another state. I had evaluated her daughter, with other members of an autism evaluation team, 6 months earlier. "I was worried about her transition to the new school and was nervous about the planning meeting with the staff," her mother continued. "So I sent them a copy of your report before the meeting. When I got there, they'd all read it and we were able to jump right into how they could put your recommendations in place for her."

"That's great to hear. I'm glad the report was helpful. So how is the move working out so far?" I asked.

"Very well," she replied. "The best part was when they met Helena, they asked her questions about her pet rabbit and asked her to draw a picture of the *Powerpuff Girls* because they'd read about her interests in the report."

"I still have the picture she drew for me of Buttercup, the green *Powerpuff* girl."

She laughed. "Her favorite."

Again Helena's mother referred back to the evaluation report. "The report did such a nice job of describing her. The recommendations were so simple and clear that we were able to talk about getting the key supports in place before school started last week."

Helena's mother reflected a reaction most parents experience when they receive a narrative report that describes their child.

THE STRUCTURE OF THE NARRATIVE REPORT

The narrative report is a written conversation about the child and is the final piece in the formal evaluation process. The emphasis is placed on writing qualitative descriptions of the child's behavioral profile and linking those descriptions to the child's specific diagnosis. It includes information gathered by the evaluation team during the conversations with the child, the parents, and the teacher. Practical suggestions are included as natural extensions of the child's individual behavioral profile.

The narrative report style is intended to help evaluators include qualitative descriptions of the child in their comprehensive evaluation report. Three distinct sections of the report lend themselves to being written as a conversational narrative: Background Information, Behavioral Observations and Results, and Summary and Recommendations. Within each section, an emphasis is placed on information relevant to the three key areas of language and communication, social relationships and emotional responses, and sensory use and interests.

The *Background Information* section provides a narrative of the child's developmental history and includes specific details about the child provided by the parents and teacher during their conversations with members of the evaluation team. This section also describes the child's reported behavior at home and at school with respect to the three key areas.

The *Behavioral Observations and Results* section lays out the qualitative description of the child's behavioral profile in each of the three key areas and links them to the specific diagnosis in a compelling way. Specific examples from the neuro-atypical conversation between the child and the evaluation team are described in this section of the narrative. The section is explicitly organized into the three key areas of language and communication, social relationships and emotional responses, and sensory use and interests. The same nontechnical but specific descriptive language that was used during the diagnostic feedback conversation with the parents is used in the written conversation of the report.

The *Summary and Recommendations* section provides a place for the evaluation team to reiterate the diagnosis and describe how the diagnosis reflects the child's pattern of developmental differences in the three key areas. This section gives parents and teachers a common framework to organize their discussion about the child's educational program. General recommendations for the child's educational supports can be written into the narrative report in a way that makes intuitive sense to parents and educators.

The team member responsible for writing the evaluation summary report varies, depending on the evaluation team. In general, one team member assumes primary responsibility for organizing the information and compiling the report. Some teams prefer to divide the report sections among team members. For example, they may have the psychologist complete the Behavioral Observations and Results section, while the educational diagnostician writes the Background Information and Recommendations sections. The important thing is for teams to discuss and decide upon the process they will use to complete the evaluation summary report in a timely and efficient way.

The process of writing a quality narrative report can be time consuming, requiring several hours of concentrated writing to summarize the information about the child. The writing process is most efficient when teams have taken the time to write detailed notes during each stage of the evaluation process. If thorough notes are taken during the parent and teacher interviews, writing the Background Information section basically consists of translating those notes into a written narrative. The structure of the interview questions should provide the structure for that section of the report. Similarly, if the evaluation team takes notes during the sensory-based diagnostic interview with the child and documents their discussion about the child's behavioral profile by completing an individualized descriptive triangle for the child, then writing the Behavioral Observations and Results section should follow the structure provided by that documentation. When suggestions for educational supports are included and documented using the descriptive triangle as part of the team discussion, that structure can be used to write the Summary and Recommendations section of the report.

Most evaluation teams set up a writing template for their narrative reports. To create a report template, they use the general descriptive terms outlined in this chapter. The structure created by the report template gives teams a starting point each time they sit down to create an individual report for a child following his or her autism evaluation.

The goal of this chapter is to provide you with information on how to create a written conversation relevant to autism spectrum disorders as part of a comprehensive evaluation report. Keep in mind that a comprehensive evaluation report also includes other information, such as the quantitative results of past testing and any current standardized tests and checklists that are completed as part of the evaluation process. The nature of the other sections of the report depends on the specific case and the requirements of the report. Additional information typically included in a comprehensive evaluation report is intentionally omitted from the example in this chapter to help you focus on the narrative aspects of the written conversation.

> *Keep in mind that a comprehensive evaluation report also includes other information, such as the quantitative results of any standardized tests that are completed as part of the evaluation process.*

There are many possible ways to structure written reports that are comprehensive and descriptive of individual children. If a team has developed a report writing format that works well for them, they should continue to use that format. The suggestions in this book are designed to help autism evaluation teams develop a structure for the narrative report.

Teams who have already developed a report writing format may find that using some of the information in this book will enhance their existing report structure.

Let's begin by looking at excerpts from a written conversation about Gabriela, a 4-year-old child with autism. Gabriela was referred for an autism evaluation by her parents, preschool teacher, and pediatrician due to concerns about her communication skills, social development, and sensory issues. At the time of this evaluation, she was enrolled in a developmental preschool program through her local school district and had been identified as a child with speech and language delays. This was her first evaluation to specifically address autism.

AN EXCERPT FROM GABRIELA'S NARRATIVE REPORT

The following excerpt from Gabriela's narrative report provides an example of a written conversation about a child who has received a diagnosis of an autism spectrum disorder. The evaluation team used the information from their conversations with the parents and teacher to complete the Background Information section of the written narrative. The Behavioral Observations and Results section of the report was written with information from the sensory-based diagnostic interview, after the team had discussed Gabriela's behavioral profile and organized their behavioral descriptions using the visual framework of developmental differences. The evaluation team used their notes from their discussion of the educational supports for Gabriela to write the Summary and Recommendations section of the report. Visual depictions of the team's discussion of Gabriela's behavioral profile and recommended educational supports are provided in Figures 12 and 13, respectively.

BACKGROUND INFORMATION

Gabriela is a 4-year, 1-month-old child who lives with her parents, Mr. and Mrs. R., and 2-year-old sister. Mrs. R. stated that she had been eager to complete this evaluation process ever since the pediatrician mentioned the possible diagnosis of autism for Gabriela. Mr. and Mrs. R. noted that they hoped this evaluation would provide a comprehensive way to understand Gabriela's developmental differences and help plan for the best ways to teach Gabriela so she can learn and grow to the best of her abilities. Gabriela's mother described her daughter as a bright child who can take anything apart and put it back together again. Her father remarked that he has to hide his tools because Gabriela will use them to dismantle household objects. They described Gabriela as an active, curious child who prefers to do things on her own rather than follow the lead of others.

Mrs. R. reported that she did not experience any pregnancy or birth difficulties and that her daughter met all of her developmental milestones on time. She recalled that Gabriela began to say a few words when she was 18 months old, but then stopped talking until after her third birthday. Gabriela has a history of chronic ear infections but is in excellent health following surgery to remove her adenoids and insert tubes prior to her third birthday. Her parents stated that the results of hearing tests showed full hearing abilities following the surgery. Her parents reported that Gabriela does not take medications on a routine basis. They stated that there are no individuals in their families who have been formally diagnosed with learning or social differences.

> *Begin the narrative by describing the parents' general concerns and their expectations regarding the autism evaluation. Include specific examples of the child's behavior given by the parents. Discuss the child's developmental history after the parents' overall concerns have been covered.*

Mrs. R. stated that at home one of Gabriela's favorite activities is to look in the mirror and watch herself as she acts out scenes from videos and cartoons. Mrs. R. noted that Gabriela will look in the mirror for extended periods of time without becoming tired of this activity if she is left on her own. Gabriela constantly talks and sings to herself. She has an excellent memory for music, and although she mixes the use of jargon with actual words, she has an uncanny ability to mimic the exact cadence and vocal style of songs and dialogue from the children's movies she watches. Mrs. R. stated that she recently bought a dollhouse for Gabriela, and Gabriela is playing with the dolls and the furniture. She noted that Gabriela tolerates having her mother play beside her with the dollhouse people and furniture, but resists her mother's attempts to direct the play. Mrs. R. commented that Gabriela is beginning to watch and incorporate some of the play modeled for her during their joint exploration of the dollhouse.

Gabriela's speech and language skills have improved over the past year, and Mrs. R. noted that her daughter can now tell her when she wants or needs something. Gabriela will seek out her mother and tell her when she hurts herself. Mr. and Mrs. R. remarked that much of Gabriela's language consists of labeling objects and repeating phrases from preferred programs. They stated that much of the time Gabriela seems to organize her world through her attention to visual details. Mr. and Mrs. R. remarked that since their daughter began attending the developmental preschool several months prior to this evaluation, her ability to communicate and her use of meaningful words has increased a great deal.

> *Organize the narrative to describe the child's behavior in the three key areas of communication, social relationships, and sensory issues.*

Mr. and Mrs. R. described Gabriela as a child who prefers to do things on her own rather than follow the suggestions of others. Her mother stated that Gabriela becomes upset and agitated by changes in her routine. Since her baby sister was born 2 years ago, Gabriela has had some difficulty adjusting to the unpredictable element her sister brings to family life.

FIGURE 12
Gabriela's Autistic Disorder Behavioral Profile

AUTISTIC DISORDER

MILD — SIGNIFICANT

Language and Communication

- Speaks with lilting, high-pitched intonation and inflection
- Whispered to herself, but shouted in response to questions or other verbal input
- Speech was self-directed rather than directed toward a listener
- Speech was a mixture of meaningful words and jargon
- Asked for help only when necessary to gain access to a preferred object
- Labeled many objects during the diagnostic interview session
- Organized language best when she had visual contextual cues
- Telegraphic syntax
- Speech intelligibility poor at times
- Rote quality to her speech; used scripted phrases
- Soothed herself by repeating "it's okay" and rubbing her hands together
- Did not initiate or respond to our attempts at social conversation
- Nonverbal language, such as eye contact and changes in facial expression, was limited

Sensory Use and Interests

- Sensory-seeking drive to her play
- Used materials to create repetitive visual and movement routines
- Attention span best with manipulative materials
- Idiosyncratic intrinsic and tangible motivation
- Captured by visual details and reflections in mirror
- No hand dominance yet
- Flinched involuntarily in response to sudden visual and auditory input
- Strong imitation skills and memory for songs
- Used peripheral eye gaze and held things close to her face
- Applied a light touch to most objects
- Body tensing and darting across the room

Social Relationships and Emotional Responses

- Neutral expression most of the time
- Facial grimacing when watching her reflection in the mirror
- Anxious about social exchanges
- Unresponsive to social praise
- Limited tolerance for input from other people; tolerance increased as session progressed
- Aware of and interested in our actions
- Social interactions with peers very limited; watches at times, but does not actively participate in play
- Agitated by demands to follow our agenda

FIGURE 13
Suggested Educational Supports for Gabriela

Language and Communication

- Use visual organization and predictable routines
- Use a visual picture and word schedule to signal transitions
- Pair verbal requests with visual prompts
- Pair visual requests with music prompts
- Limit access to mirrors
- Use visual cues to signal sequence of events ("first" and "then" mini-schedules)
- Continue to systematically build language skills through therapy and applied practice

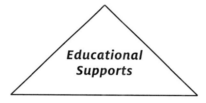

Sensory Use and Interests

- Use her natural drive for visual and auditory input as a teaching tool
- Use a visually structured work system with manipulative materials, left-to-right sequences, and a place to put her finished work
- Develop systematic sensory routines and breaks

Social Relationships and Emotional Responses

- Use visual social scripts to expand language skills beyond labeling
- Develop awareness of the use of photo books with narrative captions
- Develop social language and social skills with visual scripts and guided practice with peers
- Use object-focused play to expand her play skills

Mrs. R. noted that although Gabriela is somewhat bothered by her little sister when the baby touches Gabriela's things, she tends to ignore the baby most of the time. The baby, however, approaches Gabriela often and tries to involve her in social baby games, which Gabriela resists.

Gabriela's parents noted that although she can be affectionate with them at times, she approaches them for cuddling and attention on her own terms. She can be resistant to social contact when her parents or other family members initiate social time with her. The exception is when her father gets home from work and he follows a routine of having some rough and tumble play with her. Gabriela runs to her father and wants him to pick her up and spin her around the room. She likes to have her mother rub her back at night before she falls asleep. When something is upsetting her, Gabriela approaches her mother to rub her back.

Mr. and Mrs. R. reported that during family gatherings and other social events, Gabriela typically ignores or avoids the other children. They noted that when family friends and their children become familiar to Gabriela through repeated visits, Gabriela becomes more tolerant of playing next to them and sometimes watches the actions of the other children. Her parents have noticed that Gabriela later imitates play sequences when the children are gone and she is alone.

> *Use the names of the child and the parents throughout the course of the narrative. Include details about the child's strengths and positive attributes in addition to descriptive information about developmental differences.*

Mr. and Mrs. R. reported that Gabriela has a history of pronounced sensory sensitivities, including an aversion to wearing clothes. She used to constantly remove her clothes but has learned to keep them on all day. She does not like to wear socks or shoes and takes them off when she is at home. She is an extremely picky eater who loves salt so much that her mother has to hide the salt containers. Gabriela's mother reported that Gabriela likes to eat only bacon and chicken nuggets. Gabriela becomes anxious and bothered by unexpected sounds. Her parents recalled that Gabriela becomes distraught when she hears air brakes on a bus. There are certain scenes from her Disney movies and some television commercials that make Gabriela anxious, and she responds by hiding behind the couch until the specific scene or commercial is over. At times Gabriela covers her ears and rocks while she sits under the table.

Crowds of people are a source of agitation for Gabriela, and her parents reported that she cries and pulls on their arms to try to get them to leave when they are in a crowded store. Mrs. R. noted that at home, when Gabriela becomes agitated or when she needs to unwind, she twirls her body and runs back and forth for extended periods of time. Mr. and Mrs. R. stated Gabriela sleeps well at night and wakes up around 5:30 every morning. She entertains herself by talking and singing, and stays in her bed until her mother gets her up.

Mr. and Mrs. R. stated that they have done some reading about autism spectrum disorders and recognize some of the characteristics in Gabriela. They remarked that they have been more acutely aware of Gabriela's developmental differences since their younger daughter was born and they have experienced her development. When asked what words best describe Gabriela, they remarked that she is an intelligent, curious, and happy child. They stated that they hoped this evaluation would provide them with a better understanding of their daughter and give them suggestions for how best to teach her.

> *Include a narrative description of the child's behavioral profile in the school setting.*

In the school setting, Gabriela's teacher reported the same pattern of behaviors described by Mrs. R. Gabriela has responded well to the routines in the classroom and learns new language and skills through incidental learning rather than through direct participation in group activities. Gabriela is resistant to direct teaching and is quite driven to follow her own agenda. Her teacher stated that Gabriela is fascinated by mirrors and likes to watch her reflection as she talks to herself and gestures. Since her teacher began covering up the mirrors in the room to visually signal when they are off limits, Gabriela has been less resistant during class activities. She is aware of her peers in the classroom but does not interact with them and prefers to play by herself. One of her preferred areas is the kitchen center, where Gabriela has started labeling items as she plays with them.

In general, her teacher noted that it is difficult for Gabriela to attend to tasks and shift from her agenda to the agenda of the teacher. She has been responsive to hand-over-hand prompting to engage in activities for brief periods of time. In other words, Gabriela needs the structure of having an adult physically guide her actions to successfully focus on and complete activities. Her teacher commented that when Gabriela attends to a task, she learns very quickly. However, Gabriela becomes quickly frustrated during activities that require her to follow the teacher's lead.

Gabriela has acquired a larger vocabulary since starting in the preschool program because her imitation and recall skills are excellent once her attention is focused on a task. Routines are important to her and she does best when she can anticipate what is coming next. Waiting in line and waiting for a turn were noted to be difficult routines for Gabriela. Her teacher reported that Gabriela enjoys the group activities that involve music and movement. She appears most aware of her peers during the group music lessons when she watches the actions of her peers, and later she repeats what she saw.

Her teacher described Gabriela as a child who learns quickly once her attention is directed away from her interests and she is able to focus on the teaching activity. She noted that she hoped this evaluation would provide some suggestions for additional ways to structure Gabriela's school day so Gabriela becomes less resistant to following the daily routine and flow of the preschool classroom.

BEHAVIORAL OBSERVATIONS AND RESULTS

Gabriela is an appealing girl who was active and alert during the course of this evaluation. It is felt that this evaluation provides a reasonable estimate of her current behavioral profile.

> *State the diagnosis at the beginning of the* Behavioral Observations and Results *section and link the diagnosis to the three key areas. This sets the structure for the supporting qualitative behavioral profile in the subsequent narrative. Since the parents have already heard the diagnosis from the team during the diagnostic feedback conversation, they will be familiar with the diagnosis given to their child prior to reading the report.*

Gabriela demonstrated a profile of behaviors consistent with a diagnosis of Autistic Disorder. The degree of involvement was moderate. She showed a pervasive pattern of developmental differences in the areas of language and communication, social relationships and emotional responses, and sensory use and interests—differences that are characteristic of children with Autistic Disorder. To obtain a qualitative picture of Gabriela's language, social, and sensory profile, a structured diagnostic team-based interview was completed at her school. A description of Gabriela's behavioral profile, broken down into the three key areas, is detailed in the following sections.

> *The individual behavioral profile developed during the team discussion provides the information for this section of the report. Gabriela's individual triangle of developmental differences is depicted in Figure 12.*

Language and Communication

> *A general statement at the beginning of each section that discusses one of the three behavioral areas gives the reader a context for the qualitative descriptions of behavior that follow.*

Gabriela's language and communication profile showed a pattern of disruptions that is typically seen in children with autism. Her overall intonation and inflection were marked by a lilting, high-pitched cadence, and her speech often had a driven quality to it. Gabriela tended to mix meaningful speech with jargon, and she did not direct her utterances to the listener except on a few occasions when she needed the examiner's help to take a toy that was out of her reach off the shelf.

It is important to note that Gabriela frequently imitated what the examiner said and did and that her imitation skills are well developed. However, it was difficult at times for Gabriela to attach functional meaning to the phrases she repeated. She had a large vocabulary of nouns, and with prompting she was able to label many objects throughout the testing session. Gabriela's use of syntax was often telegraphic, and her speech intelligibility was poor at times because she was not motivated to include the listener in her conversation. Occasionally, Gabriela engaged in some perseverative use of phrases, and her speech had an overall rote quality to it.

When Gabriela made the transition from her classroom to the evaluation room, she managed her anxiety by rubbing her hands together and repeatedly saying "it's okay" to herself. When Gabriela was allowed to look in a mirror, she became focused on watching herself as she held up toys and labeled them. Even when she handed several toys to the examiner, including a wind-up caterpillar and a puzzle piece she was having trouble getting into place, Gabriela preferred to address her request for help to her own image in the mirror. She frequently whispered to herself, but shouted in response to verbal requests from the examiner. This pattern of shouting is often seen with children who find language demands to be highly stressful.

Gabriela's communication was focused primarily on commenting on her activities or areas of preoccupation. She responded best to verbal requests and comments when they were accompanied by visual, contextual cues.

Social Relationships and Emotional Responses

Gabriela demonstrated a pattern of developmental differences in the area of social relationships and emotional responses. Her overall facial expression was generally neutral, and she did not use eye contact to register social cues. When she was captivated by watching her reflection in the mirror, Gabriela engaged in some facial grimacing. She was generally aware of the presence of others, but it was difficult for her to initiate or sustain spontaneous social interactions. Social praise is not yet established as a consistent source of motivation for her. When novel toys and materials were used, including some SpongeBob SquarePants figures that Gabriela particularly liked, she was cooperative for brief periods of time.

It was quite difficult for Gabriela to shift from her agenda to the agenda of the examiner. Once she made the shift and complied with a request, it was difficult for Gabriela to sustain her attention to the task established by the examiner. Gabriela's tolerance for input from others is limited at the present time. She preferred to either abandon the materials or move away from the source of demands rather than tolerate intrusions from the examiner into her play routines.

Despite Gabriela's need to drive the agenda, it was apparent that she was aware of and interested in the actions of the examiner. The longer the session went, the more Gabriela was able to tolerate the examiner's attempts to model play with various toys and participate in simple play routines with the examiner. This pattern of wanting a connection with others but having tremendous difficulty shifting to a reciprocal agenda is oftentimes seen in children with autism.

Sensory Use and Interests

Gabriela's pattern of play and interests showed the types of developmental differences that are oftentimes seen in young children with Autistic Disorder. Gabriela's use of materials was sensory-seeking rather than social in nature, and she used the toys and materials to create visual and movement routines that she could repeat to create satisfying sensory input for herself. She was visually captured by details of the testing materials and was also visually distracted by objects in her environment. Gabriela was best able to organize her behavior when she was provided with visual structure and manipulative materials. Her attention span was also most sustained for tasks involving manipulative materials. Gabriela showed an understanding of both tangible and intrinsic rewards, but neither is yet established as a consistent source of motivation for her.

It is important to note that Gabriela was selective about the types of toys or tasks she was willing to explore. She preferred playing with materials that either provided her with opportunities to create familiar visual routines, such as the cartoon figures, or objects that provided an interesting and novel visual cause-and-effect routine, such as the expanding sphere and the spinning light-up toys. She is not yet showing the use of a dominant hand and she explored the toys using her hands interchangeably.

Gabriela asked the examiner for help on several occasions. Her play routines consisted of setting up a routine and then repeating it multiple times with a few minor variations. She flinched in response to the sound and the sudden appearance of light when the examiner squeezed the handle of a kinetic flashlight. At times, when Gabriela was completely focused on the visual aspects of materials, she held her breath for an extended period of time. She displayed some unusual body movements and mannerisms, including peripheral eye gaze, holding objects close to her face, touching objects lightly, body tensing, and darting back and forth across the room.

SUMMARY AND RECOMMENDATIONS

Gabriela is an appealing 4-year, 1-month-old girl who demonstrated a profile of behaviors consistent with a diagnosis of Autistic Disorder. Gabriela showed the pattern of disruptions in the areas of language and communication, social relationships and emotional responses, and sensory use and interests that are typically seen in young children with Autistic Disorder. The degree of involvement was moderate. Gabriela's imitation skills are an area of strength for her. To help her make a better transition to learning on the agenda of others, she would benefit from having her preferred area of focus used as a teaching modality. Since Gabriela organizes her world visually, she would benefit from the use of visual structure to teach her to use her language, play with others, and tolerate the direct teaching of key skills and developmental concepts.

> *A summary of Gabriela's diagnosis and a general statement about her learning style precedes the recommendations section of the narrative report. A visual depiction of the team's suggestions for educational supports is provided in Figure 13.*

The following are specific suggestions for Gabriela's parents and instructional team.
1. Although Gabriela showed an innate capacity to learn, her autism learning profile gets in the way of her being able to effectively organize her behavior and follow the social and play flow of a preschool environment. Transition times are highly stressful for Gabriela because she is resistant to direction from others. Gabriela would benefit from being taught to use a system that provides visual organizational aides and predictable routines. This system should have the following features:
    a. Since Gabriela seeks out visual details, she would benefit from the use of a visual picture and word schedule to signal each transition period throughout her preschool day. By having a visual schedule, Gabriela will be able to scan her routine at any time during the day and also be able to better self-regulate what she is supposed to be doing at any given time. The visual schedule would provide her teacher with a way to prompt Gabriela to redirect herself back to the activity at hand instead of having to be constantly verbally or physically redirected by her teacher.
    b. Gabriela has a strong drive to seek out mirrors wherever she goes. Once she begins her routine of watching her actions in a mirror, it is difficult for her to redirect her attention to her surroundings in a functional way. Continuing to limit her access to mirrors is recommended. If Gabriela is able to retreat into the familiar and highly rewarding routine of blocking out the world by focusing on the mirror, she will be less available to learn the adaptive routines she currently lacks. She has responded well to the visual cue of having the mirrors in the classroom covered so they are off limits to her.

> *The recommendations section of the narrative report typically addresses the following support areas: visual communication supports, classroom instruction, social skills and emotion regulation, sensory routines, and school-home collaboration.*

2. Since Gabriela resists direct instruction, she would benefit from a visually structured direct teaching work system. This would consist of having her "learning tasks" organized in work bins or folders beside her table space and giving her visual cues to indicate that she is to complete two or three tasks before she can do a preferred activity (e.g., use computer, free play). Gabriela will learn quickly that she must work with her teacher to complete the tasks in her work bins, and she will be able to see the scope of what is expected of her during each session. After she completes each task, it will be helpful to have Gabriela place the task in a "finished" basket on the other side of her work space. By having this predictable visual structure in place, Gabriela will become less resistant toward direct teaching times and better able to learn in a school setting.
3. Gabriela is beginning to show more of an interest in the actions of her peers as well as adults. However, her autism spectrum disorder interferes with her ability to discriminate basic social cues and participate in successful social and reciprocal interactions with others. She needs to learn to use statements to greet people when she meets them and also when she exits a situation. She needs help with "hellos" and "good-byes." Gabriela also needs to learn to ask joint attention questions and to check for cues from others regarding interactive play. Gabriela

has acquired quite a bit of labeling language, but she has difficulty using it without visual contextual cues.
   a. The use of a visual schedule will help Gabriela retrieve and organize her language so she can apply it in more functional contexts. Because Gabriela is a visual learner, she would respond well to the use of visual social scripts to target specific social skill sets. A combination of visual social scripts consisting of photographs and captions, and guided practice with an adult walking Gabriela through the enactment of the skills, will help her develop the social skills she needs to eventually function to the best of her abilities in the classroom setting.
   b. Gabriela also would benefit from the development of a book about herself and her life, consisting of photographs and captions. Words highlighting her interests and talents as well as photographs of her during appropriate social interactions with significant others would be helpful in getting Gabriela to develop a better sense of herself as well as the people around her.

> Each recommendation links a narrative description of the child's developmental differences to practical suggestions for instructional supports.

4. Like many young children with Autistic Disorder, Gabriela organizes her world around sensory-seeking behaviors and routines. Her drive to establish sensory routines during the day interferes with her ability to follow the agenda of the teacher and participate in classroom activities along with her peers.
   a. Gabriela would benefit from the addition of some systematic sensory routines and breaks during the day. Presenting Gabriela with sensory breaks on a systematic basis will help her better organize her behavior, become less resistant to direct instruction, and focus better on tasks. Integrating sensory breaks into her classroom routine, in the form of physical movement, access to preferred activities, solitary play, and regrouping on the computer, is a strategy that will help Gabriela split up her day and manage the stress of following the teacher's agenda in a productive way. Consultation with the school district's occupational therapist to develop specific sensory routines is highly encouraged.
   b. Gabriela has strong imitation skills and is able to apply them best when she watches others manipulate materials and perform actions. She would benefit from systematic, structured, object-focused play sessions. These sessions would consist of an adult and Gabriela playing with similar toys in a parallel way. The adult would model play routines that extend what Gabriela is doing with the toys. Representational play, social language, and interactive play can be taught using this sensory entry point.
5. Gabriela's parents are doing an outstanding job of understanding their daughter's unique language, social, and sensory challenges. They would benefit from close collaboration with Gabriela's school team to maximize the use of effective strategies across settings. Specifically, assistance in developing visual structure, social photo stories, and sensory routines in the home setting would be helpful for her parents.

REPORT WRITING ESSENTIALS

Now that you've read an excerpt from the narrative report about Gabriela, I'd like to give you some guidelines to follow when you are preparing to write a report following a team evaluation. The structure provided in this section can be used as a general organizational framework to help you write individual narrative reports. Report writing essentials for narrative reports are described for each of the three main sections: *Background Information, Behavioral Observations and Results,* and *Summary and Recommendations.* Since the requirements for comprehensive evaluation reports vary considerably, the guidelines provided here are intended to help you write only the specific narrative portions of your report.

Essentials for the Background Information Section

Goal. The goal for the Background Information section of the narrative report is to provide a description of the child as well as the main concerns expressed by the child's parents and teacher. Refer to your detailed notes from the parent interview to create a narrative description of the child's behavioral profile at home. Use your notes from the teacher interview to describe the child's behavior at school. While you will want to include information collected from the child's medical and educational records, the focus should be on writing detailed information collected during your conversations with the parents and the teacher.

Keep in mind that in a comprehensive evaluation report, this section also includes the results of previous tests and other collateral information that may have been collected.

Sources of information. The sources are the parent interview, the teacher interview, and information collected from a review of the child's medical and educational records. Two possible sources for interview questions include the Parent and Teacher Interview from the *Monteiro Interview Guidelines for Diagnosing Asperger's Syndrome* (MIGDAS; Monteiro, 2008) and the *Autism Diagnostic Interview–Revised* (ADI-R; Rutter, LeCouteur, & Lord, 2003). Information from the school observation of the child, if completed, could be included in this section as well; alternatively, that information may fit best in the Behavioral Observations and Results section.

Specifics. Organize your narrative to describe the child's behavioral profile in each of the three key areas of language and communication, social relationships and emotional responses, and sensory use and interests. Use the names of the child and the parents throughout the narrative. Make it clear when you are including information given to you by the parents during the parent interview. Do this by prefacing the content of your narrative with sentences that clearly define information collected directly from the parents. Consider using the following terminology:

> Mr. and Mrs. R. *stated...*
> Gabriela's parents *noted...*
> Her parents *remarked...*

Include specific details provided by the child's parents as you organize their comments using the visual framework. Describe the child's relationship with others, as reported to you by the parents. Include information about the child's positive attributes. If you asked the parents to think of three words to describe their child during the parent interview, include those descriptive words in this section.

You'll also want to include a paragraph that highlights the following information provided by the parents: their primary concerns, their knowledge about autism spectrum disorders, and their goals for the evaluation process.

The narrative should discuss pertinent medical and developmental information, and provide a brief developmental history.

If the child is in school and you completed a teacher interview, include the school information in this section. Reference the teacher in your narrative when you provide information collected during the teacher interview.

Essentials for the Behavioral Observations and Results Section

Goal. The goal for the Behavioral Observations and Results section of the narrative report is to provide a qualitative description of the child's current behavioral profile, as observed by the evaluation team. The information is organized into the explicit structure of the three key areas that make up the visual framework. The child's unique behavioral profile is depicted by key sentences that describe behaviors typically seen in children with autism spectrum disorders and by examples specific to the child. This section of the report begins with a brief description of the child and a comment regarding the validity of the present evaluation, followed by a statement describing the child's diagnosis and the degree of involvement of the diagnosis. Descriptions of the child's behavioral profile in the three key areas complete this portion of the report.

In a comprehensive evaluation report, this section also includes the results of any other testing that was completed as part of the current evaluation, such as standardized test scores.

Sources of information. Information for this section of the report comes primarily from conversations with and observations of the child, most notably during the neuro-atypical conversation of the sensory-based diagnostic interview. The MIGDAS is helpful in structuring the sensory-based diagnostic interview. Information from the school observation of the child, if completed, could be included in this section as well; alternatively, that information may fit best in the Background Information section.

Other measures that can be helpful in understanding the autism profile of the child include those that involve specific tasks and observations structured by the examiner, such as the *Autism Diagnostic Observation Schedule* (ADOS; Lord, Rutter, DiLavore, & Risi, 1999) and the *Psychoeducational Profile, Third Edition* (PEP-3; Schopler, Lansing, Reichler, & Marcus, 2005), as well as other structured measures and checklists, such as those listed in the Appendix. In addition to autism-specific information, other sources of information include the results of cognitive and language assessments, and inventories related to adaptive functioning and general emotional and behavioral concerns. The suggested format to report formal test results is described in the administration manuals of the various tests and can be addressed in your evaluation report separately. The focus of this chapter is on teaching you how to write qualitative behavioral descriptions of the child in a narrative format.

Specifics. This section of the narrative report contains two distinct parts: the initial summary paragraph and the behavioral profile. The initial summary paragraph summarizes the diagnosis given to the child. The narrative report is given to the parents after they have personally received the specific diagnosis for their child in a meeting with the evaluation team, so at this point they are familiar with the diagnosis. Discussing the diagnosis succinctly at the beginning of this section of the report, and then again in the Summary and Recommendations section, provides the reader with ready access to the team's diagnostic conclusions. After the initial summary paragraph, the description of the child's individual behavioral profile provides supportive information regarding the stated diagnosis. The behavioral profile is broken into the three key areas of language and communication, social relationships and emotional responses, and sensory use and interests.

The initial summary paragraph. Start with a summary paragraph that briefly describes the child, provides a validity statement about the evaluation, and succinctly states the child's diagnosis and the degree of involvement of the diagnosis. Consider using a descriptive word when introducing the child; words like *appealing, engaging, energetic,* or *dynamic* convey a positive and specific impression of the child receiving the diagnosis. Use only words that are genuinely descriptive of the child.

If your team determined that the child has a diagnosis of Autistic Disorder, Pervasive Developmental Disorder Not Otherwise Specified (PDD-NOS), or Asperger's Syndrome, cite the specific diagnosis in a statement about the child's profile of behaviors. Include a sentence that links the diagnosis to the three key areas of developmental differences discussed in the visual framework and specify the degree of involvement of the diagnosis. For example:

> Zachary is an appealing 5-year, 9-month-old boy who was active and alert on the day of this evaluation. It is felt that this evaluation provides a reasonable estimate of his current behavioral profile. He demonstrated a profile of behaviors consistent with a diagnosis of a Pervasive Developmental Disorder Not Otherwise Specified (PDD-NOS), a mild form of an autism spectrum disorder. The degree of involvement was mild but significant. Zachary displayed a pattern of developmental differences in the areas of language and communication, social relationships and emotional responses, and sensory use and interests—differences that characterize children with autism spectrum disorders. His ability to initiate and seek out social interactions, combined with his mild communication and sensory differences, showed a developmental profile typically seen in children with this form of an autism spectrum disorder.

Had Zachary's diagnosis been Asperger's Syndrome, his introductory paragraph might have read as follows:

> Zachary is an appealing 5-year, 9-month-old boy who was active and alert on the day of this evaluation. It is felt that this evaluation provides a reasonable estimate of his current behavioral profile. He demonstrated a profile of behaviors consistent with a diagnosis of Asperger's Syndrome, a high-functioning form of an autism spectrum disorder. The degree of involvement was mild but significant. Zachary displayed a pattern of developmental differences in the areas of language and communication, social relationships and emotional responses, and sensory use and interests—differences that characterize young children with high-functioning autism spectrum disorders. His highly developed use of language and his focus on selected topics of interest showed a developmental profile typically seen in children with this form of an autism spectrum disorder.

Now, let's imagine that your team evaluation ruled out an autism spectrum diagnosis. You determined that Zachary's previously diagnosed language learning disability and his attention-deficit disorder provide the most compelling way to talk about his behavioral profile. In this case, your initial paragraph would clearly make a statement to that effect. For example:

> Zachary is an appealing 5-year, 9-month-old boy who was active and alert on the day of this evaluation. It is felt that this evaluation provides a reasonable estimate of his current behavioral profile. Although Zachary displayed a pattern of language and attention challenges, he did not demonstrate a pattern of the types of developmental disruptions that are typically seen in children with autism spectrum disorders. Zachary's educational challenges are best described as a function of his previously identified language, learning, and attention difficulties.

The behavioral profile. In this section of the report, you are providing the reader with a narrative description of the child's behavioral profile in each of the three key areas associated with an autism spectrum disorder diagnosis. To set the context for the narrative, begin with sentences such as the following:

> To obtain a qualitative picture of Zachary's language, social, and sensory profile, a structured diagnostic team-based interview was completed at his school. A description of his behavioral profile, broken down into the areas of language and communication, social relationships and emotional responses, and sensory use and interests, is detailed below.

Once you've provided the context sentences, you're ready to write a qualitative description of the child's behavioral profile in each of the three key areas. The process of writing this section of the narrative report will proceed best if you use the visual organizational tool of the triangle of developmental differences. Take the time to list the child's behaviors under each of the three headings during your team conversations so you can refer to the list as you write this section of the narrative report. If you've organized your observations of the child's behavioral profile using the triangle format, you can compose a compelling and individualized narrative by expanding upon those observations in the report. Be sure to include a sentence emphasizing the child's positive attributes and strengths when describing the child's behavioral profile in each of the three key sections.

Language and communication. Start this section with a global statement about how the child's use of language and communication showed the pattern of developmental differences associated with autism spectrum disorders. Specify the form of autism spectrum disorder that represents the child's diagnosis. For example:

> Zachary showed a pattern of differences in his use of language and communication that is often seen in children with Asperger's Syndrome.

If Zachary had a diagnosis of Autistic Disorder or PDD-NOS, the introductory sentence would reflect that diagnosis. Conversely, if a diagnosis of an autism spectrum disorder was being ruled out, the introductory sentence would reflect that the child did not show the pattern of differences in the use of language and communication associated with autism spectrum disorders.

What if the child receiving the diagnosis of an autism spectrum disorder is nonverbal? Listed here are some key developmental language and communication differences that should be addressed in the narrative report about a child who has not yet developed verbal language skills.

- If the child is nonverbal, or uses words only on a random and self-initiated basis, include a sentence describing the child as being "functionally nonverbal." Using language on a self-initiated basis refers to a pattern of spontaneous labeling, with limited or no ability to consistently use language when prompted to do so.

- Because even children who are functionally nonverbal may eventually develop language, include the phrase "at the present time" in your description.

You can address other aspects of nonverbal communication in this section of the narrative, including:

- Are vocalizations used with clear communicative intent?
- Are any of the following nonverbal communication functions used?
  - Taking an adult by the hand and leading him or her to a desired object
  - Pointing
  - Eye contact
  - Change in facial expression
  - Orienting body toward a listener or speaker
  - Responsive to verbal requests without visual contextual cues

Children who have an autism spectrum disorder and who have developed verbal communication skills will show a pattern of differences in their use of language and communication. A list of the general language and communication areas to include in your narrative report is presented in Table 6. Within each general area, commonly seen differences between neuro-atypical and neuro-typical children are described.

For children who do not have a diagnosis of an autism spectrum disorder, describing their neuro-typical use of language in each of the listed areas in Table 6 provides a compelling descriptive narrative.

Social relationships and emotional responses. Just as you did with the previous section on language and communication, you'll want to start this section with a global statement describing how the child's understanding of social relationships and emotions did or did not show the pattern of developmental differences associated with autism spectrum disorders. A list of the general social and emotional areas to include in your narrative report, with respect to commonly seen differences between neuro-atypical and neuro-typical children, is presented in Table 7.

Sensory use and interests. After writing a global sentence describing the child's pattern of developmental differences in his or her sensory use and interests, describe the child's pattern of sensory-seeking behaviors and areas of sensory sensitivities. A list of the general areas of sensory use and interests to include in your narrative report, with respect to commonly seen differences between neuro-atypical and neuro-typical children, is provided in Table 8.

Essentials for the Summary and Recommendations Section

Goal. The goal for this section of the narrative report is twofold. In the summary portion the child's diagnosis is restated, while the recommendations portion provides teaching suggestions in five key areas.

In a comprehensive evaluation report, this section would also include recommendations specific to any other concerns raised by the referral question or test results.

Sources of information. Educational recommendations are generated during the team conversation about the child's behavioral profile. During the team dialogue, suggestions for the child's educational plan are organized under the three key areas of developmental differences. Since new program developments constantly emerge in the field of autism spectrum disorders, evaluation team members and teachers need to keep current in their knowledge and understanding of instructional techniques.

Specifics. This section of the narrative report can be organized to address five basic areas: visual communication supports, classroom instruction, social skills and emotion regulation, sensory routines, and school-home collaboration.

The recommendations should be global in scope and yet specific to the individual child. The global nature of the five basic educational areas helps the reader link the program suggestions to the pattern of developmental differences inherent in the diagnosis of an autism spectrum disorder. The specific suggestions in each area address the needs of the individual child.

For each of the five basic areas, begin your narrative with a sentence that provides a rationale for why the recommended suggestions are relevant for the child. Follow the introductory sentence with a brief narrative that describes the global suggestion. The text should then include information on the specific supports you are recommending.

A list of the five basic educational areas to include in your narrative report is presented in Table 9. A rationale is listed for each area, along with several global strategies.

Table 6
Language and Communication:
General Areas to Include in the Narrative Report

AREA	NEURO-ATYPICAL	NEURO-TYPICAL
Intonation and inflection	Intonation and inflection often have a nasal, rote, scripted, pedantic, or rehearsed quality. Although speech may sound robotic, avoid such a description in the narrative, as it comes across as cold and dehumanizing.	Intonation and inflection vary and match the circumstances.
Use of jargon	Speech composed of jargon interspersed with meaningful words.	Speech is meaningful.
Echolalic speech	Repeats words or phrases immediately when hears them spoken by others (immediate echolalia) and/or repeats words or phrases heard at an earlier time (delayed echolalia).	Words are not used in a repetitive way (no echolalia).
Flow of speech	Speech has a rote or scripted quality; note if speech is used in a functional way.	Speech has a natural flow to it.
Word-finding difficulties	Evidence of word-finding difficulties; for example, a child referring to his or her favorite "species" of food.	Although speech may include some searching for words, it lacks a pattern of unusual phrasing.
Use of syntax	May display telegraphic syntax, such as using nouns but omitting connecting words.	Although very young children may display some telegraphic syntax, their speech is not accompanied by the rote quality of delivery found in children with autism spectrum disorders.
Use of pronouns	The use of pronouns may be confused; for example, uses the third person to refer to himself or herself; uses the words "he" and "she" interchangeably.	In young children, speech may include some pronoun confusion, but usually self is referred to as "me" and others arereferred to as "you."
Nonverbal communication	Does not orient toward a listener when speaking. Does not check to see if his or her utterances are understood by others.	Looks at adults and orients his or her body toward the listener. Waits for the listener's response and acknowledges the response through a combination of eye contact, changes in facial expression, proximity, and verbal comments.
Spontaneous communication	Primarily uses words to label objects in his or her visual environment. Spontaneous communication is not socially reciprocal. May initiate a social conversation, but has difficulty reciprocating or extending the conversational exchange.	Makes attempt to secure the attention of the listener by looking at the person, making comments, and watching to see how the listener responds. Offers social information about self, and asks social questions about others.
Need for visual contextual cues	Needs visual contextual cues to help process language requests.	Responds to social language and requests even when there are no clear visual contextual cues.

Table 7
Social Relationships and Emotional Responses: General Areas to Include in the Narrative Report

AREA	NEURO-ATYPICAL	NEURO-TYPICAL
Facial expressions	Words that may describe facial expressions include *neutral, anxious, perpetual smile, occasional facial grimacing, self-directed spontaneous laughter.* Avoid terms such as "flat affect," which are technical and dehumanizing.	Displays a range of facial expressions, such as smiling, grinning, frowning, looking puzzled, and displaying satisfaction when completing a task. Includes others by looking at them and watching for responses.
Use of eye contact	Use of eye contact tends to be fleeting and is used only to check in with the examiner to see what is coming next. This checking in helps the child gauge information about the source of demands being made on him or her, and helps regulate the distress created by the adult imposing a demand on the child. Eye contact is not used to engage others in a social exchange or regulate social exchanges. The child is usually unresponsive to others' use of social smiles and comments.	Uses eye contact as a way to encourage and participate in social exchanges. Is responsive when adults use social smiles and eye contact.
Awareness of and response toward others	Aware of others, but not interactive. May seem to ignore others and resist attempts to engage in social play.	Spontaneously initiates and responds to social play with others. Seeks out others to watch them play or participate in play routines.
Pattern of social interactions		
Initiation of social contact	Has difficulty initiating social contact.	Spontaneously initiates social contact through the use of eye gaze, change in facial expression, making comments, and physical proximity.
Reciprocation or extension of social contact	May be able to initiate, but has difficulty reciprocating or extending social play or social exchanges.	Uses reciprocal gaze, body orientation, and conversational comments in an interactive way during social exchanges.
Response to social contact	Has difficulty responding to social contact, praise, or attention.	Responds to social contact in a fluid way by smiling, frowning, moving closer or farther away, and by increasing or decreasing his or her responses while watching the adults for their reactions.
Response to social demands	Becomes more disorganized or agitated when social demands are made.	Responds in a generally positive way to social demands, and does not become more disorganized in his or her routines.
Asking for help	May ask for help by taking the examiner by the hand, but does not include eye gaze as part of the request process.	Uses eye gaze and searches the faces of adults when asking for help.
Response to difficult tasks	May ignore the examiner and abandon a task when help is needed.	Asks for help or comment on his or her decision to abandon a difficult task.
Ability to cooperate with requests and tolerate interruptions in a set routine	Resists the examiner's attempts to interact and direct activities, and becomes agitated or distressed when adults attempt social play. May abandon an activity or leave an area when interrupted.	Tends to be responsive to, and usually enjoys, having adults participate in play routines. May abandon an activity when interrupted, but in general he or she solicits input and participation of the adult in the alternative activity.

Table 8
Sensory Use and Interests:
General Areas to Include in the Narrative Report

AREA	NEURO-ATYPICAL	NEURO-TYPICAL
Sensory-seeking behaviors	Displays sensory-seeking behaviors in one or more of the following areas. *Visual:* Attention to visual details, close inspection of objects, use of peripheral eye gaze. *Tactile:* Attention to tactile input, such as repeatedly applying deep pressure to the sensory stress balls, pressing objects to his or her face or lips. *Auditory:* Seeking out repetitive sounds that are in his or her immediate control, such as vocalizing or talking to self, or repeatedly creating sounds with objects that create noise. *Olfactory and gustatory:* Smelling or placing objects in the mouth. *Physical movement:* A need for repetitive physical movement, such as pacing or roaming across the room, standing instead of sitting while exploring toys and completing tasks, perching or climbing on furniture.	Shows an absence of repetitive, self-involved, sensory-seeking behaviors, even when presented with a range of sensory toys and materials.
Sensory sensitivities	Shows a pattern of anxiety, agitation, and subsequent avoidance of sources of sensory input. Behaviors include moving away from the source of agitation, placing hands over ears, and vocalizing in a distressed way. Some examples are becoming frightened by or anxious about sudden, unexpected visual movement or sounds, being sensitive to touch or resistant to touching certain textures, and finding certain smells or tastes off-putting.	Does not display a pronounced or heightened pattern of sensory sensitivities, even when presented with a range of senory toys and materials.
Play routines		
Nature of play routines	Engages primarily in sensory-seeking, solitary play routines.	Engages in a range of solitary, parallel, and shared or reciprocal play, but play routines are primarily social. Even when engaged in solitary play, frequently checks in with adults for social praise and includes adults in his or her exploration of toys and materials.
Extension of play routines	Has difficulty extending social play routines once started.	Seeks out extended play with adults and introduces play variations spontaneously.
Use of toys in play routines	Does best with routines that involve cause-and-effect toys and manipulative materials.	Shows an interest in a wide range of toys and materials. Introduces imaginative elements in his or her play. Sustains interest in toys longer when adults provide attention and praise.
Unusual or repetitive movements	Displays unusual or repetitive movements, including body tensing, hand posturing, peripheral eye gaze, hand flapping, hand wringing, picking at lips, running back and forth, and walking on the balls of the feet or on the toes.	Does not engage in sustained, repetitive, unusual body movements.

Table 9
Five Basic Educational Areas to Include in the Narrative Report

VISUAL COMMUNICATION SUPPORTS

Rationale: Children with autism spectrum disorders often struggle with the use of language to communicate their wants and needs. Visual supports help the child organize, retrieve, and use language. Anxiety and stress levels are significantly reduced when visual communication supports are added to a child's daily routine.

Global strategies:

- Communication schedules include using representational objects, pictures, words, icons, photographs, or a combination of these in conjunction with verbal prompts.
- The method of delivery for the visual communication supports includes any of the following: a portable notebook, a schedule mounted on the wall or desk, left-to-right or top-to-bottom sequencing.
- Keep in mind that the system should be readily accessible and close to the child's body.

CLASSROOM INSTRUCTION

Rationale: Children with autism spectrum disorders often struggle with their ability to follow the agenda of the teacher during instruction. A visually structured work system helps the child organize behavior, understand the scope of the tasks, focus on relevant information, work independently, and cooperate with the agenda of the teacher.

Global strategies:

- The following general strategies are suggested for use with students on the autism spectrum: organizational notebook, job card or sequence checklist, word banks, written instructions, left-to-right sequence of activities, manipulative materials, and a consistent place to put completed work.
- Address the need for adult supervision and coaching to use the organizational and instructional supports.
- Emphasize the link between preferred interests and vocational skill-building opportunities.

SOCIAL SKILLS AND EMOTION REGULATION

Rationale: Children with autism spectrum disorders often struggle with their ability to interpret and respond to social situations, and with emotion understanding and regulation. The child may have an awareness of others and an interest in social relationships but needs direct teaching and guided practice to learn to recognize and use social skills and identify and discriminate emotions in himself or herself and others.

Global strategies:

- Describe the tools needed to teach social routines and emotion identification, expression, and management strategies. Tools include social scripts that target specific skills and adaptive replacement strategies for maladaptive behaviors, sequenced visual guides depicting social routines, and photograph books with a first-person narrative. Systematic sensory routines can also help with the regulation of anxiety and distress.
- Address the need for visual supports, direct teaching, and guided practice to learn and generalize skills.

continued on next page...

Table 9 (continued)
Five Basic Educational Areas to Include in the Narrative Report

ROUTINES

Rationale: Children with autism spectrum disorders often struggle with managing sensory stimulation and input. The use of systematic sensory routines helps children with autism spectrum disorders organize their behavior, focus on their surroundings and relevant activities, reduce their general level of anxiety, lower their agitation and distress, and regroup throughout the day in an adaptive way. The idea here is to provide the child with planned opportunities to obtain needed sensory input so he or she is better able to focus and comply during instruction or social activities.

Global strategies:
- Provide general suggestions on ways to use the child's sensory-seeking behaviors and interests as regrouping strategies.
- Plan brief times for the child to take sensory "breaks."
- Use visual social scripts to teach self-regulation skills.
- Combine direct teaching and guided practice to help the child develop self-regulation skills.
- Consult with the school occupational therapist for specific sensory suggestions.

SCHOOL-HOME COLLABORATION

Rationale: Children with autism spectrum disorders do best when there is consistency between home and school interventions. School-home collaboration helps ensure that consistency. Emphasize how close collaboration between home and school is necessary to ensure that effective strategies are applied across settings.

Global strategies:
- Make a statement about how well the parents understand their child or how devoted they are to their child. In other words, acknowledge the observed bond between the parents and their child in this section of the report.
- Suggest the use of a notebook communication system between school and home. Consider suggesting a communication system for both the teacher to communicate information and for the child to share information about his or her day. Two-way home-school communication can be established as well by designing a notebook that allows for ongoing, back-and-forth correspondence between parents and teachers. Including the child in the use of the notebook communication system provides a structured way for the child to have visual prompts to share information about his or her school day after arriving home at the end of the day.
- Emphasize the need for consistency between school and home in the areas of communication, social and emotional regulation skills, and sensory routines.

Written Conversations: Report Writing Essentials

The Background Information section...

- Provides a description of, and cites main concerns about, the child as expressed by the child's parents and teacher during their conversations with members of the evaluation team.
- Includes details of the child's developmental history.
- Emphasizes the child's observed and reported behavior in the home and school settings within the three key areas of language and communication, social relationships and emotional responses, and sensory use and interests.

The Behavioral Observations and Results section...

- Lays out the qualitative description of the child's behavioral profile in each of the three key areas and links them to the specific diagnosis in a compelling way.
- Uses specific examples taken from the "neuro-atypical" conversation between the child and the evaluation team.
- Uses the same nontechnical but specific descriptive language that was used during the diagnostic feedback conversation with the parents.

The Summary and Recommendations section...

- Reiterates the diagnostic conclusions and describes how the diagnosis reflects the child's pattern of developmental differences in the three key areas.
- Gives parents and teachers a common framework to organize their discussion about the child's educational program.
- Provides general recommendations in the areas of visual communication supports, classroom instruction, social skills and emotion regulation, sensory routines, and school-home collaboration.

A Final Conversation

This book was written to help you have more effective conversations concerning autism spectrum disorders and to highlight the integral role that these conversations play in the context of a best practices autism evaluation. Throughout this book, we've discussed conversations with children, parents, teachers, and one another as part of the autism evaluation process. The narrative report provides parents and teachers with the written summary of those conversations.

The children you evaluate will respond to your ability to participate in a neuroatypical conversation. Their parents will appreciate being able to share their stories with you. Teachers will know they are part of the evaluation process. As you develop the skills to understand and discuss autism spectrum disorders using the visual framework, you will have more effective conversations with one another as well.

Remember that when you make a diagnosis of autism, or an autism spectrum disorder, you are talking about a unique individual. If you apply the evaluation strategies discussed in this book, you will be able to effectively discuss a child's pattern of developmental differences while describing the child in genuine and authentic terms. Your evaluation report will provide a record of the child's worldview and family life. You will provide the child's teacher with the understanding necessary to use the recommended instructional strategies.

If you are an evaluator, my goal in writing this book was to help you participate in effective conversations as you evaluate children with autism spectrum disorders. I hope this book helped you learn to recognize the pattern of developmental differences that distinguish autism spectrum disorders in a range of children and that you gained the necessary tools to help you evaluate children, have productive team discussions, and have more effective, collaborative conversations with parents and teachers. Finally, I hope that reading this book helps you write compelling narrative reports.

If you are the parent of a child suspected of having an autism spectrum disorder, my hope is that reading this book has helped you understand the nature of the developmental differences that make up autism spectrum disorders. I also hope it helped you know what to expect from an autism evaluation performed with quality and care. Share your stories. Your children will benefit when their stories are told and their worldview is understood.

APPENDIX

Questionnaires Specific to Autism Spectrum Disorders

The questionnaires listed below are designed to be completed by parents, teachers, and/or professionals who are concerned about children and adolescents with suspected autism spectrum disorders.

For general autism-related concerns:
    Gilliam Autism Rating Scale–2 (GARS-2)
    Social Communication Questionnaire (SCQ)
    Social Responsiveness Scale (SRS)

For Asperger's Syndrome:
    Asperger Syndrome Diagnostic Scale (ASDS)
    Australian Scale for Asperger's Syndrome (ASAS)
    Gilliam Asperger's Disorder Scale (GADS)
    Krug Asperger's Disorder Index (KADI)

For young children:
    Modified Checklist for Autism in Toddlers (M-CHAT)
    Temperament and Atypical Behavior Scale (TABS)

GLOSSARY

ADI-R: See *Autism Diagnostic Interview–Revised.*

ADOS: See *Autism Diagnostic Observation Schedule.*

Agenda of the child: I use this term, or the term "on his or her own agenda," to highlight the qualitative experience of being with a child who is preoccupied with his or her own thoughts and experiences to the exclusion of referencing social information in the surrounding environment. Children with autism spectrum disorders often seem captured by their internal agenda and have difficulty scanning their surroundings for social cues and information. I talk with parents and teachers about how children on the spectrum have a difficult time shifting their focus from their internal agenda to the agenda of others.

Asperger's Syndrome: A high-functioning form of an autism spectrum disorder characterized by the specific developmental differences outlined in Figure 5 (see chapter 1). With this disorder, adequately developed cognitive and self-help skills are evident. Specific diagnostic criteria can be found in the *DSM-IV-TR.*

Autism: Used in this book as an abbreviation for the broader term *autism spectrum disorders.*

***Autism Diagnostic Interview–Revised* (ADI-R):** A standardized interview protocol designed to assist in diagnosing autism spectrum disorders. A trained clinical interviewer questions a parent or caregiver who is familiar with the developmental history and current behavior of the individual being evaluated. The standardized response coding provides categorical results relevant to the communication, social, and restricted behaviors/interests of individuals with suspected autism spectrum disorders.

***Autism Diagnostic Observation Schedule* (ADOS):** A standardized assessment designed to measure the communication and social behaviors of individuals with suspected autism spectrum disorders. Tasks are designed to span a wide range—from children with no speech up to verbally fluent adults. Cutoff scores are used to determine the likelihood that a child falls on the autism spectrum.

Autism learning profile/style: The specific worldview and approach to organizing information that are characteristic of a child with an autism spectrum disorder. Specifically, the autism learning style/profile is characterized by a drive to organize information from a sensory rather than a social perspective. Children with an autism learning style show differences in their development in the three key areas of language and communication, social relationships and emotional responses, and sensory use and interests.

Autism spectrum disorders: The continuum of developmental differences that make up a form of neurodevelopmental disorders characterized by disruptions in language and communication, social relationships and emotional responses, and sensory use and interests. The three major forms of autism spectrum disorders discussed in this book are Autistic Disorder, Pervasive Developmental Disorder Not Otherwise Specified (PDD-NOS), and Asperger's Syndrome. A detailed description of each type of autism spectrum disorder is provided in chapter 1.

Autistic Disorder: A form of an autism spectrum disorder characterized by the specific developmental differences outlined in Figure 3 (see chapter 1). Autistic Disorder is the most severe type of autism spectrum disorder and is sometimes referred to as *classic autism* or simply *autism*. Specific diagnostic criteria can be found in the *DSM-IV-TR*.

Behavioral profile: Part of the visual framework for understanding autism spectrum disorders presented in this book. The behavioral profile refers to the description of behaviors displayed by a child in each of the three key areas of developmental differences (i.e., language and communication, social relationships and emotional responses, and sensory use and interests) that characterize autism spectrum disorders. When a child's behavioral profile is organized around the descriptive triangle, each distinctive behavior is listed using nontechnical and specific language, making the profile accessible to and recognizable by the child's parents and teachers.

Best practices autism evaluation: See chapter 1 for a description, as well as information about how the visual framework is applied within that context.

CARS2: See *Childhood Autism Rating Scale, Second Edition*.

***Childhood Autism Rating Scale, Second Edition* (CARS2):** An assessment instrument completed by trained raters based on direct observation of a child with a suspected autism spectrum disorder. Scores are provided to help clinicians identify children with such a disorder.

Conversational approach: The qualitative process of approaching an evaluation by having informal but structured conversations with parents, teachers, children, and each other. The essence of the conversational approach is conveyed throughout this book.

Degree of involvement: The severity with which an individual is affected by an autism spectrum disorder. Autism spectrum disorders can interfere with a child's ability to learn anywhere from a mild to a significant degree.

Descriptive triangle: Part of the visual framework for understanding autism spectrum disorders presented in this book. The descriptive triangle provides a visual way to understand the pattern of differences in development that make up autism spectrum disorders. The center of the triangle uses the words

Differences in Development to organize thinking around the idea that a child displays a pattern of differences, disruptions, or atypicalities in his or her development. The three points of the triangle are used to organize a child's behavioral profile, highlighting developmental differences in the three key areas of language and communication, social relationships and emotional responses, and sensory use and interests. The triangle can be used as a visual aid in understanding the different forms of autism spectrum disorders (see chapter 1) and in discussing a child's diagnosis with parents and teachers (see chapter 6), and as an organizational tool for teams as they discuss their observations, determine their diagnostic conclusions, and write the narrative report (see chapters 5 and 7).

Diagnostic and Statistical Manual of Mental Disorders, Fourth Edition, Text Revision (DSM-IV-TR): A classification manual of psychiatric disorders published by the American Psychiatric Association. It includes diagnostic criteria for Autistic Disorder, Pervasive Developmental Disorder Not Otherwise Specified (PDD-NOS), and Asperger's Syndrome.

Diagnostic feedback conversation: The conversation between the child's parents and the evaluation team to discuss the outcome of the autism evaluation. The child's teacher and additional school staff may also participate in the meeting, when appropriate. See chapter 6 for detailed information about the diagnostic feedback conversation.

Diagnostic label: The specific diagnosis given to a child by the evaluation team. On the autism spectrum, one of three possible diagnostic labels is generally used: Autistic Disorder, Pervasive Developmental Disorder Not Otherwise Specified (PDD-NOS), or Asperger's Syndrome.

Differential diagnosis: The process of determining the most compelling diagnosis for a child's documented behavioral profile and challenges. In this book, the term *differential diagnosis* refers to the process of ruling out the presence of an autism spectrum disorder in favor of a different diagnosis.

Direct teaching: The process of actively teaching a concept to a child. During direct teaching sessions, the adult who is teaching a skill to the child usually uses structured, predictable routines so the child knows what to expect and is more likely to focus on the content of the lesson. Direct teaching is usually followed by guided practice.

DSM-IV-TR: See *Diagnostic and Statistical Manual of Mental Disorders, Fourth Edition, Text Revision*.

Echolalic speech: Speech that is characterized by the repetitive use of words or phrases; also referred to as *echolalia*. Echolalic speech can be immediate, when words or phrases are repeated immediately upon being heard, or delayed, when words or phrases that were heard at an earlier time are repeated.

Evaluation team: See *Multidisciplinary evaluation team*.

Expressive language skills: An individual's capacity to produce spoken language.

Functionally nonverbal: The use of language only on a random and self-initiated basis. Individuals who are functionally nonverbal show a pattern of language use characterized by spontaneous labeling, with limited or no ability to consistently use language when prompted to do so.

Guided practice: The process of an adult coaching and guiding a child through a social or academic routine that has been taught in a direct teaching session.

Hand and body posturing: Involuntary and ritualistic tensing of hands, fingers, limbs, or torso in response to sensory input.

High-functioning: Used to describe individuals who display a characteristic pattern of developmental differences associated with autism spectrum disorders, but who do not show a pattern of developmental delays. Individuals who are considered to be high-functioning typically have average or above-average intelligence.

ICD-10: See *International Classification of Diseases, 10th Revision*.

Icons: Pictures or line drawings used to depict events in the child's day. Usually the icons are paired with written words describing the picture.

Idiosyncratic motivation: The child's spontaneous motivation to complete tasks, whether intrinsic or tangible, does not follow a predictable pattern.

IEP meeting: A formal, legal meeting at which a child's individualized education plan, or IEP, is discussed. The IEP is an educational plan designed to meet a specific child's unique needs.

Individualized Education Plan: See *IEP meeting*.

***International Classification of Diseases, 10th Revision* (ICD-10):** The World Health Organization's international standard diagnostic classification system for diseases and disorders, including autism spectrum disorders.

Intrinsic motivation: Motivation of the child to complete tasks due to a natural and inherent drive to explore materials and learn. Intrinsic motivation can be contrasted with *tangible motivation*.

Intrinsic reward: The child's reward for completing a task based on the internal satisfaction provided by the learning experience. Intrinsic reward can be contrasted with *tangible reward*.

Jargon: Nonsense syllables used as part of the child's language profile. Although jargon is a neuro-typical part of language development, children with autism use jargon in a self-directed and repetitive way that is distinctively neuro-atypical. Their jargon is usually not directed toward a listener and is not used as a social communication substitute for limited language.

Job card: A written list of the sequence of steps involved in completing an academic task. It is usually placed close to the child and the child's required task materials. The child can be instructed to cross off each step listed on the job card as each step in the assigned task is completed.

MIGDAS: See *Monteiro Interview Guidelines for Diagnosing Asperger's Syndrome*.

Mirroring responses: During the sensory-based diagnostic interview, one of the ways the evaluators can convey familiarity to the child on the autism spectrum is to "mirror" or subtly assume the child's mannerisms and way of speaking. My experience has been that when I mirror the child's way of speaking, the child relaxes and has an experience of sharing information with someone who is an extension of his or her worldview. Because children with autism spectrum disorders have difficulty taking in the perspective of others, I have found that assuming their perspective increases their comfort level and results in longer and more detailed conversational samples.

***Monteiro Interview Guidelines for Diagnosing Asperger's Syndrome* (MIGDAS):** A systematic, three-step approach to diagnosing Asperger's Syndrome, based on parent, teacher, and child interviews. Designed to be used by evaluation teams, the MIGDAS provides a qualitative description of the child in the three key areas of language and communication, social relationships and emotional responses, and sensory use and interests. Evaluation teams are guided to conduct a sensory-based diagnostic interview using sensory toys and topics of interest to the child with suspected Asperger's Syndrome. The MIGDAS is designed to be used with school-aged children and adolescents, as well as with verbal preschool-aged children. It is appropriate for use with high-functioning children with suspected Asperger's Syndrome, Autistic Disorder, or PDD-NOS.

Multidisciplinary evaluation team: A team of professionals from various backgrounds (e.g., psychology, speech-language pathology, occupational therapy), all of whom have training and experience relevant to autism spectrum disorders. A best practices evaluation for an autism spectrum disorder includes assessment of the child by a multidisciplinary evaluation team.

Narrative report: The written conversation about the child. It is the final piece of the formal evaluation process and includes information gathered during the conversations with the child, parents, and teacher. The emphasis is on linking qualitative descriptions of the child's behavioral profile with the child's specific diagnosis. Recommendations for educational supports are included as well. See chapter 7 for detailed information on writing the narrative report.

Neuro-atypical conversation: A conversation with a child that opens with the child's preferred topics of interest or the introduction of sensory toys. Because the adult does not focus on establishing a series of social questions or comments to start the conversation, I refer to this as starting the conversation "in the middle." See chapter 2 for a more detailed explanation of a neuro-atypical conversation.

Neuro-atypical development: In this book, the terms *neuro-atypical* and *neuro-atypical development* are used to describe individuals who display a distinctive pattern of developmental differences that are characteristic of autism spectrum disorders, specifically, differences in language and communication, social relationships and emotional responses, and sensory use and interests.

Neurodevelopment: The development of the nervous system.

Neurodevelopmental disorder: A brain-based disorder that causes disruptions in a child's development. The disorder may have a genetic, environmental, or unknown cause. Autism spectrum disorders are neurodevelopmental disorders characterized by disruptions in language and communication, social relationships and emotional responses, and sensory use and interests.

Neuro-typical development: In this book, the terms *neuro-typical* and *neuro-typical development* are used to describe individuals who do not display the characteristic pattern of developmental differences in the three key areas (i.e., language and communication, social relationships and emotional responses, and sensory use and interests) that are affected in autism spectrum disorders.

Nonfinite grief: The dual processes of confronting the fear response caused by a threat to an individual's well-being and the eventual acceptance of that threat. In the case of parents of a child who receives an autism spectrum disorder diagnosis, the threat that triggers the nonfinite grief process is the child's diagnosis. Also referred to as *ambiguous grief*. See chapter 6 for a more in-depth discussion of the nonfinite grief process.

Nonverbal language: Language and communication features that are expressed without words, such as gestures, posture, facial expressions, and eye contact.

Object-focused play: Engaging in play with a child by focusing attention on a shared toy or object. The emphasis is on the toy or object rather than on the social or language aspects of relating to the child. For children with autism spectrum disorders, object-focused play provides a less stressful entry point for a shared experience than language- or social-based exchanges.

Organizational notebook: A place for a child to keep track of his or her daily schedule, social reminders, and academic work.

PDD-NOS: See *Pervasive Developmental Disorder Not Otherwise Specified.*

PEP-3: See *Psychoeducational Profile, Third Edition.*

Peripheral eye gaze: The use of side vision to examine the visual details of objects. Children on the autism spectrum often use peripheral eye gaze to gain visual sensory input by tilting their head and looking at objects from a side angle or by placing objects close to the corner of their eye.

Pervasive Developmental Disorder Not Otherwise Specified (PDD-NOS): A form of an autism spectrum disorder characterized by the specific developmental differences outlined in Figure 4 (see chapter 1). This disorder, often abbreviated as PDD-NOS, is a milder form of an autism spectrum disorder than Autistic Disorder. Specific diagnostic criteria can be found in the *DSM-IV-TR*.

Photograph book with a first-person narrative: A book about a child and his or her social world. The photographs selected for the book might focus on showing the child's family and family events or might target school routines or social situations with peers. Once the photographs are organized in a narrative sequence, a few first-person narrative sentences are written below the pictures to create a social script for the child. Sometimes it is helpful if the book includes an interactive feature, such as matching photographs with sentence strips or text with pictures. The action of matching while hearing the narrative text being read helps the child absorb the content of the book. Reviewing the book can also help the child develop a vocabulary of feelings and a sense of identity.

***Psychoeducational Profile, Third Edition* (PEP-3):** A standardized test designed to assess the developmental skills and behaviors of children with suspected autism spectrum disorders. The test helps to identify learning strengths and is useful in designing educational programming, including individualized education plans. The test also provides quantitative scores that help clinicians categorize the likelihood that a child displays behaviors characteristic of an autism spectrum disorder.

Qualitative: Used in this book to characterize descriptive, nonnumerical information. Evaluation teams are encouraged to develop a qualitative vocabulary—that is, nontechnical but specific language—to describe a child. In the visual framework, qualitative language is used to describe the child's behavioral profile in the three key areas of communication, social, and sensory development. Qualitative language can be directly contrasted with *quantitative* (numerical) language.

Quantitative: Used in this book to describe the numerical information provided by standardized tests. Although it is important for evaluation teams to have a quantitative vocabulary in order to understand test results, teams are encouraged to organize their discussions about children and provide diagnostic feedback using qualitative, rather than quantitative, language.

Receptive language skills: An individual's capacity to comprehend spoken language.

Representational objects: Objects used to represent events about which the child needs to communicate. For example, a visual schedule that uses representational objects might have a cup to signal snack time, a miniature book to signal work time, and a small ball to signal break time. In general, representational objects are used when a child has not yet developed the ability to associate pictures with events. (Once a child can associate pictures with events, then pictures can replace the representational objects in the visual schedule.) When representational objects are used as part of a child's visual schedule, the child begins to attach meaning to the object when he or she has a routine of carrying the object to the designated area where the event is to occur, matching the object with an identical one located at the site of the activity, and promptly beginning the activity. The close association of hearing the spoken words that communicate the activity with matching the object helps the child develop an understanding of the communication function of the objects and the associated words.

Representational play: Using toys and objects in an imaginative and representational, or abstract, way. For example, feeding a baby doll, using a toy telephone to have a conversation, and using plastic food to create a shared meal are common ways children engage in representational play.

Self-regulation: The process of helping a child become aware of his or her level of agitation or distress while linking that awareness to practical self-calming strategies.

Sensory-based: Used in this book to emphasize a focus on sensory, as opposed to social, information. When a child's needs are sensory-based, that child is naturally driven to seek out and respond to sensory input, as opposed to social input. When evaluators use conversational techniques that are sensory-based, they enter the child's worldview through a sensory, as opposed to social, route.

Sensory-based conversation/sensory-based conversational techniques: See *Sensory-based diagnostic interview*.

Sensory-based diagnostic interview: A conversation between a child and a team of evaluators. Sensory-based toys and preferred topics provide the entry point for the interview. This interview format provides evaluators with a powerful, qualitative experience of the child's worldview. See chapter 2 for detailed information about the sensory-based diagnostic interview.

Sensory breaks and routines: See *Sensory-seeking*; see also *Systematic sensory breaks and routines*.

Sensory-seeking: Refers to the child's drive to search for and respond to sensory input, either in his or her internal world or the external environment. Children who are sensory-seeking display behavior and routines focused on several sensory areas, including auditory, visual, tactile, and movement. In contrast to children who are sensory-seeking, children without autism spectrum disorders are socially driven, meaning that their behavior is motivated by social relationships as opposed to sensory needs.

Sensory-seeking play: Refers to a child's preoccupation with gaining repetitive sensory input from toys and materials during the sensory-based diagnostic interview. Usually when the child is engaged in sensory-seeking play, he or she is resistant to attempts by others to share in the play routines. This type of play stands in contrast to socially driven play, which is typically seen in children who do not have an autism spectrum disorder.

Sensory sensitivities: A pattern of processing sensory input, characteristic of individuals with autism spectrum disorders, in which ordinary sensations are experienced more intensely than is typical. Due to such sensory sensitivities, individuals with autism spectrum disorders often feel anxious when presented with unexpected sensory input unless they are allowed to be in control of the input.

Sensory topics: The preferred topics and areas of interest of a child with an autism spectrum disorder. When a child becomes caught up in talking about a preferred topic during the sensory-based diagnostic interview, the qualitative experience the evaluators have is sensory rather than social. The experience typically includes the sense that the child is actually watching the events unfold as he or she describes details about a preferred topic.

Sensory toys: Toys that provide some form of clear sensory input. Usually the toys provide a way for the child to set up repetitive sensory routines to obtain visual, auditory, or tactile input. Additionally, sensory toys allow evaluators to observe when the child has an aversion or sensitivity to sensory input.

Sequenced visual guides depicting social routines: A visual sequence of steps depicting the words and actions associated with a specific social routine. For example, if the goal is to teach a child to approach a friend to initiate play on the playground, the sequenced visual guide would depict the steps of choosing a friend, selecting an activity, and deciding on the words and actions to start the play exchange. Guiding the child through the entire visual guide prior to the child's entering the natural situation in which he or she will act out the steps is a powerful teaching tool.

Social photo stories: See *Photograph book with a first-person narrative.*

Social scripts: Descriptions of the words and actions that comprise social behavior. Social scripts can be written narratives, pictorial representations of social events, or a combination of the two. Usually they are tailored to the age of the individual child, as well as his or her developmental and cognitive functioning level.

Systematic sensory breaks and routines: Planned sensory breaks and routines during a child's day. Examples include opportunities for planned movement, time to engage in a preferred activity, and access to sensory toys. The idea is to provide the child with needed sensory input so he or she can remain less stressed, more focused, and better organized during instructional times.

Tangible motivation: Motivation of the child to complete tasks in order to gain a tangible reward, such as food or access to preferred toys or activities. Tangible motivation can be contrasted with *intrinsic motivation*.

Tangible reward: An external, concrete object or experience, such as food or access to preferred objects or activities, given to a child as a reward for completing a task. Tangible reward can be contrasted with *intrinsic reward*.

Telegraphic syntax: A pattern of speech characterized by the use of nouns and the omission of connecting words; also referred to as telegraphic speech. Children display telegraphic syntax as a normal part of their speech development, usually between the ages of 18 and 36 months. Children with autism spectrum disorders may show delayed development of telegraphic syntax, continue to display such syntax past the ages at which it is typically seen, and/or display a rote quality of delivery in their use of telegraphic syntax.

Visual contextual cues: Information provided visually that helps a child on the autism spectrum understand the meaning of language. For example, holding up a set of car keys while standing by the front door provides the child with visual contextual cues to understand the language in the statement "Time to go."

Visual discrimination sheet: A visual schematic that depicts the words and actions the child used to say and do and contrasts them with the words and actions the child is learning to use as adaptive replacement behaviors.

Visual framework: The system of organizing information about autism spectrum disorders described throughout this book. In the visual framework, the key behavioral features of autism spectrum disorders that are described in traditional diagnostic categorization systems are organized into the three key areas clinicians look at when evaluating children for suspected autism spectrum disorders: language and communication, social relationships and emotional responses, and sensory use and interests. The three key areas form a behavioral profile, organized around a descriptive triangle, that provides an accessible way to understand the challenges associated with autism spectrum disorders.

Visual supports: Visual schedules, written social scripts, and other forms of visual prompts that help children organize their behavior and follow a sequence of directions in a functional way. Sometimes referred to as visual communication supports.

REFERENCES

American Academy of Child and Adolescent Psychiatry. (n.d.). *Practice parameters.* Retrieved December 31, 2008, from http://www.aacap.org/cs/root/member_information/practice_information/practice_parameters/practice_parameters

American Psychiatric Association. (2000). *Diagnostic and statistical manual of mental disorders* (4th ed., text rev.). Washington, DC: Author.

Gilliam, J. (2001). *Gilliam Asperger's Disorder Scale (GADS).* Austin, TX: Pro-Ed.

Lord, C., Rutter, M., DiLavore, P. C., & Risi, S. (1999). *Autism Diagnostic Observation Schedule (ADOS): Manual.* Los Angeles: Western Psychological Services.

Monteiro, M. J. (2008). *Monteiro Interview Guidelines for Diagnosing Asperger's Syndrome (MIGDAS): Manual.* Los Angeles: Western Psychological Services.

Rutter, M., LeCouteur, A., & Lord, C. (2003). *Autism Diagnostic Interview–Revised (ADI-R): Manual.* Los Angeles: Western Psychological Services.

Schopler, E., Lansing, M. D., Reichler, R. J., & Marcus, L. M. (2005). *Psychoeducational Profile: TEACCH Individualized Psychoeducational Assessment for Children with Autism Spectrum Disorders, Third Edition (PEP-3).* Austin, TX: Pro-Ed.

Schopler, E., Van Bourgondien, M.E., Wellman, G.J., & Love, S.R. (2010). *Childhood Autism Rating Scale, Second Edition (CARS2): Manual.* Los Angeles: Western Psychological Services.

World Health Organization. (1993). *The ICD-10 classification of mental and behavioral disorders: Diagnostic criteria for research.* Geneva, Switzerland: Author.